THE ROUGH

MAUI

Forthcoming titles include

The Algarve • The Bahamas • Cambodia
The Caribbean • Costa Brava
New York Restaurants • South America • Zanzibar

Forthcoming reference guides include

Children's Books • Online Travel • Videogaming
Weather

Rough Guides online

www.roughguides.com

Rough Guide Credits

Text editors: Mary Callahan, Don Young
Series editor: Mark Ellingham
Production: Rachel Holmes
Cartography: Melissa Baker
Proofreading: Derek Wilde

Publishing Information

This second edition published November 2001
by Rough Guides Ltd,
62–70 Shorts Gardens, London WC2H 9AH

Distributed by the Penguin Group

Penguin Books Ltd, 80 Strand, London WC2R ORL
Penguin Putnam, Inc. 375 Hudson Street, New York 10014, USA
Penguin Books Australia Ltd, 487 Maroondah Highway,
PO Box 257, Ringwood, Victoria 3134, Australia
Penguin Books Canada Ltd, 10 Alcorn Avenue,
Toronto, Ontario, Canada M4V 1E4
Penguin Books (NZ) Ltd,
182–190 Wairau Road, Auckland 10, New Zealand

Typeset in Bembo and Helvetica to an original design by Henry Iles.
Printed in Spain by Graphy Cems.

ISBN 1-85828-401-5

The publishers and authors have done their best to ensure
the accuracy and currency of all the information in
The Rough Guide to Maui, however, they
can accept no responsibility for any loss, injury or
inconvenience sustained by any traveler as a result of
information or advice contained in the guide.

THE ROUGH GUIDE TO

MAUI

by Greg Ward

ROUGH
GUIDES

We set out to do something different when the first Rough Guide was published in 1982. Mark Ellingham, just out of university, was traveling in Greece. He brought along the popular guides of the day, but found they were all lacking in some way. They were either strong on ruins and museums but went on for pages without mentioning a beach or taverna. Or they were so conscious of the need to save money that they lost sight of Greece's cultural and historical significance. Also, none of the books told him anything about Greece's contemporary life – its politics, its culture, its people, and how they lived.

So with no job in prospect, Mark decided to write his own guidebook, one which aimed to provide practical information that was second to none, detailing the best beaches and the hottest clubs and restaurants, while also giving hard-hitting accounts of every sight, both famous and obscure, and providing up-to-the-minute information on contemporary culture. It was a guide that encouraged independent travelers to find the best of Greece, and was a great success, getting shortlisted for the Thomas Cook travel guide award, and encouraging Mark, along with three friends, to expand the series.

The Rough Guide list grew rapidly and the letters flooded in, indicating a much broader readership than had been anticipated, but one which uniformly appreciated the Rough Guide mix of practical detail and humour, irreverence and enthusiasm. Things haven't changed. The same four friends who began the series are still the caretakers of the Rough Guide mission today: to provide the most reliable, up-to-date and entertaining information to independent-minded travelers of all ages, on all budgets.

We now publish more than 200 titles and have offices in London and New York. The travel guides are written and researched by a dedicated team of more than 100 authors, based in Britain, Europe, the USA and Australia. We have also created a unique series of phrasebooks to accompany the travel series, along with an acclaimed series of music guides, and a best-selling pocket guide to the Internet and World Wide Web. We also publish comprehensive travel information on our website: www.roughguides.com

Help us update

We've gone to a lot of trouble to ensure that this Rough Guide is as up to date and accurate as possible. However, things do change and all suggestions, comments and corrections are much appreciated, and we'll send a copy of the next edition (or any other Rough Guide if you prefer) for the best letters.

Please mark letters **"Rough Guide Maui Update"** and send to:

Rough Guides, 62–70 Shorts Gardens, London WC2H 9AH, or Rough Guides, 4th Floor, 345 Hudson St, New York, NY 10014.

Or send email to: mail@roughguides.co.uk
Online updates about this book can be found on
Rough Guides' website (see opposite)

The author

Greg Ward has worked for Rough Guides since 1985, in which time he has also written Rough Guides to Hawaii, Honolulu, the Big Island of Hawaii, Southwest USA, Las Vegas, Essential Blues CDs, and Brittany and Normandy, as well as co-authored the *Rough Guide to the USA* and the *Rough Guide to Online Travel*. He has edited and contributed to numerous other Rough Guides, and worked on travel guides for Fodors and Dorling Kindersley as well.

Acknowledgments

Thanks once again to Samantha Cook for her encouragement, support and patience, and for all the fun too. At Rough Guides, thanks to Mary Callahan for her thorough and conscientious editing, Don Young for additional editorial assistance, and to Andrew Rosenberg, Rachel Holmes, Melissa Baker, Audra Epstein and Sharon Martins for their hard work. For their generous assistance with my research for this new edition, I'd also like to thank Candy Aluli, David Castles, Captain Coon, Warren Gibson, Amy Hamilton, Charlene Kauhane, Wilmanette Oskins,

Shae Page, Alexandra Pangas and everyone who sent emails
via the Rough Guides' website.

Readers' letters

Paul Norfolk, Serena Satyasai, Michael Pratt, all the many business operators who wrote in, and those whose email addresses or signatures were totally inscrutable or just plain missing.

CONTENTS

MAP LIST

MAP SYMBOLS

═══════	Major road	🛕	Buddhist temple
▬▬▬▬▬	Minor road	∴	Ancient site
=========	Track	🏆	Museum
---------	Trail	🌴	Public gardens
▬▬┼▬▬	Railway	�►	Viewpoint
────────	Waterway	▲	Peak
✈	Airport	⅃	Waterfall
▣	Accommodation	♦	General point of interest
◉	Places to eat and drink	✚	Church (town maps)
Ⓧ	Campsite	▨	Park
⚲	Church (regional maps)	▨	National Park
✉	Post office	▨	Lava flow
ⓘ	Information office		

Introduction

Thanks to its superb beaches, ravishing tropical scenery, wide range of activities, and magnificent hotels, the island of Maui can justly claim to be the world's most glamorous vacation destination. The slogan Maui No Ka 'Oi – "Maui is the Best" – may gloss over the fact that it's both the second largest and the second youngest of the Hawaiian chain, and ranks a distant second to Oahu in terms of annual visitors, but for island inhabitants and devotees alike the "Valley Isle" has a cachet its neighbors could never match.

All the Hawaiian islands are the summits of a chain of submarine volcanoes, poking from the Pacific more than two thousand miles off the west coast of America. Each has continued to grow for as long as it remained poised above a stationary "hot spot" in the earth's crust; since Maui in its turn drifted to the northwest and lost its steady supply of fresh lava, it has begun to erode back beneath the ocean.

Maui is what's known as a "volcanic doublet", consisting of two originally separate but now overlapping volcanoes. The older of the two, known to geologists as Mauna Kahalawai, has eroded to become a serrated ridge that's usually referred to as the West Maui Mountains; it's now dwarfed by the younger Haleakalā to the southeast. Although Haleakalā is not technically extinct, but only

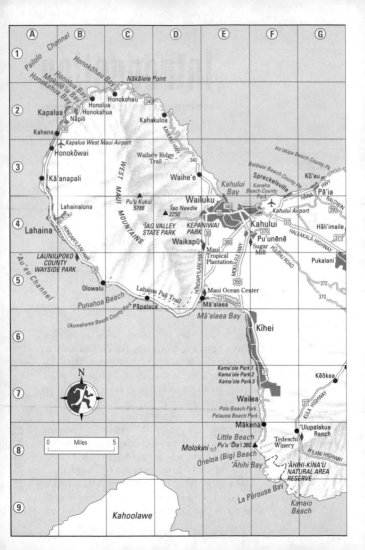

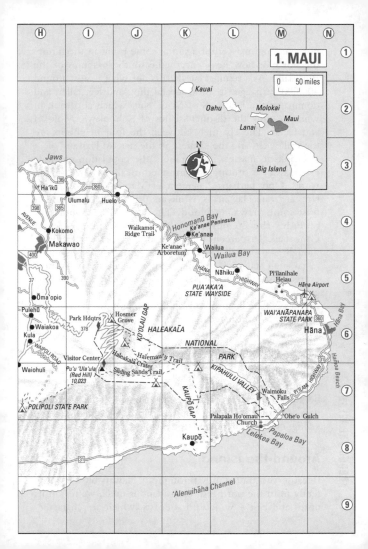

dormant, and may erupt again at some point in the future, the hot spot now lies beneath the southern shores of the Big Island. As a result, Haleakalā is not what it was: around 400,000 years ago, it stood several thousand feet taller, and dominated the landmass of Maui Nui, which also took in what are now the distinct islands of Kahoolawe, Molokai and Lanai. The channels between the four neighbors are the shallowest, and the calmest, in the state of Hawaii.

Thanks to massive immigration, the population of modern Hawaii is among the most ethnically diverse in the world. Only perhaps 2 percent of Maui's 120,000 inhabitants are pure Hawaiians, while another 20 percent claim at least some Hawaiian blood. The rest of the population includes the 26 percent who identify themselves as Caucasian, 16 percent Japanese, and 15 percent Filipino, though as over half of all marriages are classified as inter-racial such statistics are increasingly meaningless. Almost everyone speaks English, and as a rule the Hawaiian language is only encountered in the few words – such as *aloha* or "love", the all-purpose island greeting – that have passed into general local usage.

For each of its permanent citizens, Maui welcomes around twenty tourists per year – the annual total is around 2.35 million, each of whom stays on average for 6.7 days and spends at a rate of $171 per day. The island attracts a younger, more dynamic crowd than Waikīkī, principally because it offers Hawaii's most exhilarating range of vacation activities, including windsurfing, diving, sailing, snorkeling, cycling, hiking and horse-riding.

Around the island

Because the tradewinds throughout Hawaii blow consistently from the northeast, each island is much wetter on its north and east – windward – coasts, which are characterized by steep sea cliffs, inaccessible stream-cut valleys, and dense tropical vegetation, and has a drier and less fertile aspect on the west and south – leeward – sides. Maui is somewhat exceptional, in that each of its two distinct volcanoes has its own wet and dry sides. Nonethless, like its neighbors, Maui has concentrated almost all of its tourist development on its sunbaked leeward shorelines, with its major resorts either lying north of historic Lahaina in West Maui, like Kā 'anapali and Kapalua, or along the southwestern flanks of Haleakalā in what's known as South Maui, like Kīhei, Wailua and Mākena.

These resorts offer safe sandy beaches, ideal conditions for watersports, and all the amenities the modern holiday-maker could ask for. However, there's plenty to explore elsewhere on the island should you become tired of endlessly meandering between beach and brunch. To get a sense of Maui's history, the best place to start is strolling the streets of old **Lahaina**, once the capital of Hawaii and the rendezvous for the wild-living Pacific whaling fleet. The central isthmus or "neck" of the island, between the volcanoes, holds **Kahului**, the main commercial center, and the faded but somehow appealing town of **Wailuku**, standing guard over the once-sacred **'Īao Valley**.

To the east, Upcountry Maui, on the lower slopes of Haleakala, is an unexpected idyll, its cool green meadows and flower farms offering a pastoral escape from the bustle below. Higher up, beyond the clouds, you can look out across the many-hued volcanic wasteland of the vast Haleakala Crater, or dwindle into cosmic insignificance by hiking down into it.

Tortuous, demanding roads wind right around the windward coasts of both halves of the island. The better known of the two, the road to **Hāna** in the east, does not quite merit its legendary status, but its countless waterfalls and ravines make for a wonderful day-trip, culminating at lush

'Ohe'o Gulch. West Maui's equivalent, **Kahekili Highway**, enables visitors to explore the remote **Waihe'e Valley**, and offers a glimpse of how Maui must have looked before the tourists arrived.

Climate and when to go

Although Maui's high season for tourism is mid-December to March, when typical room rates rise by perhaps $25 per night, its climate remains pretty constant year-round.

Throughout the year, sea-level thermometers rarely drop below the low seventies Fahrenheit (around 22°C) in the daytime, or climb beyond the low eighties (around 28°C); at night the **temperature** seldom falls below the low sixties. The only reason to bring warm clothing is if you plan to drive up to the summit of Haleakalā; at dawn, the most popular time to visit, temperatures regularly drop below freezing point. In principle the **rainiest months** are from December to February, but where you are on the island makes far more difference than what time of year it is, and the main leeward tourist areas seldom receive more than the occasional light shower even then. The highest peak, in the West Maui Mountains – a place you almost certainly will never glimpse, let alone visit – is deluged by over 400 inches of rain per year, but all the coastal resorts, including Kā'anapali, barely five miles away, get less than twenty inches.

The only seasonal variation of any great significance for tourists is the state of the **ocean**. Along protected stretches of the shoreline, you can expect to be able to swim all year round in beautiful seas where the water temperature varies from 75°F to 82°F (24–28°C). Between October and April, however, high surf can render unsheltered beaches dangerous in the extreme, and some beaches even lose their sand altogether. Conditions on specific beaches are indicated throughout this book; see also the "Sea Sports and Safety" section on p.44.

Other factors that might influence the timing of your visit include the annual sojourn of migratory humpback whales in the offshore waters, between late November and late March; the peak season for the flowering trees along the Hāna Highway, in June; the blossoming of the extraordinary silversword plants of Haleakalā in July and August; and the island's various annual festivals, as detailed on p.41.

Despite the much-publicized onslaught of Hurricane Iniki on Kauai in September 1992, **hurricanes** are very rare in Hawaii. Similarly, **tsunamis** (often erroneously called tidal waves) hit perhaps once every fifty years, generally as a result of earthquakes or landslides caused by volcanic eruptions. Civil defense procedures adopted in such events are posted widely throughout the island.

BASICS

BASICS

Getting there from the US and Canada

O f the three airports on Maui, the one outside Kahului on the central isthmus is by far the largest and is the only one capable of handling trans-Pacific flights. In addition to receiving about ten daily nonstop flights from the US mainland, it also welcomes about fifty inter-island services each day from the state's principal airport, at Honolulu on Oahu, and a limited number of flights from the other Hawaiian islands. The travel time from LA or San Francisco to Honolulu is roughly five and a half hours, while flying from Honolulu to Kahului takes 25 minutes.

The lesser airport near **Kapalua** in West Maui receives about eight commuter flights each day from Honolulu, while even fewer flights go to and from the third, tiny airstrip, just north of remote **Hāna** on the east coast; for details on both airports, see p.16.

FARES

There is no high or low season for flights to Hawaii, and fares remain relatively consistent year-round. However, at **peak periods** – June to August and around Christmas, New Year's Day and Thanksgiving – services tend to be booked long in advance, and you might have to pay a slight premium. Flying on a weekday rather than a weekend saves anything from $50 to $200 on a round-trip.

The simplest way to save money is to buy a **package** deal including both flight and accommodation; see p.6 for a rough idea of what you're likely to pay. If you buy a flight only, through a **specialist flight agent**, aim to pay around $350 for a round-trip to Maui from the West Coast, and around $700 from New York.

AIRLINES AND FLIGHT AGENTS IN NORTH AMERICA

Airlines

Air Canada ⓣ 1-888/247-2262;
  ⓦ www.aircanada.ca
Aloha ⓣ 1-800/367-5250;
  ⓦ www.alohaairlines.com
American Airlines ⓣ 1-800/
  433-7300; ⓦ www.aa.com
American Trans Air ⓣ 1-800/
  435-9282; ⓦ www.ata.com
Continental ⓣ 1-800/523-3273;
  ⓦ www.continental.com

Delta ⓣ 1-800/221-1212;
  ⓦ www.delta.com
Hawaiian ⓣ 1-800/367-5320;
  ⓦ www.hawaiianair.com
Northwest ⓣ 1-800/225-2525;
  ⓦ www.nwa.com
TWA ⓣ 1-800/221-2000;
  ⓦ www.twa.com
United ⓣ 1-800/241-6522;
  ⓦ www.ual.com

GETTING THERE FROM THE US AND CANADA

Flight agents

Airhitch ☎ 1-800/326-2009;
  Ⓦ www.airhitch.org
Cheap Tickets ☎ 1-888/
  922-8849;
  Ⓦ www.cheaptickets.com
Council Travel ☎ 1-800/
  226-8624;
  Ⓦ www.counciltravel.com
Expedia Ⓦ www.expedia.com
High Adventure Travel
  Ⓦ www.airtreks.com
Hotwire Ⓦ www.hotwire. com

Orbitz Ⓦ www.orbitz.com
Priceline Ⓦ www.priceline.com
Qixo Ⓦ www.qixo.com
STA Travel ☎ 1-800/777-0112;
  Ⓦ www.sta-travel.com
TicketPlanet
  Ⓦ www.ticketplanet.com
Travelocity
  Ⓦ www.travelocity.com
Travelscape
  Ⓦ www.travelscape.com

FLIGHTS FROM THE WEST COAST

The number of nonstop flights between Kahului and the West Coast has increased greatly in recent years. Most come from **Los Angeles**; Hawaiian Airlines flies the route four times daily, United and American twice, and Delta once. Daily service from **San Francisco** is provided by United (twice daily) and American (once), while Hawaiian also flies once daily from Seattle. In addition, during peak season, Midwest-based charter airline American Trans Air offers regular flights to Kahului from both San Francisco and Los Angeles.

Nonetheless, the great majority of flights to Hawaii from the West Coast still arrive in **Honolulu**. Hawaiian, United, American, Continental, Northwest, and Delta fly to Honolulu from LA; Hawaiian, United, American, and Delta from San Francisco; Hawaiian and Northwest also fly from Seattle, as does American from San Jose. Hawaiian has services from Las Vegas, San Diego, and Portland as well.

FLIGHTS FROM THE EAST COAST

There are no scheduled nonstop flights from the **East Coast** to Hawaii (although American Trans Air has in recent years offered once-weekly nonstop flights during the busiest parts of the year between New York's JFK airport and Honolulu), so most visitors fly via California. American, however, flies direct to Honolulu **from Chicago** and **Dallas**, Northwest **from Minneapolis**, Delta **from Atlanta**, and TWA **from St Louis**; all take eight to ten hours.

PACKAGE DEALS FROM THE US AND CANADA

Buying your flight, accommodation and perhaps car rental as well as part of a package deal, as opposed to paying for each component separately, can bring down the cost of your vacation enormously – especially as Maui is small enough to explore in its entirety from a single base. A straightforward flight-and-hotel deal with one of the operators listed below can cost as little as $800 a week traveling from the West Coast, $1000 a week from New York. Anything more specialized is likely to be much more expensive, however: for example, Crane Tours and the Sierra Club both run week-long backpacking trips for around $1000 excluding airfare. Bear in mind also that most of the larger hotels listed in this book can arrange all-inclusive packages.

NORTH AMERICAN TOUR OPERATORS

American Airlines Vacations
📞 1-800/321-2121;
🌐 www.aa.com

Continental Airlines Vacations
📞 1-800/634-5555;
🌐 www.coolvacations.com

Crane Tours 📞 1-800/653-2545

Delta Certified Vacations 📞 1-800/654-6559;
🌐 www.deltavacations.com

Earthwatch 📞 617/926-8200;
🌐 www.earthwatch.org

Elderhostel 📞 1-877/426 8056;
🌐 www.elderhostel.org

Globus and Cosmos
🌐 www.globusandcosmos.com

Pacific Quest, Hale'iwa, HI 96712 📞 1-800/776-2518

Pleasant Hawaiian Holidays, Westlake Village, CA 📞 1-800/7HAWAII;
🌐 www.2hawaii.com

Questers Worldwide Nature Tours, New York, NY
📞 212/251-0444 or 1-800/468-8668;
🌐 www.questers.com

Sierra Club, San Francisco, CA
📞 415/977-5522;
🌐 www.sierraclub.org

Tauck Tours, Westport, CT
📞 1-800/788-7885;
🌐 www.tauck.com

TWA Getaway Vacations 📞 1-800/GETAWAY;
🌐 www.twa.com

United Vacations 📞 1-800/328-6877;
🌐 www.unitedvacations.com

World of Vacations, Etobicoke, ON 📞 416/620-8050;
🌐 www.macktravel.ca

FLIGHTS FROM CANADA

Getting to Hawaii from any **Canadian** city apart from Vancouver will almost certainly require you to change planes on the US mainland. United offers routings from **Toronto** via San Francisco for around CDN$1250, or from **Vancouver** for CDN$700–850; better from Vancouver is Northwest, with fares starting at CDN$650, via Seattle. Flying from either **Toronto** or **Montréal**, you can go via

Chicago or Dallas with American (CDN$1300); via Detroit or Minneapolis on Northwest (CDN$1250); or via Atlanta on Delta (CDN$1350).

Air Canada flies daily to Honolulu from **Toronto** (CDN$1200) via **Vancouver** (CDN$700). Canadian has daily nonstop flights to Honolulu from **Vancouver**, with fares around CDN$700, and flights three times weekly (Tues, Wed & Fri) from **Toronto** starting around CDN$1000. Through trips from **Montréal**, via Vancouver, start at around CDN$1050.

Canadians flying to Hawaii need passports, but not visas.

TRAVEL INSURANCE

Your existing insurance may offer full cover when you're away from home. Some homeowners' policies are valid on vacation, and credit cards such as American Express often include medical or other insurance, while most Canadians are covered for medical mishaps overseas by their health plans. If you're not already covered, either contact a specialist travel insurance company, or consider Rough Guides' own travel insurance, customized for our readers and available for anyone, of any nationality, traveling anywhere in the world.

Rough Guides offers two main plans: Essential, for basic, no-frills cover, and Premier, which offers more generous benefits. You can also take out annual multi-trip insurance, which covers you for any number of trips (maximum sixty days each) throughout the year. If you intend to be away for the whole year, the Adventurer policy will cover you for 365 days. Each plan can be supplemented with a "Hazardous Activities Premium" if you plan to indulge in sports considered dangerous, such as scuba diving.

For a policy quote, call the Rough Guide Insurance Line on US toll-free ☎1-866/220-5588, UK toll-free ☎0800 015 09 06, or, if you're calling from elsewhere ☎44 1243/621 046. Alternatively, get an online quote at Ⓦwww.roughguides.com/insurance.

Getting there from Australia and New Zealand

To get to Maui **from Australia and New Zealand**, you must fly via **Honolulu**. Flights are numerous, with little difference in prices. Five airlines provide daily service, with travel times of about nine hours.

Fares vary seasonally by around AUS/NZ$200–300. **Low** season counts as mid-January through February, and all of October and November; **high** season runs from mid-May to August and December to mid-January; and **shoulder** season is the rest of the year.

From Australia, most flights to Honolulu are out of **Sydney**, with daily nonstop service on Qantas, American Airlines and Air Canada for about AUS$1500 in low season or AUS$1750 in high season. For about the same price, United flies via Auckland.

From New Zealand, the best deals to Honolulu are on varying combinations of the United/Air New Zealand partnership out of Auckland, costing from NZ$1599 in low season up to NZ$1899 in high season, whether you fly nonstop, or via Fiji, Tonga or Papeete. Air Canada also flies nonstop, while Qantas can take you via either Sydney or Western Samoa.

PACKAGE DEALS

All the tour operators listed below specialize in providing **package deals** that include your flights, accommodation and car rental, at rates which will almost certainly work out cheaper than arranging things yourself.

AIRLINES, AGENTS AND TOUR OPERATORS IN AUSTRALIA AND NEW ZEALAND

Airlines

Air New Zealand ☎ 13/2476 (Aus); ☎ 0800/737 000 (NZ); ⓦ www.airnz.com

Air Pacific ☎ 1-800/230 150 (Aus); ☎ 09/379 2404 (NZ); ⓦ www.airpacific.com

Cathay Pacific ☎ 13/1747 (Aus); ☎ 09/379 0861 (NZ); ⓦ www.cathaypacific.com

Qantas ☎ 13/1313 (Aus); ☎ 0800/808 767 (NZ); ⓦ www.qantas.com.au

Singapore Airlines ☎ 13/1011 (Aus); ☎ 0800/808 909(NZ); ⓦ www.singaporeair.com

Flight agents

Anywhere Travel, Sydney
  ⊤ 02/9663 0411,
  ⓔ anywhere@ozemail.com.au
Budget Travel, Auckland
  ⊤ 09/366 0061
Destinations Unlimited,
  Auckland ⊤ 09/373 4033
Flight Centre, Sydney
  ⊤ 02/9235 3522; Auckland

  ⊤ 09/358 4310;
  ⓦ www.flightcentre.com.au
Northern Gateway, Darwin
  ⊤ 08/8941 1394,
  ⓔ oztravel@norgate.com.au
STA Travel ⊤ 1-300/360 960
  (Aus); ⊤ 09/366 6673 (NZ);
  ⓦ www.statravel.com.au

Specialist agents

Creative Holidays, Sydney
  ⊤ 02/9386 2111; ⓦ www
  .creativeholidays.com.au
Hawaiian Island Golf Tours,
  Sydney ⊤ 02/968 1778
Padi Travel Network, Sydney
  ⊤ 02/9417 2800;
  ⓦ www.padi.com.au

Surf Travel Co, Sydney
  ⊤ 02/9527 4522;
  ⓦ www.surftravel.com.au
**Sydney International Travel
  Centre**, Sydney ⊤ 02/9299
  8000; ⓦ www.sydneytravel
  .com.au

ENTRY REQUIREMENTS

Under the visa waiver policy, Australian and New Zealand passport holders who stay less than ninety days in the US **do not require visas** if they have an onward or return ticket. For longer stays, a twelve-month US tourist or business visa costs AUS$85.50/NZ$108. You'll need an application form – available from the US visa information service (⊤ 1-902/262 682) – one signed passport photo and your passport. For details, contact the US Embassy (Aus: 21 Moonah Place, Canberra ⊤ 02/6214 5600; NZ: 29 Fitzherbert Terrace, Thorndon, Wellington). In either country, apply and pay for US visas at any post office.

GETTING THERE FROM AUSTRALIA AND NEW ZEALAND

11

INSURANCE

Travel insurance, including medical cover, is essential in view of the high cost of health care in the US. For details of Rough Guides' own policies, see p.8.

Getting there from Britain and Ireland

Much the quickest and cheapest route from the UK or Ireland to Hawaii is via the mainland United States or Canada, so your options are more or less the same as they are for North Americans. A ten-hour flight across the Atlantic to the West Coast and a five-hour flight over the Pacific make for a very long journey. On the other hand, it is just possible to get to Maui on the same day you set off, thanks to the ten- or eleven-hour time difference.

Three airlines can get you **from London** to Maui in a single day – United, Virgin and Continental via Los

Angeles, or United only via San Francisco. In each case, you must connect with a United flight on to Kahului. If you're happy to fly **via Honolulu**, you can also take Delta via Atlanta, Air Canada via Toronto, or British Airways, in conjunction with Air New Zealand, via Vancouver.

From Ireland, Delta provides same-day connections from Dublin to Maui via Atlanta and Los Angeles, and from Shannon to Maui via New York and Los Angeles. Aer Lingus and American also offer daily services to Los Angeles, where you can join other carriers for the onward leg to Maui.

A typical round-trip ticket from London to Maui **costs** about £475 between January and March and up to as much as £800 in July and August.

PACKAGE DEALS

Several operators offer **package deals**, including flights, accommodation and car rental, that will definitely work out cheaper than anything you can arrange yourself. The Hawaiian Travel Center, for example, can arrange two weeks in a top Maui hotel for a little more than £1000 a head, including flights.

AIRLINES AND FLIGHT AGENTS

Airlines

Aer Lingus ☎ 020/8899 4747, ☎ 01/705 3333 (Dublin); Ⓦ www.aerlingus.ie
Air Canada ☎ 08700/524 7226; Ⓦ www.aircanada.ca

Air New Zealand ☎ 020/8741 2299; Ⓦ www.airnz.co.uk
American Airlines ☎ 0845/778 9789; Ⓦ www.aa.com
British Airways ☎ 0845/773

3377; Ⓦ www.britishairways
.com

Continental Ⓣ 0800/776464;
Ⓦ www.flycontinental.com

Delta Ⓣ 0800/414767,
Ⓣ 1800/414 767 (Dublin);
Ⓦ www.delta.com

Hawaiian Airlines
Ⓣ 01753/664406;

Ⓦ www.hawaiianair.com

KLM/Northwest Ⓣ 08705/074
074; Ⓦ www.klmuk.com

United Airlines Ⓣ 0845/844
4777; Ⓦ www.ual.com

Virgin Atlantic
Ⓣ 01293/747747;
Ⓦ www.virgin-atlantic.com

Agents

Bridge The World Ⓣ 020/
7911 0900;
Ⓦ www.bridgetheworld.com

STA Travel Ⓣ 0870/160 6070;
Ⓦ www.statravel.co.uk

Trailfinders Ⓣ 020/7628 7628;
Ⓦ www.trailfinders.com

Travel Bag Ⓣ 0870/900 1350;

Ⓦ www.travelbag.co.uk

USIT Campus Ⓣ 0870/240 1010;
Ⓦ www.usitcampus.oo.uk

USIT Now Belfast Ⓣ 028/9032
7111, Dublin Ⓣ 01/602 1777
or 677 8117, Cork Ⓣ 021/270
900, Derry Ⓣ 028/7137 1888;
Ⓦ www.usitnow.ie

TOUR OPERATORS IN BRITAIN AND IRELAND

Bon Voyage Ⓣ 0800/316 3012;
Ⓦ www.bon-voyage.co.uk

Contiki Tours Ⓣ 1-
888/CONTIKI;
Ⓦ www.contiki.com

Destination Pacific
Ⓣ 020/7400 7003

The Hawaiian Dream
Ⓣ 020/8552 1201

Hawaiian Travel Center
Ⓣ 020/7706 4142

North America Travel Service
Ⓣ 0845/766 0209

Page & Moy Ⓣ 0870/010 6250;
Ⓦ www.page-moy.co.uk

ENTRY REQUIREMENTS

Passport-holders from **Britain**, **Ireland** and most European countries do not require visas for trips to the United States of less than ninety days. Instead you simply fill in the **visa waiver form** handed out on incoming planes. Immigration control takes place at your point of arrival on US soil, which, if you're flying from Britain, will not be in Hawaii. For further details, contact the **US embassy** in Britain (24 Grosvenor Square, London W1A 1AE; ☎020/7499 9000; premium-rate visa hotline ☎0906/820 0290) or Ireland (42 Elgin Rd, Ballsbridge, Dublin; ☎01/668 8777). There is no British or Irish **consulate** in Hawaii.

INSURANCE

Travel insurance, including medical cover, is essential in view of the high cost of health care in the US. For details of Rough Guides' own policies, see p.8.

Inter-island travel

T he only way to reach Maui from any of the Hawaiian islands other than its closest neighbors Lanai and Molokai (each of which has a ferry service; see p.102) is to fly. In fact, the route between Honolulu and **Kahului** ranks as the busiest domestic route in the entire United States, with more than three million passengers each year. Both of the two major local airlines, **Hawaiian** and **Aloha**, fly this route about twice an hour, all day every day. In addition, Hawaiian operates two daily nonstop flights between Kahului and both **Hilo** and **Kona** on the Big Island, as well as one to **Kauai**, while Aloha serves the same Big Island cities and has two nonstop flights each day to and from Kauai. Aloha's affiliate, Island Air, also connects Kahului three times daily with **Molokai**. Pacific Wings (☎248-7700 or 1-888/575-4546; ⓦwww.pacificwings.com) operates one or two scheduled flights each day between Molokai and Kahului, while Paragon Air (☎1-800/428-1231), an on-demand charter service, connects Molokai with any airport on Maui.

Kapalua in West Maui – see p.131 – receives around eight Island Air flights from Honolulu each day. Scheduled flights to and from **Hāna**, the third, tiny airport, are currently only available on Pacific Wings (see above), which operates three or four daily round-trip flights between

Kahului and Hāna, and also one or two nonstop flights between Honolulu and Hāna.

No airline offers any flights later than 8pm.

FARES AND DISCOUNTS

Both Hawaiian and Aloha have standard one-way **fares** on all inter-island routes of about $85, although Hawaiian sells cut-price seats on early-morning and late-evening flights daily for more like $50. Both airlines offer all sorts of **discount packages**. The most common deal is a "book" of six tickets valid for any inter-island flight; these cost about $380 on Hawaiian or Aloha, and $420 on Aloha affiliate Island Air. Hawaiian's Hawaiian Inter-Island Pass allows unlimited travel for five days ($321), one week ($345), ten days ($409), and two weeks ($469), while Aloha's similar Visitor Seven-Day Island Pass costs $321.

Many **discount travel agents** in Hawaii sell airline coupons over the counter, offering individual tickets rather than entire "books" for about $65. Remember also that virtually all the resorts, hotels, B&B agencies and even hostels in Hawaii can arrange discounts on inter-island flights.

DISCOUNT TRAVEL AGENTS IN HAWAII

Cheap Tickets Inc,
US ☎ 1-888/922-8849, Oahu ☎ 947-3717, Maui ☎ 242-8094 or 244-7782;
ⓦ www.cheaptickets.com

Cut-rate Tickets,
US ☎ 1-800/297-5093, Kailua ☎ 326-2300, Hilo ☎ 969-1944, Kahului ☎ 871-7300, Lahaina ☎ 661-5800;
ⓦ www.cutratetickets.com

INTER-ISLAND TRAVEL

INTER-ISLAND CARRIERS

	Aloha	Island Air	Hawaiian
Web site	Ⓦ www.alohaair.com		Ⓦ www.hawaiianair.com
US & Can	Ⓣ 1-800/367-5250	Ⓣ 1-800/323-3345	Ⓣ 1-800/367-5320
Oahu	Ⓣ 484-1111	Ⓣ 484-2222	Ⓣ 1-800/882-8811
Big Island	Ⓣ 935-5771	Ⓣ 1-800/652-6541	Ⓣ 1-800/882-8811
Kauai	Ⓣ 245-3691	Ⓣ 1-800/652-6541	Ⓣ 1-800/882-8811
Lanai		Ⓣ 1-800/652-6541	Ⓣ 1-800/882-8811
Maui	Ⓣ 244-9071	Ⓣ 1-800/652-6541	Ⓣ 1-800/882-8811
Molokai		Ⓣ 1-800/652 6541	Ⓣ 1-800/882-8811

PACKAGE DEALS FROM HONOLULU

Waikīkī travel agents such as Magnum Tickets & Tours,
2134 Kalākaua Ave (Ⓣ923-7825), or Aloha Express, 2464
Kalākaua Ave (Ⓣ924-4030), offer inexpensive **package
tours** to Maui. Designed to suit short-stay visitors keen to
see more of Hawaii than just Oahu, they are available on
short notice. All-inclusive flight, accommodation and
rental-car deals cost about $100 per person for one night,
$130 for two nights, and $30 for each extra night. Fly-drive
deals typically start at about $40 per person one way.

Information and maps

A vast amount of information is available about Hawaii. Tourism is big business, and plenty of people and organizations are eager to assist you. The **Hawaii Visitors Bureau** has offices (known as "chapters") on every island; the one on Maui, run by the affiliated Maui Visitors Bureau, is responsible for promoting all of Maui County, which includes Molokai and Lanai as well as Maui itself. In addition to their two free glossy brochures – the statewide *Islands of Aloha* and Maui's own *Maui Travel Planner* – ask also for the annual *Connections Hawaii* booklet, which contains detailed listings for accommodation, restaurants and island activities.

In hotels, malls and airports, racks contain leaflets and free magazines such as *This Week* and *Maui Gold*. Resort areas such as Lahaina and Kīhei are full of **activities desks**, kiosks that act as information booths but are primarily concerned with selling tickets for cruises, horse rides, island tours, or whatever. Details on operators can be found on p.27, 49 and 55.

An ever-increasing amount of information is also available

on the **Internet** and World Wide Web, on sites such as Aloha from Hawaii, at ⓦ www.aloha-hawaii, and the official site at ⓦ www.gohawaii.com. Many Maui companies and organizations can be accessed via servers and directories such as ⓦ www.maui.net, ⓦ www.mauigateway.com, ⓦ www.westmaui .com, and ⓦ www.e-hawaii.com.

HAWAII VISITORS BUREAU OFFICES

In Hawaii

#801, Waikīkī Business Plaza, 2270 Kalākaua Ave, Honolulu, HI 96815, Admin (8th Floor) ⓣ 923-1811, ⓕ 924-0290; ⓦ www.gohawaii.com

Big Island Visitors Bureau, 250 Keawe St, Hilo, HI 96720 ⓣ 961-5797, ⓕ 961-2126; 250 Waikoloa Beach Drive, #B-15, Waikoloa, HI 96748 ⓣ 886-1655, ⓕ 886-1652; ⓦ www.bigisland.org

Kauai Visitors Bureau, 4334 Rice St, #101, Līhuʻe, HI 96766 ⓣ 1-800/262-1400 or 245-3971, ⓕ 246-9235; ⓦ www.kauaivisitorsbureau.org

Destination Lanai, PO Box 700, Lānai City, HI 96763

ⓣ 565-7600, ⓕ 565-9316; ⓦ www.visitmaui.com

Maui Visitors Bureau, 1727 Wili Pā Loop, Wailuku, HI 96793 ⓣ 244-3530 or 1-800/525-MAUI, ⓕ 244-1337; ⓦ www.visitmaui.com

Molokai Visitors Association, PO Box 960, Kaunakakai, HI 96748 ⓣ 553-3876, 1-800/800-6367 (US & Can), or 1-800/553-0404 (HI); ⓕ 553-5288, ⓦ www.molokai-hawaii.com

Oahu Visitors Bureau, 733 Bishop St, #1872, Honolulu, HI 96813 ⓣ 1-877/525-OAHU or 524-0722, ⓕ 521-1620; ⓦ www.visit-oahu.com

Elsewhere

Australia ⓣ02/9955 2619,
ⓕ9955 2171
Canada ⓣ604/669-6691,
ⓕ683-9114

New Zealand ⓣ09/379 3708,
ⓕ309 0725
United Kingdom ⓣ020/8941-
4009, ⓕ941-4011

MAPS

Much the best **map** of Maui is published by the University
of Hawaii at $3.95. Plenty of free maps are available on the
island itself – you'll get a map booklet with your rental car,
for example. These can be useful for pinpointing specific
hotels and restaurants, but only the University of Hawaii
map is at all reliable for minor roads.

INFORMATION AND MAPS

Costs, money and banks

Although it's possible to have an inexpensive vacation in Hawaii, prices on the islands are consistently higher than in the rest of the US. About 85 percent of the state's food and 92 percent of its fuel is shipped in, and the cost of living is about forty percent above the US average.

How much you spend per day is, of course, up to you, but it's hard to get breakfast for under $6, a cheap lunch easily comes to $10, and an evening meal in a restaurant, with drinks, is likely to be $25–30. Even the cheapest hotel or B&B is likely to charge well over $60 for a double room, and a rental car with gas won't cost less than $25 per day. It's easy to spend $75 per person per day before you do anything; pay for a snorkel cruise, let alone a helicopter ride, and you've cleared $100.

The state **sales tax** of 4 percent on all transactions is almost never included in the prices displayed. Hotels impose an additional 7.25 percent tax, adding a total premium of more than eleven percent to accommodation bills.

MONEY AND BANKS

US dollar **travelers' checks** are the best way to carry significant quantities of money, for both American and foreign visitors; they offer the security of knowing that lost or stolen checks will be replaced. Foreign currency, whether cash or travelers' checks, can be hard to exchange, so foreign travelers should change some of their money into dollars at home. However, Maui is absolutely bursting with **ATM machines**, which accept most cards issued by domestic and foreign banks. Call your bank before you leave home if you're in any doubt.

For many services, it's taken for granted that you'll pay with a **credit card**. Hotels and car-rental companies routinely require an imprint whether or not you intend to use it to pay.

Transport and tours

f you want to travel around Maui you're going to have to drive. It's possible to use a cab or shuttle service to get from the airport to your hotel, and there's a limited bus network, but without a car your movements will be extremely restricted.

RENTING A CAR OR MOTORCYCLE

The demand for **rental cars** in Hawaii is so great that competition among rival suppliers is fierce, and prices are among the lowest in the US. All the major rental chains are represented at **Kahului Airport**. In addition, Avis has outlets in Kīhei, Wailea and Kāʻanapali, and also at Kapalua airport; Dollar is at Hāna and Kapalua airports as well as in Kāʻanapali; Hertz and National are in Kāʻanapali and at Kapalua airport; and Alamo and Budget are represented in Kāʻanapali. Call the toll-free numbers for reservations; individual offices cannot advise on rates or availability. Local alternatives include Wheels R Us, which rents cars, motorcycles and mopeds, and accept drivers under 25, with outlets in Lahaina (℡667-7751), Kahului (℡871-6858), and Kīhei (℡875-1221). Vans adapted for carrying **windsurfing** equipment can be rented from Al West's in Kahului (℡877-0090; ⓦwww.mauivans.com).

With so much competition, it's hard to quote specific prices, but a target rate for the cheapest economy car with unlimited mileage should be around $40 per day or $200 per week. No companies rent cars to anyone under 21. Before you commit yourself to a rate, check whether the **airline** that flies you to Maui, or your **hotel, B&B** or **hostel**, can offer a discount on car rental.

Motorcycles can be rented from Island Riders (ⓦwww.islandriders.com), which has outlets in Lahaina (℡661-9966) and Kīhei (℡874-0311), or Hawaiian Riders in Lahaina (℡662-4386).

CAR RENTAL CHAINS

Alamo ☎ 1-800/327-9633 (US, Can & HI); 0870/606 0100 (UK); ⓦ www.alamo.com

Avis ☎ 1-800/331-1212 (US & Can); 1-800/831-8000 (HI); 020/8848 8733 (UK); 1-800/225 533 (Aus); 0800/655 111 (NZ); ⓦ www.avis.com

Budget ☎ 1-800/527-0700 (US, Can & HI); 0800/181181 (UK); 1-300/362 848 (Aus); 0800/ 652 227 (NZ); ⓦ www.budgetrentacar.com

Dollar ☎ 1-800/800-4000 (US & Can); 1-800/367-7006 (HI); 01895/233300 (UK); 1-800/358 008 (Aus); ⓦ www.dollar.com

Hertz ☎ 1-800/654-3001 (US & HI); 1-800/263-0600 (Can); 0870/844 8844 (UK); 1-800/550 067 (Aus); 0800/655 955 (NZ); ⓦ www.hertz.com

National ☎ 1-800/227-7368 (US, Can & HI); 0870/536 5365 (UK); 09/537 2582 (NZ); ⓦ www.nationalcar.com

DRIVING

In the absence of adequate roads to cope with its volume of tourists, the **traffic** on Maui is consistently bad. The worst area is the narrow **Honoapi'ilani Highway**, which leads south from the central isthmus to the resorts of West Maui; the universal habit of suddenly stopping en route to watch whales in the ocean doesn't help. At least the snail's pace along the **Haleakalā** and **Hāna** highways is due to the natural obstacles along the way, and gives you a chance to appreciate the scenery. Car-rental companies forbid their clients to use certain roads altogether, notably the **Kahekili Highway** in West Maui (see p.139), and the remote **Pi'ilani Highway** along the southern coast of East Maui (see p.221). Both roads are in fact passable most of the time; the ban has more to do with the difficulty of providing assistance should you happen to break down.

Keep a close eye on your fuel gauge; **gas stations** are common around the major towns and resorts, but in some areas you can drive fifty miles without seeing one. Typical prices are significantly higher than in the rest of the US.

CABS AND SHUTTLE SERVICES

Maui has less of a **public transport** system than any of the other major Hawaiian islands. However, as detailed on p.67, the Maui Airporter Shuttle (☎877-7308 or 1-800/259-2627) and TransHawaiian (☎877-0380 or 1-800/231-6984) run regular scheduled **buses** from the airport at Kahului to Kā'anapali and Lahaina. Taxis and **shuttle buses** are operated by companies such as Speedishuttle (☎875-8070) and Airport Shuttle (☎661-6667). Local bus services in the Kā'anapali and Lahaina areas are summarized on p.124 and p.101.

FLIGHTS

If you're really in a hurry, it's possible to take a fifteen-minute **flight** between Kahului and Hāna on Pacific Wings; see p.16.

CYCLING

Several companies rent out **mountain bikes**, typically at $20–25 per day or up to $100 per week. Among them are South Maui Bicycles, 1993 S Kīhei Rd, Kīhei (☎874-0068); West Maui Cycles, 840 Waine'e St, Lahaina (☎661-9005); and Island Biker, 415 Dairy Rd, Kahului (☎877-7744). Chris' Bike Adventures (☎871-2453) can arrange customized **bike tours** of Maui. A full list of operators running **downhill bike rides** on Haleakalā appears on p.180.

Be warned that neither motorbikes nor bicycles are allowed on the hiking trails in national or state parks.

BUS TOURS

The most popular **bus tours** on the island run around East Maui to Hāna (typically costing around $70 per person from South Maui, $85 from West Maui), and up the volcano to Haleakalā Crater ($30–40). Operators include Akina Aloha Tours (℡ 879-2828), Polynesian Adventure Tours (℡ 877-4242), Ekahi Tours (℡ 877-9775), and Ali'i Coach Service (℡ 871-2544).

FLIGHT-SEEING TOURS

All the **helicopter** companies listed below **run tours** from Kahului airport; none currently operates from Kapalua. Maui is large enough for a full round-island flight to take more than an hour and cost about $200; if you'd prefer a shorter flight, try a twenty- or thirty-minute loop over West Maui. For discounted rates, buy tickets through an activities operator such as Tom Barefoot's, as detailed on p.45; target prices range from $75 for a twenty-minute jaunt to $150 to fly over Haleakalā and Hāna, or more than $200 to fly over to Molokai or Lanai as well. Visibility is almost always best in the early morning.

It's also possible to take **airplane** or "fixed wing" tours. Volcano Air Tours (℡ 877-5500; ⓦ www.volcanoairtours .com) flies across to the active volcano on the Big Island from Kapalua or Kahului, for about $250. Pacific Wings (℡ 873-0877; ⓦ www.pacificwings.com) runs a full-day flying tour to Hāna from Kahului on Tuesdays only, featuring two fifteen-minute flights and a ground tour by coach, for $190, and a similar day-long tour to Kalaupapa on Molokai, on Wednesdays for $210. They even offer a private **four-hour flying lesson**, touching down at Lanai, for $322.

HELICOPTER TOUR OPERATORS

Air Maui ⓣ 877-7005;
  ⓦ www.airmaui.com
Alexair Helicopters ⓣ 871-
  0792 or 1-888/418-8458;
  ⓦ www.helitour.com
Blue Hawaiian Helicopters
  ⓣ 871-8844 or 1-880/745-
  2583;

ⓦ www.bluehawaiian.com
Hawaii Helicopters ⓣ 877-
  3900 or 1-800/994-9099;
  ⓦ www.hawaii-helicopters.com
MauiScape ⓣ 877-7272
Sunshine Helicopters ⓣ 871-
  0722 or 1-800/469-3000;
  ⓦ www.sunshinehelicopters
  .com

Accommodation

M aui is an extreme example of a typical Hawaiian
pattern, in that most of the accommodation for
tourists is situated in the drier and less scenic parts
of the island. Most of its hotels and condos are either along
the leeward coast of West Maui, in the highly developed
strip that runs from Lahaina by way of Kā'anapali up to
Kapalua, or on the southwest shores of East Maui, in Kīhei,
Wailea and Mākena. If golf or a beach is your main priority,

ACCOMMODATION PRICE CODES

Throughout this book, accommodation prices have been graded with the symbols below, covering the full spectrum of rooms in each establishment and ranging upward from the quoted rate for the least expensive double room for most of the year, not including state taxes of 11.25 percent.

Hostels, in which dorm beds are usually available for $15–20, have been coded with symbol ❶ for clarity. Both hostels and budget hotels tend to keep the same rates throughout the year, but in more expensive properties rooms that are normally priced above $70 often rise by $15–30 in peak seasons – from Christmas to Easter and June to August.

❶ up to $40	❹ $100–150	❼ $250–300
❷ $40–70	❺ $150–200	❽ $300–400
❸ $70–100	❻ $200–250	❾ over $400

that's fine; most of Maui's historic sites and most attractive landscapes are, however, a long way away. Prospective visitors who think of Hawaii as expensive won't be reassured by the official statistics showing that in 2001 the average cost of a single night's accommodation on Maui was $220, but that figure too was heavily skewed by the lavish upscale resorts of Kā'anapali and Mākena; it's perfectly possible to find a good room for less than half that.

Travelers looking for a paradise-island hideaway would do better to consider one of the many plush little **B&Bs** tucked away in the meadows of Upcountry Maui and the rainforests around Hāna in the east. (Don't expect to spot any as you drive around; county regulations forbid B&Bs to display signs.) If you're not planning to rent a car, **Lahaina** is the only place where you can stay in a real town with sightseeing, beaches and restaurants within easy walking

ACCOMMODATION

distance. For **budget travelers**, the cheapest options of all are in faded downtown Wailuku.

Few visitors bother to stay in more than one place during their time on Maui. Although it can involve a lot of driving, the island is just about small enough to make it possible to get to most places and back in a single day.

RESORTS

If you haven't visited a tropical destination before, you may not be familiar with the concept of a **resort**. These gigantic, sprawling enclaves, each holding hundreds or even thousands of rooms, are more than just hotels; often far from any significant town, they have their own restaurants, stores, swimming pools, beaches, golf courses, tennis courts, walking trails and so on, all designed to ensure that guests can spend their entire vacations without ever feeling the need to leave the property.

Prime examples on Maui include the *Sheraton*, *Marriott* and *Hyatt Regency* in **Kā'anapali**, the *Ritz-Carlton* in **Kapalua**, and the *Four Seasons* and *Kea Lani* in **Wailea**. Even if you book as part of a package, you're very unlikely to find a room in any of these for less than $200 per night.

HOTELS AND CONDOS

In terms of guest rooms, standards in the resorts are high, but you can also find high-quality rooms in the conventional **hotels**. En-suite bathrooms can be taken for granted, and most rooms have balconies (known as *lānais*). The distinction between a hotel room and a **condominium** apartment is not always clear; the same building may hold some private condos and others let by the night to casual guests. An individual condo is likely to be more comfortable and better equipped than a typical hotel room, often with a kitchenette, but conversely the building as a whole may not have a lobby, daily housekeeping service, restaurants or other amenities. Maui's main concentrations of condos are found between **Honokōwai** and **Nāpili** in West Maui, and in **Kīhei** in South Maui. Like the nearby hotels, they tend to charge upward of $100 per night for a double room.

BED AND BREAKFASTS

In Hawaii the definition of a **bed and breakfast** stretches from a simple room or two in a private home, through self-contained, self-catering cottages to luxurious fifteen-room inns. In principle, however, the standards are always very high. The cheapest rooms, perhaps sharing a bathroom, start at around $70, while for $90 or more per night you can expect your own well-furnished apartment, with all facilities.

Most small-scale B&Bs tend to be away from the beaches, in rural areas that otherwise offer little choice of accommodation. The greatest concentrations are among the meadows of Upcountry Maui, and at the start and end of the road to Hāna, along the northeastern flanks of Haleakalā. The owners are often friendly and full of advice on making the most of your vacation, but it's unusual to find a B&B run by anyone other than recent immigrants from the mainland.

For a comprehensive selection of top-quality Maui B&Bs, contact **Hawaii's Best Bed & Breakfasts** (PO Box 563, Kamuela, HI 96743; ☎885-4550 or 1-800/262-9912, ⓕ885-0559; ⓦwww.bestbnb.com).

HOSTELS

A couple of budget **hostels** in **Wailuku** – the *Banana Bungalow* and the *Northshore Inn* (both reviewed on p.76) –

ACCOMMODATION

ROUGH GUIDE FAVORITES: ACCOMMODATION

Banana Bungalow, Wailuku (**①**)	p.76
Wailana Inn, Kīhei (**③**)	p.146
Old Lahaina House, Lahaina (**③**)	p.104
Silver Cloud Guest Ranch, Kula (**③–⑤**)	p.171
The Mauian, Nāpili (**④–⑤**)	p.133
Best Western Pioneer Inn, Lahaina (**④**)	p.103
Hotel Hāna-Maui, Hāna (**⑥**)	p.212
Hāmoa Bay Bungalow, Hāna (**⑥**)	p.212
Embassy Vacation Resort, Honokōwai (**⑧**)	p.132
Kea Lani Hotel, Wailea (**⑧–⑨**)	p.156

offer dormitory beds for under $15 per night. Both are strongly geared toward young surfers, and neither offers any reduction for members of youth hostel organizations.

ACCOMMODATION

Food and drink

I f you imagine that eating in Hawaii will consist of an endless feast of fresh fruits and fishes, you'll be disappointed to find that the islands are not bountiful Gardens of Eden: the state produces less than twenty percent of the food it consumes. Polynesian cuisine can mean little more than putting a pineapple ring on top of a burger, and, amazingly, more than half of all the Spam eaten in the United States is consumed in Hawaii.

However, two strong factors work in your favor. First of all, there's the **ethnic diversity**. Immigrants from all over the world have brought their national dishes and recipes, and traditions have mingled to create intriguing new cuisines. Second, the presence of thousands of **tourists**, prepared to pay top rates for good food, means that the island has some truly superb restaurants.

Food in general is often referred to as **kaukau**, and it's also worth knowing that **pūpūs** (pronounced *poo-poos*) is a general term for little snacks, the kind of finger food that is given away in early-evening happy hours.

THE HAWAIIAN TRADITION

Cooking in ancient Hawaii was the responsibility of the menfolk, who prepared food for themselves and their wives in separate calabash gourds and ovens. Women were forbidden to eat pork, bananas or coconuts, as well as several kinds of fish, or to eat with the men.

The staple food was *poi*, a purple-gray paste produced by pounding the root of the *taro* plant. *Poi* is eaten with the bare hands and comes in three basic grades, one-finger, two-finger or three-finger, according to how many fingers it takes to scoop a satisfactory portion out of the pot – one-finger is the thickest and best.

These days, there's no such thing as an authentic "Hawaiian" restaurant; the closest you can come to eating traditional foods is at a *lū'au* or "banquet." Primarily tourist money-spinners, and always accompanied by pseudo-Polynesian entertainment, these offer the chance to sample such dishes as *kālua pork*, an entire pig wrapped in *ti* leaves and baked all day in an underground oven known as an *imu*; *poke*, which is raw fish, shellfish or octopus, marinated with soy and Oriental seasonings; and *lomi-lomi*, a dish made with raw salmon. As *lū'aus* always involve mass catering and canteen-style self-service, the food itself, however, rarely provides sufficient incentive to go.

BUDGET RESTAURANTS

Maui has its fair share of outlets of the national fast-food chains, but typical budget **restaurants**, **diners** and **takeout stands** serve a hybrid cuisine that draws on the traditions of the US mainland along with Japan, China, Korea and the Philippines, giving the resultant mixture a slight but definite Hawaiian twist.

Breakfast tends to be the standard combination of eggs, meat, pancakes, muffins or toast. At midday, the usual dish is the **plate lunch**, a molded tray holding meat and rice as well as potato or macaroni salad and costing from $5 to $8; *bento* is the Japanese equivalent, with mixed meats and rice,

MAUI LŪ'AUS

The *lū'aus* listed below charge anything from $60 to $90 per adult, and $28–60 per child; you can buy discounted tickets, offering perhaps $10 off, from activities operators all over the island. While the Feast at Lele offers the best food – see p.116 – the Old Lahaina Lū'au is generally considered to be the best value of them all.

Beachcombers Lū'au, *Royal Lahaina Resort*, Kā'anapali ℡ 661-9119. Daily 5pm. $89.

Drums of the Pacific, *Hyatt Regency Maui*, Kā'anapali ℡ 667-4420. Daily 5pm.

The Feast at Lele, 505 Front St, Lahaina ℡ 667-5353. Tues, Wed, Fri & Sat 5.30pm. $89.

Marriott Lū'au, *Maui Marriott*, Kā'anapali ℡ 661-5828. Daily 5pm.

Old Lahaina Lū'au, Lahaina Cannery Mall, Lahaina ℡ 667-1998. Daily 5.30pm. $69.

Royal Lahaina Lū'au, *Royal Lahaina Resort*, Kā'anapali ℡ 661-9119. Daily 4.45pm. $67.

Wailea Sunset Lū'au, *Renaissance Wailea Beach Resort*, Wailea ℡ 879-4900. Tues, Thurs & Sat 5.30pm. $68.

Wailea's Finest Lū'au, *Outrigger Wailea Resort*, Wailea ℡ 879-1922. Mon, Tues, Thurs & Fri 5pm. $62.

while in Filipino diners you'll be offered **adobo**, pork or chicken stewed with garlic and vinegar. Korean barbecue, **kal bi** – prepared with sesame – is especially tasty, while **saimin** (pronounced *sy-min* not *say-min*), a bowl of clear soup filled with noodles and other ingredients, has become something of a national dish. Finally, the carbohydrate-packed **loco moco** is a fried egg served on a hamburger with gravy and rice.

FOOD AND DRINK

FINE DINING

Many of Maui's best **restaurants** are in its most expensive hotels, and a meal in the showcase resorts of Kā'anapali and Wailea can cost as much as $100 per head. However, less exclusive communities such as Lahaina, Kīhei and Pā'ia all manage to support a wide range of excellent eating options at more affordable prices. In the last few years, a distinctive Hawaiian cuisine has begun to emerge, known variously as **Pacific Rim**, **Euro-Asian**, or **Hawaii Regional**. In its ideal form it consists of combining foods and techniques from all the countries and ethnic groups that have figured in Hawaiian history, using the freshest ingredients possible. Top chefs, such as Jean-Marie Josselin of the *Pacific Café* and Roy Yamaguchi of *Roy's*, preserve natural flavors by flash-frying meat and fish like the Chinese, baking it whole like the Hawaiians or even serving it raw like the Japanese. The

ROUGH GUIDE FAVORITES: EATING

These are not so much the ten best restaurants on Maui as ten very good places to eat, drawn from all price categories and arranged in ascending order of price.

FOOD AND DRINK

effect is enhanced with Thai herbs and spices, and by the inventiveness of modern Californian cooking.

Maui also has plenty of conventional **American** shrimp and steak specialists, as well as high-class **Italian**, **Thai** and **Chinese** places. Many restaurants offer all-you-can-eat **buffets** one or more nights of the week; they all sacrifice quality to quantity, so you might as well go for the cheaper ones. Lastly, to cater for that much-prized customer, the Japanese big-spender, some large hotels have very good Japanese restaurants.

HAWAIIAN FISH

Although the ancient Hawaiians were expert offshore fishermen, as well as being sophisticated fish farmers, the great majority of the **fish** eaten in Hawaii nowadays is imported. Local fishing is on too small a scale to meet the demand, and in any case many of the species that tourists expect to find thrive in much cooler waters. Thus the salmon and crab featured on menus here come from Alaska, and the mussels from New Zealand, although Maine lobsters are now being farmed in the cold waters of the deep ocean off the Big Island.

However, if you feel like being adventurous, you should get plenty of opportunity to try some of the Pacific species caught nearby. If the list below still leaves you in the dark, personal recommendations include *opah*, which is chewy and salty like swordfish; the chunky *'ōpakapaka*, which because of its red color (associated with happiness) is often served on special occasions; the succulent white *ono* (which means "delicious" in Hawaiian); and the dark *'ahi*, the most popular choice for sashimi.

FOOD AND DRINK

TYPES OF HAWAIIAN FISH

'ahi	yellow-fin tuna	*mano*	shark
a'u	swordfish or marlin	*moi*	thread fish
		onaga	red snapper
'ehu	red snapper	*ono*	mackerel or tuna-like fish
hapu'upu'u	sea bass		
hebi	spear fish	*'opae*	shrimp
kake	barracuda	*opah*	moonfish
kalekale	pink snapper	*'ōpakapaka*	pink snapper
kamano	salmon	*papio*	pompano
keme	red goat fish	*uhu*	parrot fish
lehi	yellow snapper	*uku*	gray snapper
mahimahi	dorado or dolphin fish	*ulua*	jack fish
		weke	goat fish

DRINK

The usual range of **wines** (mostly Californian, though Maui does have its own tiny Tedeschi Winery; see p.176) and **beers** is sold at Maui restaurants and bars. At some point, however, every visitor seems to insist on getting wiped out by a tropical **cocktail** or two. Among the most popular are the **Mai Tai**, which should contain at least two kinds of rum, together with orange Curaçao and lemon juice; the **Blue Hawaii**, in which vodka is colored with blue Curaçao; and the **Planter's Punch**, made with light rum, grenadine, bitters and lemon juice.

Tap **water** is safe to drink. If you're hiking, however, never drink untreated stream water.

FOOD AND DRINK

Communications
and media

Telephone connections on and between the Hawaiian Islands and to the rest of the US are generally efficient and reliable, but **mail services** can be slow.

To make an international call to Hawaii, dial your country's international access code, then 1 for the US, then 808 for Hawaii. To place an international call from Hawaii, dial 011, then the relevant country code (Britain is 44, Ireland is 353, Canada is 1, Australia is 61 and New Zealand is 64).

PHONES AND THE MAIL

The **telephone area code** for the entire state of Hawaii is ☎808. Calls from anywhere on Maui to anywhere else on the island count as local; you don't need to dial the area code and it costs a flat-rate 25¢ on pay phones. When calling any of the other islands, you must dial 1-808 before the number.

Hotels impose huge surcharges, so it's best to use a **phone card** for long-distance calls. In preference to the ones issued by the major phone companies, you'll find it simpler and cheaper to choose from the various **pre-paid** cards sold in almost all groceries and general stores.

Post offices usually open between 8.30am and 4pm on weekdays, and for an hour or two on Saturday mornings. **Mail services** are slow, because all the mail must go via Honolulu. Allow a week for anywhere in the US, two weeks or more for the rest of the world.

NEWSPAPERS

Maui's principal homegrown **newspaper** is the daily *Maui News*, while the weekly *Lahaina News* focuses on West Maui in more detail, and the bi-weekly *Haleakalā Times* concentrates on environmental issues. All can be reached on the Internet via the Maui Net Newsstand, on ⓦ www.maui.net/news.html. Both the *Honolulu Advertiser* and *Honolulu Star-Bulletin* are also widely distributed and cover island news. The literature listed on p.19 is of no use whatsoever, even for local news. As for **other US newspapers**, only *USA Today* is widely available, although the larger resorts tend to stock the major West Coast dailies. You can buy almost any publication in the world at Borders in Kahului.

Entertainment and festivals

Although it can't compete with the big-city atmosphere of Honolulu, and island residents jokingly refer to the hour of 10pm as "Maui midnight," by Hawaiian standards Maui offers visitors a reasonably lively **nightlife**.

As ever, most of the activity is confined to the tourist ghettoes, and the resort hotels in particular, but if you enjoy wandering the streets from bar to bar the oceanfront at **Lahaina** provides almost the same buzz as Waikīkī. The south coast, from **Kīhei** on down, is too spread out to have the same intensity, but it's always party-time somewhere along the strip. *Maui Brews*, in the Lahaina Center, and *Hapa's Brew Haus* in Kīhei are the likeliest venues to catch contemporary Hawaiian music. The *Tsunami* at the *Grand Wailea* resort in Wailea is renowned as Maui's glitziest nightclub.

Away from the resorts, the local community of rock exiles and ex-Californians makes *Casanova's* in Upcountry **Makawao** an amazing venue for such a tiny town, while the Maui Arts and Cultural Center by the harbor in **Kahului** attracts big-name touring bands.

MAUI HOLIDAYS AND FESTIVALS

Jan 1	New Year's Day (public holiday)
Jan	Maui Pro Surf Meet: surfing competition, Honolua Bay and Ho'okipa Beach
3rd Mon in Jan	Dr Martin Luther King Jr's Birthday (public holiday)
3rd week in Jan	Hula Bowl Football All-Star Classic: college football tournament, War Memorial Stadium
3rd Mon in Feb	President's Day (public holiday)
early March	Whale Fest Week: whale-related events, Lahaina and Kā'anapali
early March	Hawaii Pro Am Windsurfing Tournament: windsurfing contest, Ho'okipa Beach
mid-March	Maui Marathon, Kahului to Kā'anapali
March 26	Prince Kūhiō Day (public holiday)
March/April	East Maui Taro Festival, Hāna
early April	Maui O'Neill Pro Board: windsurfing contest, Ho'okipa Beach
Easter Monday	Public holiday
late April	David Malo Day, Lahainaluna High School, Lahaina
late April	Maui County Agricultural Trade Show, 'Ulupalakua Ranch
May 1	Lei Day (public holiday)
late May	Da Kine Classic: windsurfing competition, Kanahā Beach
late May	Bankoh Ho'omana'o Challenge: outrigger canoe race, Kā'anapali to Waikīkī
last Mon in May	Memorial Day (public holiday); In Celebration of Canoes, Lahaina
June 11	Kamehameha Day (public holiday)

June	Bankoh Kihoʻalu, slack-key guitar festival, Maui Arts & Cultural Center
end June	Art Night: music and arts festival, Lahaina
July 4	Independence Day (public holiday); Makawao Rodeo, Makawao
early July	Quicksilver Cup: windsurfing competition, Kanahā Beach
early Aug	Hawaii State Championships: windsurfing competition, Kanahā Beach
3rd Fri in Aug	Admission Day (public holiday)
1st Mon in Sept	Labor Day (public holiday)
mid-Sept	A Taste of Lahaina: food festival, Lahaina
late Sept	Run to the Sun: foot race, Pāʻia to Haleakalā
Sept/Oct	Aloha Festival: consecutive week-long festivals on each island
2nd Mon in Oct	Columbus Day (public holiday)
early Oct	Maui County Fair, Wailuku
Oct 31	Halloween Mardi Gras of the Pacific, Lahaina
early Nov	Aloha Classic World Wavesailing Championships: windsurfing competition, Hoʻokipa
Nov 11	Veterans' Day (public holiday)
Last Thurs in Nov	Thanksgiving (public holiday)
Dec 25	Christmas Day (public holiday)
Dec 31	First Night arts festival, Maui Arts & Cultural Center

Note that the exact dates of surfing contests, and in some cases the venues as well, depend on the state of the waves.

ENTERTAINMENT AND FESTIVALS

Sea sports and safety

Maui's tourism industry is rooted in the picture-book appeal of its endless palm-fringed sandy beaches and crystal-clear fish-filled turquoise ocean. More so than any other island, Maui also offers almost infinite opportunities for sea sports, ranging from swimming through snorkeling, scuba diving, fishing and whale-watching, to Hawaii's greatest gift to the world, the noble art of surfing. It's all too easy, however, to forget that Hawaiian beaches can be deadly as well as beautiful, and you need to know exactly what you're doing before you enter the water. As well as the general ocean safety advice in this section (see p.51), safety tips for specific beaches are given throughout this guide.

No one owns any stretch of beach in Hawaii. Every beach in the state – defined as the area below the vegetation line – is regarded as public property. That doesn't mean that you're entitled to stroll across any intervening land between the ocean and the nearest highway; always use the clearly signposted "public right of way" footpaths. Whatever impression the large oceanfront hotels may attempt to convey, they can't stop you from using "their" beaches; they can also only restrict, but not refuse to supply, parking places for non guests.

What constitutes the "**best beach**" on the island is a matter of taste, but be sure to visit **Oneloa** (or **Big**) **Beach**, south of Mākena, and the nudist enclave of **Little Beach** alongside (p.161); the resort beaches at **Kā'anapali** (p.124) and **Kapalua** (p.131); **Polo Beach** in Wailea (p.158); and the black-sand beach at **Wai'ānapanapa State Park** (p.206).

OCEAN FUN

With average water temperatures of between 75°F and 82°F (24–28°C), the sea around Maui is irresistible, and most visitors are tempted to try at least one or two **ocean sports**. **Activities operators** in all the tourist areas, especially along Front Street in Lahaina, offer **cut-price deals** well below the advertised rates. Tom Barefoot's Cashback Tours – at 834 Front St, Lahaina (☎661-8889 or 1-888/222-3601; ⓦwww.tombarefoot.com) and Dolphin Plaza, 2395 S Kīhei Rd, Kīhei (☎879-4100) – and The Activity Connection (☎661-1038; ⓦwww.beachactivityguide.com) are among the few that don't also try to sell time-shares. Both run Web sites that detail every imaginable island activity, along with the latest prices.

SNORKELING

Probably the easiest activity for beginners is **snorkeling**. Equipment is available for rent all over the island, while among the best sites are **Kā'anapali Beach** and **Honolua Bay** in West Maui, and **La Pérouse Bay** beyond Mākena in South Maui. The most popular snorkeling spot of all, the tiny islet of **Molokini**, can be reached only by boat, on one of the **snorkel cruises** listed on p.90.

SCUBA AND SNUBA

Scuba diving is both expensive and demanding, but with endless networks of submarine lava tubes to explore, and the chance to get close to some amazing marine life forms, Maui is a great dive destination. The most popular spots are in the vicinity of **Molokini Crater**, off South Maui. Learners and inexperienced divers start by exploring the sheltered, shallow "Inside Crater" area, and eventually progress to the "Back Wall" with its huge drop-offs. There's also good **shore diving** at Black Rock in Kā'anapali and in La Pérouse Bay, while the most spectacular dives of all lie off southern Lanai, within easy reach of a day's boat-trip from Maui.

Many companies arrange **diving excursions** in the waters off Maui and Lanai, with the largest operator being **Maui Dive Shop**; full listings appear on p.49. Typical prices start at around $70 for a one-tank trip, $90 for two tanks. Equipment rental works out at an additional $20–25. Almost all offer multi-day packages for beginners, leading to PADI certification; a typical price would be $220–250 for three days, and $300 for four. Note also that there's a considerable overlap with the Molokini cruise ships listed on p.90.

Be sure not to dive within 24 hours of flying, or ascending to any significant altitude. The summit of Haleakalā is certainly out of bounds, while you should ask your dive operator for advice before even driving into the Upcountry.

For a taste of what it's all about, you might like to try **snuba** – snorkeling from a boat, with a longer breathing tube.

SURFING

The nation that invented **surfing** – long before the foreigners came – remains its greatest arena. A recurring theme in ancient legends has young men frittering away endless days in the waves rather than facing up to their duties (see p.243); now young people from all over the world flock to Hawaii to follow suit. Surf aficionados rate several Maui sites as equal to anything on Oahu's fabled North Shore, with **Honolua Bay** on the northern tip of West Maui and **Jaws** off Ha'ikū in the east as the greatest of all. You need to be a real expert to join the locals who surf at these kind of places, however – beginners would do better to start out at spots such as Lahaina and Kā'anapali beaches. The peak **season** is between November and March.

Surfing lessons are offered in most tourist areas, and come with a guarantee that you'll ride a wave on your own before it's over. They're not cheap, costing perhaps $60 for a two-hour lesson in a group and more like $90 for private instruction, but they're great fun, and if you have the commitment to put in the necessary effort they really work. Operators in the Lahaina area include the **Goofy Foot Surf School** (℡244-9283) and **Soul Surfing Maui** (℡870-7873), while South Maui instructors include **Hawaiian Style Surf School** (℡874-0110) and **Maui Waveriders** (℡875-4761).

WINDSURFING

Since Robbie Naish of Kailua won the first world championships in the 1970s, at the age of 13, Hawaii has also been recognized as the spiritual home of **windsurfing**. Maui is renowned as offering the best conditions of all the Hawaiian islands, which makes it a prime goal for enthusiasts from around the world, though once again many of them find that Hawaiian waters present challenges on a vastly different scale to what they're used to at home. If you find an oceanfront parking lot filled with shiny rental cars, and bursting with tanned tourists sporting Lycra clothing

SEA SPORTS AND SAFETY

and expensive equipment, the chances are you're at a beginners' beach. Salt-caked local rust buckets and cut-off denims are the markers of demanding venues such as **Ho'okipa Beach Park**, which plays host to major championships throughout most of the year.

Strong winds rather than high surf are of most importance to windsurfers, so the peak season is the summer. Between December and February, the winds tend to drop for days on end, but even then conditions are usually good enough somewhere on the island, with Mā'alaea Bay on the south shore of the isthmus as the likeliest spot.

The best place to learn to windsurf is Kanahā Beach near Kahului, a few miles west of Ho'okipa. Expect to pay about $65 for a three-hour lesson, including equipment rental, with companies such as Action Sports Maui (☎871-5857; ⓦ www.actionsportsmaui.com), Alan Cadiz's HST Windsurfing School (☎871-5423; ⓦ www.hstwindsurfing .com), Hawaiian Island Surf & Sport (☎871-4981), or Maui Ocean Activities (☎667-2001).

Maui Windsurfing Vacations specializes in putting together all-inclusive packages for windsurfers (☎871-7766 or 1-800/736-6284; ⓦ www.maui.net/~mwvg).

PARASAILING

Parasailing, which is a bit like waterskiing except you suddenly find yourself several hundred feet up in the air, has become very popular in the waters just off Kā'anapali and Lahaina in West Maui. To avoid disturbing humpback whales during their winter migrations, however, it's only permitted between mid-May and mid-December. Expect to pay $40–50 for a fifteen-minute ride with operators such as Parasail Kā'anapali (☎669-6555), UFO Parasail (☎661-7836) and West Maui Parasail (☎661-4060).

OCEAN ACTIVITIES

Dive companies

Divers Locker, Kīhei ⓣ 280-3483; ⓦ www.diverslocker.com

Ed Robinson's Dive Tours, Kīhei ⓣ 879-3584; ⓦ www.mauiscuba.com

Extended Horizons, Lahaina ⓣ 667-0611; ⓦ www.scubadivemaui.com

Lahaina Divers, Lahaina ⓣ 667-7496; ⓦ www.lahainadivers.com

Maui Diamond, Māʻalaea ⓣ 879-9119;

ⓦ www.mauiscubatours.com

Maui Dive Shop, All over ⓣ 879-3388; ⓦ www.mauidiveshop.com

Maui Diving, Lahaina ⓣ 667-0633; ⓦ www.mauidiving.com

Maui Sun Divers, Kīhei ⓣ 879-3337; ⓦ mauisundivers.com

Mike Severn's, Kīhei ⓣ 879-6596; ⓦ severns.maui.his.us

Trilogy, Lahaina ⓣ 661-4743; ⓦ www.sailtrilogy.com

Boat tours

Atlantis Submarines ⓣ667-2224 or 1-800/548-6262; ⓦwww.atlantisadventures.com One-hour underwater excursions off Lahaina ($79).

Club Lanai ⓣ 871-1144; ⓦ www.clublanai.com. Full-day catamaran snorkeling trips from Lahaina to Lanai, with a stop at Manele Bay, for $69, or 2hr sunset dinner cruises for $75. Tues–Sat only.

Maui Princess ⓣ 661-8397; ⓦ www.whalewatchmaui.com or ⓦ www.mauiprincess.com. Dinner ($75) and whale-watching ($30) cruises from Lahaina, plus one-day excursions to Molokai, from $79 (see p.90).

Navatek II ⓣ 873-3475. Full-day snorkel cruises around Lanai, with breakfast and lunch, for $120, and 2hr sunset cruises for $87; departs from Māʻalaea.

SEA SPORTS AND SAFETY

Pacific Whale Foundation

☏ 879-8811;
ⓦ www.pacificwhale.org.
Non-profit-making 2–3hr cruises from Lahaina or Māʻalaea, offering whale-watching (Nov–April; $21–25), plus snorkeling and dolphin-watching tours to Molokini ($49) or Lanai ($79).

Reefdancer ☏ 667-2133. Sixty- or ninety-minute cruises in a semi-submersible from Lahaina, viewing the reef from an underwater cabin; $33 or $45.

Sea View ☏ 661-5550. Lahaina-based semi-submersible, which also offers passengers a chance to snorkel; 2hr cruise for $45.

Trilogy Ocean Sports ☏ 661-4743 or 1-888/628-4800; ⓦ www.sailtrilogy.com. Day-long sailing trips from Lahaina to Lanai, including snorkeling, beach barbecue and Lanai van tour; $160. They also offer diving and snorkeling at Molokini and off Lanai.

Sportfishing

Kāʻanapali Sportfishing

☏ 667-5792. Deep-sea fishing charters on six-passenger boat from Kāʻanapali.

Luckey Strike Charters

☏ 661-4606;
ⓦ www.luckeystrike.com. 4-, 6-, and 8hr fishing trips with Captain Todd Luckey from Lahaina.

Start Me Up ☏ 667-2774 or 268-2449;

ⓦ www.sportfishingmaui.com. Half- or full-day charters on six-passenger boat from Lahaina.

Kayak tours

Rainbow Kayak Tours ☏ 1-800/923-4004;

ⓦ www.travelhawaii.com/rainbow.htm. 3hr ($52) and 5hr 30min ($80) kayak tours from bases in Lahaina and Kīhei.

South Pacific Kayaks, Rainbow Mall, 2439 S Kīhei Rd (☏ 875-4848; ⓦ www.mauikayak.com). 3hr guided excursions at Mākena or Lahaina, or in season 2hr 30min whale-watch for $59; 6hr trip around La Pérouse for $89.

See also the list of Molokini snorkel cruises on p.90.

SEA SPORTS AND SAFETY

Equipment rental

Auntie Snorkel, 2439 S Kīhei Rd, Kīhei (☏ 879-6263). Snorkels and kayaks.

Boss Frog's Dive Shop, 2395 S Kīhei Rd, Kīhei (☏ 875-4477); 150 Lahainaluna Rd, Lahaina (☏ 661-3333); 4310 Lower Honoapiʻilani Rd, Kahana (☏ 669-6700); and Nāpili Plaza, Nāpili (☏ 669-4949). Activity center that also rents out scuba, snorkeling and surf gear.

Maui Dive Shop, 1455 S Kīhei Rd, Kīhei (☏ 879-3388); Honokōwai Marketplace, 3350 Lower Honoapiʻilani Hwy (☏ 661-6166); and five other Maui locations. Dive specialists who rent scuba and snorkeling equipment.

Maui Ocean Activities, Whaler's Village, Kāʻanapali (☏ 667-2001). Kayaks, windsurfing equipment, and two-person "Seacycles."

Rental Warehouse, Azeka Place II, 1279 S Kīhei Rd, Kīhei (☏ 875-4050), and 602 Front St, Lahaina (☏ 661-1970). Pretty much anything, from golf clubs and snorkel gear up to a Harley Davidson.

Snorkel Bob's, 2411 S Kīhei Rd, Kīhei (☏ 879-7449); 1217 Front St, Lahaina (☏ 661-4421); and *Nāpili Village Hotel*, Nāpili (☏ 669-9603). Snorkel gear, for return on any island.

South Pacific Kayaks, as above. Kayaks, surfboards, snorkels, boogie-boards, beach chairs and the like, for rent.

West Maui Cycles, 840 Waineʻe St, Lahaina (☏ 661-9005). Snorkels, mountain bikes, boogie-boards and surfboards.

OCEAN SAFETY

When in or near the ocean, you must be aware of **safety issues**. Maui is one of the most remote islands on earth, so waves have two thousand miles of the misnamed Pacific Ocean to build up their strength before they come crashing in. People born in Hawaii are brought up with a respect for the sea and learn to watch out for all sorts of signs before they swim. You'll be told to throw sticks into the waves to see how they move, or to look for disturbances in the surf that indicate powerful currents; unless you have local expertise, however, you're better off sticking to the official beach parks and most popular spots, especially those shielded by offshore reefs. Not all beaches have lifeguards and warning flags, and unattended beaches are not necessarily safe. Look for other bathers, but whatever your experience elsewhere don't assume you'll be able to cope with the same conditions as the local kids. Always ask for advice, and above all *never turn your back on the water*.

The beaches that experience the most **accidents and drownings** are those where waves of four feet or more break directly onto the shore, such as Oneloa or Big Beach, south of Mākena. Conditions often vary according to the season, so what in summer is an idyllic beach can be a storm-tossed deathtrap between October and April. If you get caught in a rip current or undertow and are dragged out to sea, stay calm and remember that the vast majority of such currents disappear within a hundred yards of the shore. Never exhaust yourself by trying to swim against them, but allow yourself to be carried out until the force weakens, and swim first to one side and then back to the shore.

Sea creatures to avoid include *wana* – black spiky **sea urchins** – Portuguese men-of-war **jellyfish** and **coral** in general, which can give painful, infected cuts. **Shark attacks** are much rarer than you might think; those that do occur are usually due to "misunderstandings," caused by surfers who idle on their boards and look a bit too much like turtles from below.

SUN SAFETY

Only expose yourself to the harsh tropical **sun** in moderation; a mere fifteen to thirty minutes is the safe recommendation for the first day. The hours between 10am and 3pm are the worst, and be aware that even on overcast days human skin still absorbs harmful UV rays. Use plenty of **sunscreen** – doctors recommend Sun Protection Factor (SPF) 30 for Hawaii – and always reapply after swimming, whatever it says on the bottle.

Hiking, riding and camping

Well-maintained **hiking trails** in all parts of Maui guide walkers through spectacular scenery that ranges from dense tropical rainforest to desert-like landscapes atop a ten-thousand-foot volcano. If you're planning to do any hiking, however, it's essential to remember that Hawaii is more than a vacation playground, and you may find yourself in some pretty uncompromising **wilderness**.

CAMPING

Opportunities to **camp** on Maui are very limited, with the best sites being in **Haleakalā National Park**, up near the crater (see p.182), and also at Kīpahulu on the southeast shore (see p.220). Cabins and tent camping are also available at Maui's two **state parks**, Polipoli (see p.172), and the much nicer Wai'ānapanapa (see p.206); $5 permits are issued, by mail or in person, by the Department of Land and Natural Resources, 54 S High St, Wailuku, HI 96793 (Mon–Fri 8am–noon & 1–4pm; ☎984-8109). When this book went to press, no **county parks** were open to campers; for the latest information, contact the Department of Parks and Recreation, 1580 Ka'ahumanu Ave, Wailuku, HI 96793 (Mon–Fri 8am–4pm; ☎270-7389).

HIKING

All the best **hiking trails** on Maui are described in detail in the relevant chapters of this book. Favorites include the rainforest hikes along the **Waihe'e Ridge Trail in West Maui** (p.87) and the **Pīpīwai Trail** up 'Ohe'o Gulch (p.219), and the coastal walks north of Hāna, in **Wai'ānapanapa State Park** (p.206) and along **'Ula'ino Road** (p.205).

However, Maui's most unusual and fascinating feature has to be the crater of **Haleakalā**, at the top of the island. It's possible to get into and out from the crater in a single long and energetic day-hike, but there's also potential for countless longer backpacking expeditions. See Chapter Six for full accounts.

EQUIPMENT AND SAFETY

Like all the Hawaiian islands, Maui is basically a large pile of rough lava, and any **footwear** except sturdy boots is likely to be torn to shreds. Other equipment should include rain gear, a flashlight, insect repellent, sunscreen and sunglasses and a basic first-aid kit; if you're backpacking, you'll need a waterproof tent and sleeping bag, and if you're heading up Haleakalā take warm clothing as well.

Never drink untreated water. **Leptospirosis**, a bacterial disease carried by rats and mice in particular, can be contracted through drinking stream water (filtering alone will not purify it) or even from wading through fresh water. Symptoms range from diarrhea, fever and chills through to kidney or heart failure and appear in anything from two to twenty days.

HORSE-RIDING

Adventures on Horseback
  ☎ 242-7445 or 572-6211;
  Ⓦ www.mauihorses.com. 6hr expeditions to swim in Ha'ikū Falls, including picnic, for $185.
Ironwood Ranch ☎ 669-4991. Riding excursions up to the forest above Kapalua, at $78 for 1hr 30min, or $104 for 2hr.
Mākena Stables ☎ 879-0244;
  Ⓦ www.makenastables.com. Mon–Sat 2–3hr morning or evening rides from 'Āhihi Bay along coastline to La Pérouse,

or 5hr 30min trips up to Tedeschi Winery, with tour; $110–175. No credit cards.
Mendes Ranch ☎ 871-5222. Mon–Sat half-day tours of cattle ranch in East Maui's Waihe'e Valley, with barbecue lunch; $130 per person or $219 with a 30min helicopter flight. Shorter 2hr tours cost $85.
'Ohe'o Stables ☎ 667-2222. 3hr rides from Kīpahulu, up to 'Ohe'o Gulch waterfalls; 10.30am $119, 11.30am (with lunch) $139.

Pony Express Tours ⓣ 667-2200; ⓦ www.ponyexpresstours .com. Mon–Fri 1hr ($55), 2hr ($80), and 2hr 30min (with picnic; $95) tours of Haleakalā Ranch, Maui's largest cattle ranch. Mon–Sat 5hr 30min descent to Ka Moa O Pele junction in Haleakalā Crater ($145) or 8hr trip to Kapalaoa Cabin ($180), both with picnic lunch.

Thompson Ranch ⓣ 878-1910. Half-day, full-day and overnight rides through Haleakalā Crater; $120 and up.

Golf

Maui is renowned for its **golf courses**, a full list of which appears below. Those at the major resorts, such as Kā'anapali and Wailea, are designed to tournament specifications, and have both the highest reputations and also the highest **green fees** – all cost well over $100 for a round, and the reductions for hotel guests are not all that significant.

The annual *Hawaii Golf Guide*, published by the Aloha Section PGA (#715, 770 Kapi'olani Blvd, Honolulu, HI 96813; ⓣ 593-2230), carries complete listings. Stand-By

Golf (☎ 1-888/645-2265) specializes in finding discounted and short-notice golfing opportunities.

Golf 4-Less, at 3350 Lower Honoapi'ilani Hwy, in the Honokōwai Market Place (☎ 662-8044 or 1-877/895-GOLF), offers equipment rental and sales, and can also arrange single-round discounts.

COURSES AND GREEN FEES

Dunes at Maui Lani
Kahului; $85 ☎ 873-0422
Elleair
Kīhei; $75 ☎ 874-0777
Grand Waikapū Country Club
Waikapū; $200 ☎ 244-7888
Kā'anapali Golf Course
North Course, Kā'anapali; $150 ☎ 661-3691
South Course, Kā'anapali; $142 ☎ 661-3691
Kapalua Golf Club
Bay Course, Kapalua; $180 ☎ 669-8820
Plantation Course, Kapalua; $220 ☎ 669-8877
Village Course, Kapalua; $180 ☎ 669-8835
Mākena Golf Club
North Course, Mākena;

$110 ☎ 879-3344
South Course, Mākena; $110 ☎ 879-3344
Maui Country Club
Pā'ia; $65 (9 holes) ☎ 877-7893
Pukalani Country Club
Upcountry; $55 ☎ 572-1314
Sandalwood Golf Course
Waikapū; $75 ☎ 242-4653
Wai'ehu Municipal Golf Course
Wailuku; $26 ☎ 243-7400
Wailea Golf Club
Blue Course, Wailea; $140 ☎ 875-7450
Emerald Course, Wailea; $160 ☎ 875-7450
Gold Course, Wailea; $150 ☎ 875-7450

GOLF

●

Crafts and shopping

I f you have come to Hawaii specifically to **shop**, the stores of Maui may not meet your needs. The state's premier malls are concentrated in Honolulu on Oahu, and unless you go there as well, you may fly home with fewer gifts and souvenirs than you expected. The prints, posters and T-shirts on sale in Lahaina and the major tourist areas are OK if you think that whales are interplanetary voyagers from another dimension, or that a gecko on a surfboard is real neat, but stores and galleries selling high-quality indigenous arts and crafts are few and far between. Maui's largest malls are the **Ka'ahumanu Mall** and the **Maui Marketplace** in Kahului, though the most upmarket individual stores are in the new **Shops at Wailea** mall, or in individual resort hotels.

HAWAIIAN CRAFTS AND PRODUCE

Some of the most attractive **products of Hawaii** are just too ephemeral to take home. That goes for the orchids and tropical flowers on sale everywhere, and unfortunately it's also true of *leis*.

Leis (pronounced *lays*) are flamboyant decorative garlands, usually consisting of flowers such as the fragrant *melia* (the plumeria or frangipani) or the Big Island's own bright-red *lehua* blossom (from the *'ō'hia* tree), but sometimes also made from feathers, shells, seeds or nuts. Both men and women wear them, above all on celebrations or gala occasions. The days are gone when every arriving tourist was festooned with a *lei*, but you'll probably be way-*leied* at a *lū'au* or some such occasion, while on Lei Day (May 1) everyone's at it.

Colorful Hawaiian clothing, such as aloha **shirts** and the cover-all "Mother-Hubbard"-style *mu'umu'u* dress, is on sale everywhere, though classic designs are quite rare and you tend to see the same stylized prints over and over again. Otherwise, the main **local crafts** are *lau hala* **weaving**, in which mats, hats, baskets and the like are created by plaiting the large leaves (*lau*) of the spindly-legged pandanus (*hala*) tree, and **wood turning**, with fine bowls made from native dark woods such as *koa*.

Directory

Area code The telephone area code for the state of Hawaii is ⓣ808.

Climate For details on the climate in Hawaii, see the Introduction on p.xvi.

Electricity Hawaii's electricity supply, like that on the US mainland, uses 100 volts AC. Plugs are standard American two-pins.

Fishing For full details of Hawaii's fishing regulations, write to Division of Aquatic Resources, Dept of Land and Natural Resources, Kalanimoku Building, 1151 Punchbowl St, Room 330, Honolulu, HI 96813.

Gay and lesbian life Much the greatest concentration of gay activism in Hawaii is in Honolulu, though the state as a whole is liberal on gay issues. It's one of 25 states to allow consensual "sodomy," with no criminal laws against private sex acts and a guarantee of privacy in the constitution. *Pacific Ocean Holidays* (PO Box 88245, Honolulu, HI 96830-8245; ⓣ923-2400 or 1-800/735-6600, ⓕ923-2499; ⓦwww.gayhawaii.com/vacation/index.html) organizes all-inclusive **package vacations** in Hawaii for gay and lesbian travelers. It also publishes the thrice-yearly *Pocket Guide to Hawaii*, a useful booklet of gay listings throughout the state (available free in Hawaii, or by mail for $5 per issue, one year's subscription $12). Other useful sources of **information** include Matthew Link's *Rainbow Handbook*

(Ⓦ www.rainbowhandbook
.com), a self-published guide
book to all the Hawaiian
islands available from local
bookstores for $15, and the
various Web pages gathered
on gayhawaii.com. Maui's
largest gay organization, the
Gay & Lesbian 'Ohana Maui
(Ⓣ 244-4566; Ⓦ maui-tech
.com/glom/), can supply
contacts and information on
forthcoming events.

Hospitals Maui hospitals can
be contacted on the following
numbers: Wailuku Ⓣ 244-
9056; Kula Ⓣ 878-1221; Hāna
Ⓣ 248-8294. In emergencies
call Ⓣ 911.

Inoculations No inoculations or
vaccinations are required by
law in order to enter Hawaii,
though some authorities
suggest a polio vaccination.

Public toilets Some public
toilets are labeled in Hawaiian:
Kanes means Men, *Wahines*
means Women.

Quarantine Very stringent
restrictions apply to the
importation of all plants and
animals into Hawaii. Cats and
dogs must stay in quarantine
for 120 days; if you were
hoping to bring an alligator or

a hamster into the state,
forget it. For full regulations
call Ⓣ 871-5656.

Senior travelers US residents
aged 50 or over can join the
American Association of
Retired Persons, 601 E St NW,
Washington, DC 20049 (Ⓣ 1-
800/424-3410;
Ⓦ www.aarp.org), for
discounts on accommodation
and vehicle rental.

Time Unlike most of the United
States, Hawaii does not
observe Daylight Saving
Time. Therefore, from 2am on
the last Sunday in April until
2am on the last Sunday in
October, the time difference
between Hawaii and the US
West Coast is three hours,
not the usual two; the
difference between Hawaii
and the mountain region is
four hours, not three; and the
islands are six hours later
than the East Coast, not five.
Hawaiian time is from ten to
eleven hours behind the UK.
In fact it's behind just about
everywhere else; although
New Zealand and Australia
might seem to be two and
four hours, respectively,
behind Maui time, they're on

DIRECTORY

61

the other side of the International Date Line, so are actually almost a full day ahead.

Tipping Waiting staff in restaurants expect tips of fifteen percent, in bars a little less. Hotel porters and bellhops should receive around $1 per piece of luggage and housekeeping staff $1 per night.

Travelers with disabilities Copies of the *Aloha Guide to Accessibility in the State of Hawaii* and additional information on facilities for travelers with disabilities on Oahu can be obtained from the State Commission on Persons with Disabilities, 919 Ala Moana Blvd, #101, Honolulu, HI 96814 (☎ 586-8121). Accessible Vans of Hawaii (186 Mehani Circle, Kīhei, HI 96753; ☎ 879-5521; ⓦ www.accessiblevans.com) rent out wheelchair-accessible vans and also run island tours and shuttle services.

Weddings To get married in Hawaii, you must have a valid state licence, which costs $50 from the Department of Health, Marriage License Office, 1250 Punchbowl St, Honolulu, HI 96813 (Mon–Fri 8am–4pm; ☎ 586-4545; ⓦ www.hawaii.gov), and is valid for thirty days. You also need proof of rubella immunizations or screening, which can be arranged through the Department of Health. Most resorts offer their own marriage planners, or you can pick up a full list of companies that specialize in arranging weddings by visiting the Maui Wedding Association online (ⓦ www.maui.net /~hwpa). Their members include A Beautiful Hawaii Wedding (☎ 661-6655; ⓦ www.oldlahaina.com), Marry Me Maui (☎ 1-800/745-0344; ⓦ www.marrymemaui .com), and Enchanted Weddings of Maui (☎ 1-800/648-8697; ⓦ www .mauiweddingvows.com).

DIRECTORY

THE GUIDE

THE GUIDE

Central Maui

The plains of **central Maui**, overshadowed by mighty
Haleakalā to the east and the West Maui mountains
to the west, form a narrow "neck" that links the
island's two volcanic massifs. Measuring just seven miles
north to south, and so flat you sometimes feel the ocean
could wash right over it, this is the economic heartland of
Maui.

Kahului, the main town, is home to the island's principal
airport, as well as its major harbor, the bulk of its com-
merce and industry, and around half of its 120,000 inhabitants – the workers who keep the rest of the fantasy island
going. Largely a modern creation, Kahului is, however, a
characterless sprawl of malls and warehouses that's no one's
idea of a vacation destination.

In ancient times, **Wailuku**, its neighbor to the west, was
far more significant. From a royal enclosure at the mouth of
the stunning **ʻĪao Valley**, its chiefs ruled a region known as
Nā Wai ʻEhā, watered by four rivers that flowed down from
the peaks of West Maui. ʻĪao Valley remains one of the
most scenic spots in all Hawaii, but toward the end of the
twentieth century Wailuku experienced a severe economic
downturn, retreating into itself as Kahului crept ever closer.

The few beaches near Wailuku and Kahului are exposed
strips of scrubby sand, far too inferior to have inspired the

construction of major hotels or resorts. However, they do offer ideal conditions for **windsurfing**. As a result, the former plantation town of **Pā'ia**, east of Kahului, has reinvented itself as a year-round hangout for surf-bums and hippies, and a mecca for young budget travelers.

The rest of the isthmus, stretching south, consists of a patchwork of sugar and pineapple fields, dotted with the occasional rusting refinery. It was described by the nineteenth-century British traveler Isabella Bird as "a Sahara in miniature, a dreary expanse of sand and shifting sandhills, with a dismal growth of thornless thistles and indigo." Only since nineteenth-century sugar barons created irrigation channels to carry water from the eastern flanks of Haleakalā has it been capable of supporting the agriculture that now makes it so green.

Kahului

Although **KAHULUI** is the largest town on Maui, holding the island's chief harbor and airport, and most of its main shopping centers, it's not an interesting, let alone historic, place to visit. It's arguably worth considering as a convenient central base, but there's next to nothing to see here, and you could miss Kahului altogether with a clear conscience.

Having started the nineteenth century as a small cluster of grass shacks, Kahului grew in tandem with the expansion of commercial agriculture. A major spur was the opening of the Kahului and Wailuku Railroad in 1879, which channeled the sugar and pineapple crops of central Maui down to the wharves of Kahului. At first Kahului was an insanitary place: an outbreak of plague in 1900 forced the authorities to burn down the oceanfront Chinatown district and ring the whole town with ratproof fences. When it was rebuilt, the harbor was greatly expanded and dredged, to provide the only deep-water anchorage on the island.

Kahului thereafter supplanted Lahaina as Maui's main port and has remained so ever since. It was further boosted after World War II, when newly built low-cost housing in "Dream City," as it was optimistically promoted, lured laborers away from plantation towns such as Pā'ia with the promise of owning their own homes.

ARRIVAL AND INFORMATION

The majority of visitors to Maui arrive at **Kahului Airport**, a couple of miles east of town. The main lobby area is surprisingly small, though it does hold a **Hawaii Visitors Bureau information booth** that's open to greet all flights. For a snack or a drink, you have to pass through the security checks and head for the departure gates.

See p.3 onwards for details of trans-Pacific flights
to and from Kahului Airport; inter-island
services to Maui are summarized on p.16.

All the national **rental-car** chains (see p.24) have offices immediately across from the terminal. In addition, Speedishuttle (☏875-8070) and Airport Shuttle (☏661-6667) run shuttle vans on demand to all destinations, charging about $20 to Kīhei, $32 to Lahaina and $45 to Nāpili. Both the Maui Airporter Shuttle (☏877-7308 or 1-800/259-2627) and TransHawaiian (☏877-0380 or 1-800/231-6984) run regular scheduled **buses** to Kā'anapali by way of Lahaina, for $13 one way or $19 round-trip.

Kahului's **post office** is on Pu'unēnē Avenue (Mon–Fri 8.30am–5pm, Sat 8.30am–noon; zip code HI 96732).

ARRIVAL AND INFORMATION

67

ACCOMMODATION

If you plan to spend most of your time on Maui touring the island or windsurfing at Ho'okipa just down the coast (see p.92), Kahului's pair of aging hotels may suit your needs. Although both are right in the center of town, Kahului is not a place you'd choose to stroll around and doesn't make a lively overnight stop.

Maui Beach Hotel

170 W Ka'ahumanu Ave, Kahului, HI 96732 ⓣ877-0051, ⓕ871-5797, or reserve through Castle Resorts, ⓣ591-2235, 1-800/367-5004 (US & Can) or 1-800/272-5275 (HI); ⓦwww.castleresorts.com. Somewhat faded seafront hotel in the heart of Kahului, offering 150 or so run-down but bearable rooms. Available through the main lobby are cheaper, even less appealing rooms in the unattractive *Maui Palms* next door – Maui's second-oldest hotel, which opened in 1954 and is now only partly operational. Daily buffets of mostly Asian dishes are offered by both *Maui Beach's Rainbow Dining Room* and the *Red Dragon* restaurant; the latter also has live entertainment and dancing nightly. Both hotels offer a free sixth night or rental car. ❸/❹.

Maui Seaside Hotel

100 W Ka'ahumanu Ave, Kahului, HI 96732 ⓣ877-3311 or 1-800/560-5552 (US & Can), ⓕ877-4618; ⓦwww.mauiseasidehotel.com. Good-value waterfront hotel, facing the harbor in central Kahului. Rooms are cheaper in the older of its two wings, but the whole place has been modernized, with a swimming pool and its own artificial beach. The location, across from the main shopping malls, is hardly romantic, but at least it is by the sea, and the *Seaside* makes a convenient and relatively inexpensive central base. Discounts available on car rental. ❹.

ACCOMMODATION PRICE CODES

All accommodation prices in this book have been graded with
the following symbols; for a full explanation, see p.29.

1 up to $40   **4** $100–150   **7** $250–300

2 $40–70   **5** $150–200   **8** $300–400

3 $70–100   **6** $200–250   **9** over $400

DOWNTOWN KAHULUI

Kahului is one of the few towns in all Hawaii to have taken
shape since the invention of the automobile, and is consequently devoid of anything that feels like a downtown.
Neither is the ocean ever particularly conspicuous, with the
waterfront screened away behind rows of factories and load-
ing areas.

Instead, your abiding impression of Kahului is likely to
be of the succession of aging shopping malls along
Ka'ahumanu Avenue, which parallels the sweep of the
shoreline. Only the ever-expanding **Ka'ahumanu
Center** itself is worth visiting, for its standard array of
generic upmarket stores and a few more distinctive craft
outlets. It also holds one or two good restaurants – see
p.73 – while its second-floor food court offers distant
views of Kahului Bay.

Kahului's newest shopping mall, the **Maui Marketplace**,
further back on Dairy Road, is noteworthy as the home of
the island's best **bookstore** – a giant Borders (Mon–Thurs
9am–11pm, Fri & Sat 9am–midnight, Sun 9am–10pm;
℡877-6160).

Maui Arts and Cultural Center

Map 2, D3

Just off the busy Kahului Beach Road, which curves around Kahului Harbor, the **Maui Arts and Cultural Center** (☏242-ARTS, box office ☏242-7469; ⓦwww.mauiarts.org) opened in 1994 as Maui's most important venue for the visual and performing arts. In addition to a 4000-seat open-air amphitheater, it houses two separate indoor theaters and an art gallery that hosts changing temporary exhibitions. Those big-name musicians who make it as far as Maui – more than you might expect, as it's a favorite final stop for trans-America touring bands – play here, and the Maui Symphony Orchestra (☏244-5439) puts on half a dozen concerts each winter.

Kanahā Pond State Wildlife Sanctuary

Map 2, G3

Half a mile west of Kahului Airport, just before Hwy-36A meets Hwy-36, a tiny roadside parking lot marks the only public access to the **Kanahā Pond State Wildlife Sanctuary**. This marshy saltwater lagoon – used as a fish-pond until it was choked by the mud dredged up from Kahului Harbor – is now set aside for the protection of endangered bird species such as the *ae'o* (black-necked stilt) and the *'auku'u* (night heron).

There are no official opening hours; visitors simply make their way through the gate and follow a pedestrian causeway for fifty yards out to a windy, open-sided viewing shelter. It's not a very prepossessing spot; the factories of Kahului Harbor are clearly visible off to the left, while the waters are tinged an unsavory green, with a layer of scum swelling around the edges. Nonetheless, the sanctuary lives up to its title, and you're almost certain to see plenty of wading birds picking their way through the mire.

Kanahā Beach County Park

Map 2, H1

Amala Place runs due east of central Kahului through an industrial area behind Kanahā Pond. Even before it joins Alahao Street on the ocean side of the airport, there are plenty of places where you can park beside the road and walk through the trees to find a long strip of empty beach.

However, the most popular oceanfront spot is the large **Kanahā Beach County Park**, which despite its proximity to the runways is completely undisturbed by all the comings and goings and feels comfortably far from Kahului. Its shallow, choppy turquoise waters are ideal for novice **windsurfers**, who come from all over the world to swirl back and forth against the backdrop of ʻĪao Valley and the West Maui mountains. Among companies offering windsurfing lessons here (at around $65 for two and a half hours, including equipment rental) are Action Sports Maui (☏871-5857; ⓦwww.action sportsmaui.com) and Alan Cadiz's HST Windsurfing School (☏871-5423; ⓦwww.hstwindsurfing.com).

For its full length, the beach is fringed by pine trees, with countless shoots sprouting from the dunes, and fallen needles creating a soft forest floor just behind. The lawns under the trees have picnic tables, though to buy food or drink you have to drive back into Kahului. In principle, good facilities make this one of the best **campgrounds** on Maui. The seven individual sites are available for $5 per night, with a three-night maximum stay. As this book went to press, however, the campground was closed, supposedly temporarily, due to health and sanitation concerns; call the county parks office (see p54) for the latest information.

Windsurfers ready for the big time graduate to
Hoʻokipa, just a few miles east but light years
away in terms of difficulty; see p.92.

DOWNTOWN KAHULUI

Alexander & Baldwin Sugar Museum

Map 2, G6. Mon–Sat 9.30am–4.30pm; adults $4, under-18s $2.

There's no missing the rusty red hulk of the **Puʻunēnē Sugar Mill**, which forces Hwy-350 to make a sharp right turn a mile south of Kahului. Still belching smoke as it consumes the cane from the surrounding fields, this was the largest sugar mill in the world when it was built in 1902. Only two such mills are still operational in the state of Hawaii; the other is on Kauai. Easily overlooked, however, is the smaller building just across from the mill, at the intersection with the minor Hansen Road, which houses the **Alexander & Baldwin Sugar Museum**.

The museum relates the history of sugar production on Maui, a tale of nineteenth-century scheming and skulduggery that, more than a century later, may not hold your interest for all that long. Alexander & Baldwin was one of the original "Big Five" companies at the heart of the Hawaiian economy – see p.236 – and remains a prominent island name to this day. **Samuel T. Alexander** (1836–1904) and **Henry Baldwin** (1842–1911) started growing sugar at Pāʻia in 1869 and were responsible for constructing the first irrigation channel in 1878 to carry water from East Maui to the central isthmus. Their great rival was **Claus Spreckels** (1828–1908), who used his royal connections (he underwrote King Kalākaua's gambling debts) to acquire land and water rights at "Spreckelsville" near Pāʻia. He all but controlled the Hawaiian sugar industry before losing favor with the king and being forced to return to California. Alexander and Baldwin were then free to expand their operations across Maui, centered on the processing facilities at Puʻunēnē.

The cinder cone for which Puʻunēnē ("Goose Hill") was named was leveled to surface the roads between the fields.

Scale models in the museum include a typical plantation house, a whirring but incomprehensible re-creation of the main mill machinery, and a relief map of the whole island. More illuminating displays focus on the daily lives of the plantation laborers, showing the thick clothes they wore to work, despite the heat, as protection against the dust and poisonous centipedes, and the numbered *bango* tags by which they were identified in place of names. No bones are made of the fact that the multiethnic workforce was deliberately, but ultimately unsuccessfully, segregated to avoid solidarity. The museum store is well stocked with books on ethnic and labor history, as well as souvenir packets of raw sugar.

RESTAURANTS

Kahului is disappointingly short of **restaurants**, and few people would choose to drive here from elsewhere on Maui in search of a good meal. There are, however, a few alternatives scattered around the town's lesser malls, while the breezy **Queen's Market** area, upstairs at the front of the **Ka'ahumanu Center**, holds a wide assortment of fast-food counters. As well as a few juice and coffee bars, these include the Japanese *Edo*, the Chinese *Panda Express*, and the Greek *Athens*, plus *Yummy Korean B-B-Q* and *McDonald's*. There's also a *Starbucks* (Mon–Thurs 6am–10pm, Fri & Sat 6am–11pm, Sun 6.30am–9pm), but not much else, at the Maui Marketplace.

Ichiban The Restaurant

Kahului Shopping Center, 47 Ka'ahumanu Ave ☎ 871-6977. Large, old mall eatery, which serves American and continental breakfasts, then devotes itself to Japanese cuisine. For lunch there's *saimin* for $5, *donburi* bowls for $6 and teriyakis for $6–8; at dinner you can get shrimp or chicken stir-fries, *udon* noodles and sushi rolls, as well as most items from the lunch menu, for under $10. Mon–Fri 6.30am–2pm & 5–9pm, Sat 10.30am–2pm & 5–9pm.

Kaka'ako Kitchen

Ka'ahumanu Center, Ka'ahumanu Ave ☏ 893-0366. High-quality Hawaiian-style fast-food diner, run by renowned Honolulu restaurateur Russell Siu, at the front of the Ka'ahumanu Center mall. Takeout and eat-in orders alike are placed at the counter. Lunch and dinner prices are the same, with pretty much everything, from the hamburger stew to the signature dish chicken linguine, costing $6–9. The daily $7.25 specials include pot roast and seafood marinara, always with a vegetarian alternative. Mon–Fri 8–10am & 11am–9pm, Sat & Sun 8am–9pm.

Marco's Grill & Deli

444 Hāna Hwy ☏ 877-4446. Large, lively Italian restaurant, in a modern mall not far from the airport on the corner of Dairy Road. Once the breakfast omelets, pancakes and espressos have finished, the lunch and dinner menus feature deli sandwiches, pizzas with a choice of toppings from $10, and rich meat and seafood pastas, including rigatoni with prosciutto served in a vodka sauce for $16. Daily 7.30am–10pm.

Maui Coffee Roasters

444 Hāna Hwy ☏ 877-2877. This relaxed espresso bar with hand-painted tables is a popular hangout for windsurfers from the nearby beaches. Vegetarian wraps and sandwiches, like focaccia with mozzarella, are $6–7; try the fabulous raspberry-and-white-chocolate scones. Mon–Fri 7am–6pm, Sat 8am–5pm, Sun 8am–2.30pm.

Pizza in Paradise

60 E Wakea Ave ☏ 871-8188. Dependable, inexpensive, but not exceptional pizzas, baked up in a warehouse-style, backstreet setting. Industrial-sized 18-inch pizzas, with the usual toppings, cost from $10, and there are daily $5 lunch specials. Sun–Thurs 11am–9pm, Fri & Sat 11am–10pm.

Wailuku

The center of **WAILUKU** is barely two miles west of Kahului, and there's no gap in the development along Ka'ahumanu Avenue to mark where one town ends and the other begins. However, situated as it is at the mouth of the fertile 'Īao Valley, and within a few miles of the lush valleys that line the windward coast of West Maui, Wailuku has a very different geography and a much more venerable history. This was what might be called the *poi* bowl of Maui, at the heart of the largest *taro*-growing area in Hawaii, and was home to generations of ancient priests and warriors.

Well into the twentieth century, Wailuku was the center of the island's nascent tourist industry, housing the few visitors Maui received and equipping their expeditions up Haleakalā. Much of its administrative and commercial role was then usurped by Kahului, and Wailuku went into something of a decline. These days, with the construction of various new county offices and even a few stores, Wailuku appears to be on the way back, but it remains a sleepy sort of place, easily seen in less than half a day. Nonetheless, it's one of the few towns on Maui that still feels like a genuine community and can serve as a welcome antidote to the sanitized charms of the modern resorts.

INFORMATION

You can't help suspecting that the main Maui office of the **Hawaii Visitors Bureau** (Mon–Fri 8am–4.30pm; ☎244-3530 or 1-800/525-MAUI) was tucked away at 1727 Wili Pa Loop to deter casual visitors. If you do find your way there – it's in a modern development off Mill Street, half a mile northeast of central Wailuku – they can provide lots of printed material on all of Maui County, which also includes

WAILUKU

the islands of Molokai and Lanai. Wailuku's **post office** is nearby at 250 Imi Kala St (Mon–Fri 8.30am–5pm, Sat 9am–4pm; zip code HI 96793).

Camping permits for Maui's state parks are available from the Department of Land and Natural Resources, opposite Ka'ahumanu Church at 54 S High St (Mon–Fri 8am–noon & 1–4pm; ☎984-8109), while the county parks office is at Baldwin High School, just east of central Wailuku at 1580 Ka'ahumanu Ave (Mon–Fri 8am–4pm; ☎243-7389).

For more details of camping on Maui, see p.54.

ACCOMMODATION

Because Wailuku has Maui's only **hostels** – and no hotels – the only people who spend the night here tend to be backpackers and surfers. A drawback for budget travelers is that the nearest beaches are several miles away, but the *Banana Bungalow* runs inexpensive minivan trips.

Note that while a couple of other places on Vineyard Street often rent out hostel-style rooms, neither is recommended.

Banana Bungalow

310 N Market St, Wailuku, HI 96793 ☎244-5090 or 1-800/846-7835, ⓕ244-3678, ⓔbungalow@gte.net; ⓦhome1.gte.net/bungalow.htm. Friendly unofficial hostel, open to non-Hawaiian residents only, in an unattractive area a short walk from the center of Wailuku. Beds in two- and three-bed dorms ($16), and several basic private rooms from $29. Guests hang out in the gardens and living rooms. Not only are there free shuttles to the airport and to Kanahā beach, but there's also a changing daily

rotation of free excursions to all parts of the island. The hostel also offers free Internet access and a free Jacuzzi. ❶.

Northshore Inn

2080 Vineyard St, Wailuku, HI 96793 ⓉT 242-1448 or 1-866/946-7835;
Ⓦwww.hawaii-hostel.com. Budget accommodation in downtown Wailuku, behind the blue balcony above the *Mushroom Restaurant*. Beds in plain, four- and six-bed dorms for $16, plus equally plain private rooms – each holds just a bed or two bunks – for just under $40. Popular with European travelers, who leave their surfboards propped against the giant banyan in the courtyard. Free seventh night

but five percent credit-card surcharge. Kitchen facilities and cheap car, moped and surfboard rental, but no free shuttles. ❶.

Old Wailuku Inn at Ulupono

2199 Kahoʻokele St, Wailuku, HI 96793 ⓉT 244-5897 or 1-800/305-4899;
Ⓦwww.mauiinn.com. Spacious plantation-style home, set in landscaped gardens a short walk south of central Wailuku, that's been converted to become a luxurious seven-room B&B. All rooms have private *lānais* and baths and are equipped with VCRs; some also have whirlpool spas. Guests share use of a living room and wide verandah. ❹–❺.

CENTRAL WAILUKU

The heart of Wailuku is where **Main Street**, the continuation of Kaʻahumanu Avenue, crosses **Market Street**. Both streets hold a small assortment of shops, the most interesting of which are the fading **antique** and **junk stores** along Market Street to the north, just before it drops down to cross the ʻĪao Stream. Also look for the 1929 **ʻĪao Theater**, an attractive little playhouse on Market Street that puts on six shows each year (season runs Sept–June; ⓉT 242-6969).

Ka'ahumanu Church, at the intersection of Main and High streets just west of the center, was founded in 1832. Naming it after Queen Ka'ahumanu, a convert to Christianity who was largely responsible for the destruction of the old Hawaiian religion (see p.208), was the idea of the Queen herself. The current building, whose four-story white spire has a clock face on each side, dates from 1876. It's not usually open to visitors, but you're welcome to attend the Hawaiian-language services at 9am on Sunday mornings.

Bailey House

Map 3, A7. Mon–Sat 10am–4pm; adults $5, under-13s $1; ☏ 244–3326.

The **Bailey House**, to the left of Main Street as it starts to climb west out of Wailuku as 'Īao Valley Road, is the best **museum of general history** on Maui. It sits on what was once the most highly prized plot of land on the island: the site of a royal compound that controlled access to the sacred 'Īao Valley. Local chiefs donated it during the 1830s so the Central Maui Mission could build day schools to teach both adults and children to read. From 1837 until 1849, it was also the site of the **Wailuku Female Seminary**, a boarding school designed to produce "good Christian wives" for the male graduates of the Lahainaluna Seminary (see p.110).

The first occupant of the house was Reverend Jonathan Green, who resigned from the mission in 1842 to protest the fact that the American Board of Commissioners for Foreign Missions accepted money from slave owners. For the next fifty years, it was home to Edward Bailey and his wife Caroline Hubbard Bailey. He was a minister, schoolmaster, carpenter and amateur painter, while she is remembered in the name of the long "Mother Hubbard" dresses, also known as *mu'umu'us*, that she made for local women.

After an entertaining introductory talk, visitors can wander through rooms filled with period furniture, none of which originally belonged here. The largest room focuses on ancient Hawaiian history, with archeological finds from Maui, Lanai and Kahoolawe including bones, clubs, shark's-tooth weapons, and *leis* of shells and feathers. One large wooden platter was used for serving boiled dog – a popular dish for women, who were forbidden to eat pork. There's also a copy of the only carved temple image ever found on Maui, an image of the pig-god Kamapua'a discovered in a remote sea cave. As the label points out, both the Baileys and the ancient Hawaiians alike would be appalled to see it on public display. On the wall there's a portrait of the unruly chief Boki, who sailed to the South Seas in 1829 in search of sandalwood to replace Hawaii's vanished crop and died in an explosion at sea.

A separate gallery downstairs is reserved for local land-scapes painted by the white-bearded Edward Bailey in his old age, while the upstairs rooms are preserved more or less as the Baileys would have known them, though presumably they'd disavow the opium pipe and paraphernalia display. A very solid wooden surfboard that once belonged to legendary Waikīkī surfer and "Beachboy" Duke KaHānamoku hangs outside the restrooms in the garden.

Haleki'i and Pihana heiaus

Map 2, B2. Daily 7am–7pm; free.

A mile from central Wailuku – but more than three miles by road – the twin ancient temples of **Haleki'i** and **Pihana** guard the Wailuku Plain from two separate hillocks near the mouth of the 'Īao Stream. They can only be reached via a very convoluted route; follow Hwy-333 all the way out of Wailuku to the north, double back south along Waiehu Beach Road, turn inland at Kūhiō Place, and take the first left, Hea Place.

With rows of low-budget housing to the north, and the industrial area of Kahului to the south, this is not the most evocative of sites, but raising your gaze toward the horizon provides fine views of the ocean and the turquoise waters of the **harbor**, and in the early morning mighty Haleakalā can often be seen in its entirety. The short trail from the parking lot leads through scrubby soil – these hillocks are in fact lithified sand dunes – to **Haleki'i Heiau**. Maui's ruling chief, Kahekili, lived at this "house of images" during religious ceremonies in the 1760s, when its uppermost platform would have held thatched huts interspersed with carved effigies of the gods. The hilltop is now bare, with the lower stone terraces of the *heiau* dropping down the side toward Kahului.

Both Haleki'i and **Pihana Heiau**, on the far side of the gulch to the west, were *luakinis*, or temples dedicated to the war god Kū that were the site of human sacrifice. Such temples were not necessarily always in use; they might well be dedicated or rededicated in the hope of ensuring victory in a particular military campaign. Pihana seems to have been originally constructed between 1260 and 1400 AD, and enlarged during the eighteenth century, at which time it was reoriented to face toward the Big Island, presumably at a time when the chiefs of Maui were preparing an attack. When Kamehameha the Great's Big Island warriors finally conquered Maui, they celebrated their victory at 'Īao Valley (see p.82) with a rededication ceremony at Pihana, one of many held here over the centuries.

Maui Tropical Plantation

Map 1, E4. Daily 9am–5pm; free.

The **Maui Tropical Plantation**, two miles south of Wailuku below the entrance to Waikapū Valley, is a principal stop on round-island bus tours, but it's of minimal interest. Visitors are free to walk into the main "Marketplace," where the stalls are piled with plants, fruits and souvenirs, and then pass into the lackluster gardens beyond to explore pavilions describing the cultivation of macadamia nuts, sugar, coffee and other local crops. You can see a few more unusual plants on the forty-minute tram tours (daily 10am–4pm, every 45min; $9.50), while the nursery near the entrance sells and ships spectacular orchids.

The indoor *Tropical Restaurant* (daily 9am–3pm) serves unremarkable $14.50 buffet lunches between 11am and 2pm (expect long lines), and sandwiches and salads for the rest of the day.

RESTAURANTS

Wailuku may not have any particularly outstanding **restaurants**, but budget travelers can choose from a wide assortment of inexpensive options. Most are downtown, with the rest strung along Lower Main Street as it loops down toward Kahului Harbor – too far to walk from the center.

Café Marc Aurel

28 N Market St ☎ 244-0852. Smart little sidewalk espresso café, serving coffees and pastries and providing Internet acces. Daily 7am–8pm.

Maui Bake Shop & Deli

2092 Vineyard St ☎ 244-7117. Healthy deli breakfasts and lunches, served close to the *Northshore Inn*. Choose from a wide assortment of soups, salads and quiches as well as wonderful fresh-baked breads, including focaccias, calzones, whole-grain loaves and sweet brioches. You can eat well for $5 or less. Mon–Fri 6am–4pm, Sat 7am–2pm.

Ramon's

2102 Vineyard St ☎ 244-7243. The menu in this down-home diner in the heart of Wailuku ranges from local to Mexican to sushi. Plate lunches, burritos, and specials like *lomi* salmon and *kālua* pork all cost under $10. Mon–Sat 7am–10pm.

Saeng's

2119 Vineyard St ☎ 244-1567. Pleasant Thai restaurant, serving high-quality food at bargain prices. Plate lunches include honey-lemon chicken and garlic shrimp for $6–8, and full dinners cost only a few dollars more. Mon–Fri 11am–2.30pm & 5–9.30pm, Sat & Sun 5–9.30pm.

A Saigon Café

1792 Main St ☎ 243-9560. Predominantly Vietnamese restaurant with an extremely wide-ranging and unusual menu, most of it extremely tasty. Hot and cold noodle dishes and soups, and a lot of seafood stews and curries, plus simpler stir-fried and steamed fish specials. All entrees come in at well under $20, appetizers like summer rolls and pancakes less than half that. Mon–Sat 10am–9.30pm, Sun 10am–8.30pm.

Tasty Crust

1770 Mill St ☎ 244-0845. Basic, cheap and very filling home cooking on the road up from Kahului Harbor. The day kicks off with bumper stacks of pancakes for $3, and the plates are piled high from then on. Mon 5.30am–1.30pm, Tues–Sun 5.30am–1.30pm & 5–10pm.

'Īao Valley

Main Street heads due west out of Wailuku to enter the high-walled cleft carved by the 'Īao Stream into the West Maui mountains. Waterfalls drop down pleated grooves in the rock to either side. For ancient Hawaiians, gorgeous **'Īao Valley** was the equivalent of Egypt's Valley of the Kings: they buried their royal dead in the long-lost Olopio cave, and access was barred to commoners.

    Kamehameha the Great conquered Maui in a battle

here in 1790. The local armies were driven back into the valley from the shoreline, where they could be bombarded with impunity by the great cannon Lopaka, directed by John Young and Isaac Davis (see p.118). While the defeated general, Kalanikūpule, the son of Maui's chief Kahekili, fled across the mountains, the bodies of his men choked the ʻĪao Stream. Hence the name by which the battle became known – **Kepaniwai**, "the water dam."

ʻĪao Valley – and especially the stunning **ʻĪao Needle**, a 1200-foot pinnacle of green-clad lava – is now one of Hawaii's most famous beauty spots. Owing to the crumbly nature of the rock, climbing the needle would be a physical impossibility, but you can admire it from various short hiking trails that meander around its base.

Tropical Gardens of Maui

Map 1, D4. Daily 9am–5pm; free.

Less than a mile out of Wailuku, the **Tropical Gardens of Maui** spread away below and to the right of what by now is ʻĪao Valley Road. This small commercial garden displays and sells a colorful assortment of tropical plants from all over the world and mails specimens to the continental US. It also holds a small snack bar.

Kepaniwai County Park

Map 1, D4. Daily dawn–dusk; free.

Just after the road crosses the ʻĪao Stream, a mile past the Tropical Gardens, **Kepaniwai County Park** is an attractive public garden set amid dramatic, curtain-like folds in the mountains. Its lawns and flowerbeds are laid out to commemorate the many ethnic groups of Hawaii, with themed areas paying tribute to Maui's Japanese, Chinese and Portuguese immigrants, among others. Structures include a traditional thatched *hale*, ornamental pavilions and minia-ture pagodas, as well as statues of anonymous sugar-cane workers and Dr Sun Yat-Sen, a sometime Maui resident who became the first President of the Republic of China (see p.174).

Hawaii Nature Center

Map 1, D4. Daily 10am–4pm; adults $6, under-13s $4; ⓣ 244-6500; ⓦ www.hawaiinaturecenter.org.

The **Hawaii Nature Center**, immediately adjoining Kepaniwai County Park, is largely an educational facility for schoolchildren and holds simple exhibitions on Hawaiian flora, fauna and handicrafts. In addition, however, staff members conduct guided **hikes** in the ʻĪao Valley area (Mon–Fri 2pm; adults $25, ages 8 to 12 $23). Because the high-mountain trails are otherwise closed to visitors, these provide the only access to the wilderness beyond the Needle. The cost of the hikes includes admission to the center and a souvenir T-shirt.

John F. Kennedy Profile

Map 1, D4.

The next stop along ʻĪao Valley Road is a wayside lookout at the mouth of a small side valley. A natural rock formation a couple of hundred yards up the valley has for many years been known as the **John F. Kennedy Profile**, although tree growth has increasingly obscured JFK's chin. Signs that formerly pointed out the likeness have recently been changed to read "A Changing Profile," and coyly avoid mentioning the assassinated president. The official line now is that the face belongs to Kūakaʻiwai, a sixteenth-century chief.

'Īao Valley State Park

Map 1, D4. Daily 7am–7pm; free.

'Īao Valley Road meanders to a dead end three miles out of Wailuku, at the parking lot for **'Īao Valley State Park**. Although you can clearly see 'Īao Needle from here, a short but steep footpath crosses the stream and climbs up a nearby knoll for even better views from a covered rain shelter. Two paved but potentially slippery trails loop down to the stream from the main footpath, one on either side of the stream. Gardens laid out with native plants line the one closer to the parking lot. The small waterlogged *lo'i* or *taro* patch here, similar to a paddy field, offers one of the best angles for photographs, as you look up past the footbridge toward the Needle.

Despite appearances, the velvety **'Īao Needle** is not free-standing, but simply a raised knob at the end of a sinuous ridge. Standing, head usually in the clouds, at the intersection of two lush valleys, it's what geologists prosaically term an "erosional residual," meaning a nugget of hard volcanic rock left behind when the softer surrounding rocks were eroded away. From this side, it's an impressive 1200 feet tall, but no higher than the ridges that surround it. With their usual scatological gusto, the ancient Hawaiians named it Kūka'emoku, which politely translates as "broken excreta."

This whole area owes its existence to the phenomenal amount of rain that falls on West Maui; the 5788-foot peak of **Pu'u Kukui**, just over two miles from here, receives more than 400 inches per year. Unless you come early in the morning, it's likely to be raining in 'Īao Valley, but even when it's pouring you can usually look straight back down the valley to see the dry sunlit plains of the isthmus. After a series of accidents, the **trails** that lead beyond 'Īao Needle are barred to unaccompanied walkers, and can now only be seen on the guided hikes run by the Hawaii Nature Center (see above).

'ĪAO VALLEY STATE PARK

Waihe'e

On the map, it might look as though driving **north from Wailuku** would be as good a way to reach Lahaina and the resorts of West Maui as heading south via Mā'alea. In fact, the northward road, **Kahekili** Highway (Hwy-340), rapidly becomes so narrow and dangerous that all the major rental-car agencies forbid their customers to use it. While that means most visitors never see the dramatic scenery en route, it has at least spared a superb stretch of coastline from the over-development that typifies much of West Maui.

To see the most spectacular segments of this little-known route, you'd do best to approach from the opposite direction, driving beyond Kapalua and Honolua Bay as detailed on p.139 onward. However, for the first few miles out of Wailuku, as it heads into the little suburb of **WAIHE'E**, the Kahekili Highway is broad and easy to drive, and the trailhead for the enjoyable Waihe'e Ridge hike lies only a short distance beyond.

WAIHE'E VALLEY

Map 1, D3.

Three-quarters of a mile after Hwy-340 passes Waihe'e School on the left, a total of four miles out of Wailuku, Waihe'e Valley Road heads half-a-mile inland into **Waihe'e Valley**. So long as you've come equipped with raingear and mosquito repellent, it's possible to do the two-hour round-trip **rainforest hike** from here.

However, ongoing disputes over public access have resulted in the trail falling into disrepair, and locals are not keen on hikers leaving vehicles on or near their property. If you're determined to try, park as close as seems wise to the T-junction at the end of the road, and set off walking uphill along the dirt road to the right, which soon deteriorates to a rutted track. After almost a mile of hiking past dense ferns, banyans and fruit trees, you have to cross the Waihe'e Stream twice in quick succession. If it's raining, or looks likely to start, turn back; flash floods render conditions extremely dangerous. Should you make it all the way, you'll be rewarded by a cool, deep swimming hole, below a small dam two miles from the start, and views of waterfalls deeper into the valley.

WAIHE'E RIDGE TRAIL

Map 1, D3.

For two miles beyond the Waihe'e Valley turnoff, Kahekili Highway climbs steadily up **Waihe'e Ridge**, leaving civilization ever further behind. Near the top of the ridge, a dirt road signposted to Camp Maluhia, a scout camp, cuts away inland, meandering across the meadows for a mile to reach the starting point for the **Waihe'e Ridge Trail**.

This gorgeous climb, best done in the morning before the clouds set in, takes you as deep into the West Maui mountains as it's possible to go; allow at least two hours for the round-trip. Follow the road until it makes a sharp curve toward the camp itself, and park in the field alongside. The trail starts off as a very clear cement path beyond a barred gate, heading straight up the hill through a field of cows. Having skirted the minor hill on the left by taking a right fork at the top, you find yourself in a pine and eucalyptus forest. You emerge to views down into Waihe'e Valley, over to a double waterfall embedded in the next ridge to the north, and back across the isthmus to Haleakalā Highway snaking up the volcano.

For the first mile and a half, it looks as if you're heading for the crest of the ridge ahead, but the path ultimately sidesteps across a brief razorback to reach an unexpected high mountain valley. The terrain here is extremely marshy, but you're soon climbing again, and the trail ends at an unsheltered picnic table in a clearing two and a quarter miles up. In principle, you can see most of northern Maui from this spot, which is the summit of Lanilili ("small heaven") Peak, but you'll almost certainly find that, by now, you're well above the cloud line.

Māʻalaea

The direct road south from Wailuku, **Honoapiʻilani Highway** (Hwy-30), is joined as it crosses the isthmus by highways from Kahului and Kīhei and carries virtually all the traffic heading for Lahaina and the West Maui resorts. At the point where it reaches the south coast, six miles out of Wailuku, **MĀʻALAEA** is a former commercial port that has been given a new lease of life as the preferred marina of Maui's flotilla of cruise and pleasure boats. The largest contingent are the Molokini snorkel boats (see p.90), so Māʻalaea is at its busiest very early in the morning, when the day's passengers assemble. At this time it also offers great views of Haleakalā, whose summit pokes out above the ring of clouds that usually obscures it from Kīhei.

Swimming anywhere near Māʻalaea is not recommended, but there are good **surfing** breaks just to the south, while **windsurfers** hurtle out into Māʻalaea Bay from the thin and unexciting strip of sand that stretches all the way east to Kīhei.

For an account of the Lahaina Pali Trail, which sets off across the southern tip of West Maui from just north of Māʻalaea, see p.120.

Maui Ocean Center

Map 1, D5. Daily 9am–5pm, adults $18.50, ages 3–12 $12.50;
ⓣ 270-7000; ⓦ www.mauioceancenter.com.

While Mā'alaea is still not a town in any meaningful sense,
it has recently acquired a center, in the guise of the
Mā'alaea Harbor Village mall. That in turn focuses on
the **Maui Ocean Center**, a state-of-the-art **aquarium**
providing a colorful introduction to the marine life of
Hawaii. It's not quite as large as you might expect from the
size of the entrance fee, but its exhibits are well chosen and
very well displayed.

The most spectacular section comes first. The coral groves
of the **Living Reef** (some of them fluorescent) hold such
species as camouflaged scorpionfish, seahorses, octopuses and
bizarre "upside down jellyfish." Eerie garden eels poke like
blades of grass from the sandy seabed, but the star, of course,
is Hawaii's state fish, the *humuhumunukunukunukuāpua'a* – literally, "the triggerfish with a snout like a pig."

Open-air terraces perched above the harbor hold tanks of
huge rays and green sea turtles. Beyond them, additional
displays cover the life cycle of **whales**, and the relationship
between **Hawaiians and the Sea**, illustrating traditional
fishing techniques and equipment. A final huge tank holds
pelagic, or open-ocean, sea creatures; its walk-through
glass tunnel means that you can stand beneath mighy sharks
and rays as they swim above your head.

Practicalities

Mā'alaea has in the past few years acquired half a dozen characterless **condo** buildings, lined up beyond the harbor along
Hau'oli Street. Most enjoy broad sea views, but Mā'alaea is a
decidedly windy and insect-prone spot, and staying here is
only likely to appeal to fanatical sailors. If you do want to

MAUI OCEAN CENTER

CHAPTER ONE

OKINI SNORKEL CRUISES

wn **snorkeling** and **diving** spot is the tiny
kini, three miles off Mākena. Created by a
some 230,000 years ago, it rises about 500ft
from the underwater flank of Haleakalā, though only the southern half of the circular crater still pokes above the waves, to a maximum height of 162ft. There's no beach, or landfall of any kind, but you see a lot of fish, including deep-water species.

Countless cruises leave early each morning from Mā'alaea Harbor; the currents off the Maui coast are too strong to allow swimming or kayaking to Molokini. For virtually all the companies listed below, you should be able to find discount prices from activities operators such as those listed on p.45. Snorkelers can pay anything from $45 to $100 for a five- to six-hour morning trip, depending on the size and comfort of the boat and the refreshments offered, and from $30 for a shorter afternoon jaunt; scuba divers pay around $40 extra. Note that between November and April, many companies stop running Molokini trips and concentrate on lucrative whale-watching cruises instead; for full details, see p.50.

Company	Phone	ⓦwww	Passengers
Blue Dolphin	ⓣ622-0075	–	40
Friendly Charters	ⓣ244-1979	mauisnorkeling.com	70
Frogman	ⓣ662-0075	bossfrog.com	52
Lahaina Princess	ⓣ667-6165	maui.net/~ismarine	100
Leilani	ⓣ242-0955	–	49
Ocean Activities Center	ⓣ879-4485	mauioceanactivities.com	75/100
Pacific Whale Foundation	ⓣ879-8811	pacificwhale.org	20/48/100
Paragon Sailing Charters	ⓣ244-2087	sailmaui.com	35
Pride of Maui	ⓣ242-0955	prideofmaui.com	149
Prince Kuhio	ⓣ242-8777	mvprince.com	149

book a condo locally, contact Māʻalaea Bay Rentals (℡244-5627 or 1-800/367-6084; ⓦwww.maalaeabay.com).

However, Māʻalaea is also home to a handful of high-quality **restaurants**. Perched above the harbor at the seaward end of Māʻalaea Harbor Village – with an ocean-view terrace that comes into its own at lunchtime – *Merriman's Bamboo Bistro* (daily 11.30am–2pm & 5.30–9pm; ℡243-7374) serves delicious Pacific Rim cuisine. Its specialty is what chef Peter Merriman calls "tropas" – a tropical version of tapas. A typical three-course dinner of goats' cheese in phyllo with strawberry and onion salad, sesame-crusted *onaga* with papaya relish, and prime rib with Japanese sauce is a bargain at $25. Nearby, the menu at the equally large and scenic *Māʻalaea Waterfront Restaurant*, 50 Hauʻoli St (daily 5–9.30pm; ℡244-9028), focuses on expensive freshly caught fish, with a *cioppino* stew priced at $35. You can also buy fish for yourself at the Māʻalaea Fish Market (Mon–Sat 10am–4pm), just around the harbor.

Pāʻia

PĀʻIA, four miles east of Kahului on the Hāna Highway, is a friendly, laid-back town whose two distinct sections both began life serving the sugar plantations in the 1870s. **Upper Pāʻia**, concentrated around the sugar mill half-a-mile inland, was built on plantation land and held the camps that housed the laborers, as well as company stores and other facilities. Meanwhile, freebooting entrepreneurs set up shop in **Lower Pāʻia**, at sea level, operating stores, theaters, restaurants and anything else that might persuade their captive clientele to part with a few pennies.

Both parts of Pā'ia declined apace with the collapse of agriculture, especially after the post-World War II drift to Kahului (see p.67). The name "Pā'ia" today refers almost exclusively to what used to be Lower Pā'ia, which has re-emerged in recent years as a center for windsurfers and beach bums. The paint-peeling wooden buildings around the bottom end of **Baldwin Avenue** are home to assorted gift stores and galleries, giving it a very similar feel to Makawao, at the top of the road (see p.166).

Narrow footpaths thread their way toward the ocean from the Hāna Highway, passing between ramshackle houses with colorful gardens, to reach a short, tree-lined and sandy **beach**. Swimming here in Pā'ia Bay is rarely appealing, thanks to shallow, murky water and abundant seaweed, so locals head instead to the **H.A. Baldwin Beach County Park**, a mile west. Named for Harry Baldwin, son of Henry Baldwin of Alexander & Baldwin fame (see p.72), this was once the official sugar-company beach, and the chimneys of the sugar mill, which closed down in 2000, remain visible for the moment a few hundred yards off the highway, across the still-active cane fields. The beach itself is reached by a short approach road lined by a graceful curve of palm trees. Perfect body-surfing waves crash onto its long unprotected stretch of sand, with safer swimming areas at either end.

Most visitors to Pā'ia are simply day-trippers,
passing through as they drive the "Road to Hāna,"
described in detail in Chapter Seven.

HO'OKIPA BEACH COUNTY PARK

Map 9, B2.

The best **windsurfing** site in Maui, if not the world, is **Ho'okipa Beach County Park**, just below the highway two miles east of Pā'ia. Thanks to a submerged rocky ledge that starts just a few feet out, the waves here are stupendous, and so are the skills required to survive in them – this is no place for beginners. The peak season for windsurfing is summer, when the trade winds are at their most consistent. By longstanding arrangement, sailboarders can only take to the water after 11am each day. In the early morning, and on those rare winter days when the wind dies down, expert **surfers** flock to Ho'okipa to ride the break known as "Pavilions" near the headland to the east.

As a beach, Ho'okipa is not hugely attractive. It's unshaded for most of its length apart from a nice big grove of trees at the western end. Picnic shelters, showers and restrooms are ranged along a platform of lava boulders raised above the small shelf of sand. In summer, the surf can be low enough for swimming, but you still have to negotiate the seaweed-covered ledge to reach deep enough water.

Ho'okipa is so busy that you can only approach it along a one-way loop road, which starts beyond its far eastern end; the auxiliary parking lot on the headland here is a great place from which to watch or photograph the action.

ACCOMMODATION IN THE PĀ'IA AREA

There's very little **accommodation** in Pā'ia itself. Windsurfers on a tight budget tend to stay at the *Banana Bungalow* in Wailuku (see p.76), while those limited to $60 per night head for Kahului or a cheap Kīhei condo. If you can pay any more, try one of the plush **B&Bs** scattered along country lanes in and around nearby villages such as **Kū'au** and **Ha'ikū**. Long-term visitors should be able to find a room through the local **bulletin boards**, which advertise rates of around $270 per week, or from $425 to $750 per month.

Both the county parks near Pā'ia that used to offer **camping** – **Baldwin Beach County Park** and **Rainbow Park**, up the road toward Hāli'imaile – no longer do so.

Golden Bamboo Ranch

1205 Kaupakalua Rd, Ha'ikū, HI 96708; reserve through Hawaii's Best B&B, PO Box 563, Kamuela, HI 96743 ⓣ 885-4550 or 1-800/262-9912, ⓕ 885-0559; ⓦ www.bestbnb.com.
Lovely, gay-friendly B&B on a gorgeous garden estate above Ha'ikū, with one self-contained cottage and another divided into three apartments. All units have kitchens and bathrooms, plus *lānais* looking across paddocks and orchards to the ocean. ❸.

Kū'au Cove Plantation

2 Wa'a Place, Kū'au, Pā'ia, HI 96779 ⓣ 579-8988, ⓕ 579-8710; ⓦ www.maui.net/~kuaubnb.
Restored plantation home, very close to the ocean a mile or so east of Pā'ia – and thus ideal for windsurfers visiting Ho'okipa. It features two en-suite bedrooms and two studio apartments. ❸.

Pilialoha

2512 Kaupakalua Rd, Ha'ikū, HI 96708 ⓣ 572-1440, ⓕ 572-4612.
Small cottage in gardens of private home above Ha'ikū, with kitchen, bathroom and space enough to sleep four comfortably. Three-night minimum stay. ❹.

PĀ'IA RESTAURANTS

Pā'ia may fall down on lodging, but as far as **restaurants** are concerned it comes up trumps. Though fresh fish is the local specialty, there's something for all tastes, including a rare vegan option.

Anthony's Coffee Co

90C Hāna Hwy ⓣ 579-8340.
Small coffee shop just west of central Pā'ia, dominated by the churning coffee roaster, and serving espressos, pastries, soups, bagels and deli sandwiches at a handful of

indoor tables. Daily
5.30am–6pm.

Charley's

142 Hāna Hwy ⓣ 579-9453.
Large, sprawling, indoor
restaurant, offering eggy
breakfasts and mac-nut
pancakes, plus lunchtime
sandwiches, burritos and
burgers for $7–10. The
dinner menu has the same
snacks, plus pasta and pizzas –
calzones are $11 – and ribs or
fish for more like $15.
Breakfast and lunch daily
7am–2.30pm, bar food
2.30–5pm, dinner 5–10pm.

Mama's

799 Poho Place ⓣ 579-8488.
Upmarket and wildly popular
fish restaurant, set in
beachfront gardens on a
headland a mile east of
downtown Pā'ia. At lunch,
there are fishy sandwiches and
burgers for $10; at dinner, the
fresh catch of the day is
around $25. The menu
credits the individual
fisherman who caught your
fish. Daily 11am–9.30pm.

Milagros

112 Hāna Hwy at Baldwin Ave
ⓣ 579-8755.
Friendly café, serving all
meals at parasol-shaded tables
on a terrace at Pā'ia's main
intersection. Salads and deli
sandwiches for around $6,
burgers, tacos and burritos for
more like $8. Daily
8am–10pm.

Moana Bakery & Café

71 Baldwin Ave ⓣ 579-9999.
Smart, tasteful café not far off
the main highway, with
mosaic tables and large
windows. Serves fancy
breakfasts, $7–8 lunchtime
sandwiches, and $9–24 dinner
entrees that range from green
or red Thai curries to chili-
seared 'ahi to 'ōpakapaka laulau
(snapper wrapped in ti leaves).
Daily 8am–9pm.

Pā'ia Fish Market

110 Hāna Hwy at Baldwin Ave
ⓣ 579-8030.
Informal, inexpensive place
with wooden benches and
tables, where fresh fish –
sashimi or blackened – is $12,
while scallops, shrimps and
calamari cost a bit more, and

a fish or meat burger is just $6. Pasta entrees include chicken for $13 or seafood for $15, and there's a sideline in quesadillas, fajitas and soft tacos. Daily 11am–9.30pm.

Pauwela Café

375 W Kuiaha Rd, Haʻikū ⓣ575-9242.

Occupying one corner of the rusting gray old hulk of Pauwela Cannery, a mile off Hwy-36 and roughly five miles east of Pāʻia, this cheerful, classy neighborhood café serves delicious, inexpensive breakfasts – try the *pain perdu* – plus salads, sandwiches, and lunch specials all priced around $5. Mon–Sat 7am–3pm, Sun 8am–2pm.

Pic-nics

30 Baldwin Ave ⓣ579-8021.
Bright yellow plantation-style

diner serving espressos plus delicious spinach-nut-burgers with cheese, and chicken, fish and beef plate lunches, for $6–8. Picnics to go cost from $8.50 per person. Daily 7am–5pm.

The Vegan

115 Baldwin Ave ⓣ579-9144.
Top-quality vegetarian cuisine, served at rattan tables in a simple yet colorful diner, well away from the mayhem a couple of hundred yards up from Pāʻia's central junction. Spicy, tofu-heavy Thai specialties, plus polenta, lasagne and Mexican dishes. Try two of the $10 daily entrees for the price of one, a soy burger for $5.50, or a tofu hot dog for $3.50. Tues–Sun 11am–9pm.

96

Lahaina

Seen from a short distance offshore, **LAHAINA**, West Maui's only real town, is one of the prettiest communities in all Hawaii. During the early nineteenth century it served as capital of the entire Kingdom of Hawaii, but it has barely grown since then, and on first impressions it could still almost be the peaceful, tropical village it once was. Its main oceanfront street is lined with timber-frame buildings; a tall-masted sailing ship bobs in the harbor; coconut palms sway to either side of the central banyan tree; surfers swirl into the thin fringe of beach to the south; and the mountains of West Maui dominate the skyline, ringed as often as not by beautiful rainbows.

Up close, however, many of Lahaina's decrepit-looking structures turn out to be mere fakes, housing T-shirt stores, galleries peddling "celebrity art" by the likes of Ron Wood and Sly Stallone, and tacky themed restaurants, and the crowds and congestion along **Front Street** can seem all too reminiscent of Waikīkī.

Note that although Lahaina is of course in West Maui, it merits a chapter to itself – use map 4 at the back of the book for easy orientation. See Chapter Three for coverage of West Maui as a whole.

Even so, Lahaina makes an attractive base, sandwiched in a long thin strip between the ever-fascinating ocean and equally spellbinding hills. Early evening is especially unforgettable, with the sun casting a rich glow on the mountains as it sets behind the island of Lanai. Lahaina is lively and by Maui standards inexpensive, with a huge range of activities and little rainfall, but above all it's the only town on the island to offer lodging, sightseeing, nightlife and an abundance of restaurants within easy walking distance of each other.

Some history

Although there's little left to show for it nowadays – you can easily see all the town has to offer in a couple of hours – Lahaina boasts a colorful past. By the time the first foreigners came to Hawaii, it was already the residence of the high *ali'i* of Maui. The name "Lahaina" is thought to derive from a Hawaiian phrase meaning "merciless sun," and was in legend suggested by a chief foolish enough to attempt a long walk through West Maui in the full heat of the day.

Kamehameha the Great sealed his conquest of Maui by sacking Lahaina in 1795, then returned in 1802, and spent a year preparing for what was to be an unsuccessful invasion of Kauai. His successors, Kamehamehas II and III, made the town their **capital** between the 1820s and 1840s, ruling from the island of **Moku'ula**, in a lake in what is now Malu'ulu o Lele Park, south of downtown.

When **whaling** ships started to put in during the 1820s, seeking to recuperate from their grueling Pacific peregrinations, fierce struggles between the sailors and Lahaina's Christian **missionaries** became commonplace. Whaling crews, incensed by missionary attempts to control drinking and prostitution, repeatedly attacked the home of Reverend

William Richards, but in due course chose to head instead for the fleshpots of Honolulu. In the 1840s, however, following the death of Maui's devout Governor Hoapili, the whalemen returned en masse. More than four hundred whaling ships docked at Lahaina in 1846, and for the next two decades, it was a lawless and rip-roaring frontier town, described by another missionary as "one of the breathing holes of Hell."

Surprisingly, Lahaina has never been a true deep-water port. Its prosperity was based on its calm, shallow roadstead, sheltered by the islands of Molokai and Lanai. For the most part, sailing ships simply anchored anything from a couple hundred yards to three miles offshore and sent their crews ashore by rowboat. During the nineteenth century, in fact, a long covered marketplace lined the banks of a canal parallel to the seafront, enabling seamen to buy all they needed without ever leaving their boats.

With the decline in whaling, Lahaina turned toward agriculture. **Sugar** arrived in 1862, when the Pioneer Mill Company was established, while **pineapples** followed early in the twentieth century. The roadstead had never been quite as safe as the sailors had liked to imagine, and a new harbor was constructed in 1922 at Māla Wharf, just north of town. Unfortunately it proved to be dangerously storm-prone, and Lahaina is no longer a port of call for ships of any size.

Devastated by a huge fire in 1919, and by the state-wide *tsunami* of 1946, Lahaina remained a sleepy backwater until the 1970s. Only with the success of the Pioneer Mill Company's resort development at neighboring **Kāʻanapali** did it return to prominence, as the hectic tourist destination of today. The mill itself, meanwhile, quietly closed down in 1999.

HISTORY

INFORMATION

Walk along Front Street and you'll be deluged with brochures and leaflets by the various activity kiosks, but dispassionate advice – together with more brochures and maps, and also email access – can be obtained at the **Lahaina Visitor Center** (daily 9am–5pm; ☎667-9193; ⓦwww.visitlahaina.com), inside the Old Lahaina Court House on Banyan Tree Square.

The main **post office** (Mon–Fri 8.30am–5pm, Sat 10am–noon; zip code HI 96761), which handles general delivery mail, is a couple of miles north of town past Māla Wharf, near the civic center, but there's a smaller branch at 132 Papalaua St, in the Lahaina Shopping Center (Mon–Fri 8.15am–4.15pm).

GETTING AROUND

With the exception of the ferries to Molokai and Lanai, and the taxi-style shuttle buses that serve all of Maui (see p.26), Lahaina has only very localized **public transport**.

While you'll be glad to have a **rental car** to get to or from Lahaina, in town it can be a real nuisance. If you're staying here, leave the car at your hotel, as the cramped streets make **parking** a terrible business. The only free public parking is at Front and Prison streets, though you can usually leave your car at one of the larger malls, like the Lahaina Shopping Center.

For details of flights to Lahaina's nearest airport, at Kapalua, see p.16; Maui's main airport is at Kahului, see p.67.

If you'd prefer to **cycle**, West Maui Cycles, 840 Waine'e St (☎661-9005), rents out mountain bikes at around $25 for 24 hours or about $100 per week; it also has snorkel equipment, boogie boards and surfboards.

Buses

The West Maui Shopping Express (℡ 877-7308) operates two **bus** routes in the Lahaina area, both connecting the Wharf Cinema Center with the Whaler's Village mall in **Kā'anapali** and both charging a flat one-way fare of $1. One runs thirteen times daily, and stops at all the major hotels in Kā'anapali. The first departure from the Wharf Cinema Center is at 10.10am and the last at 10.10pm; the first bus of the day **from Kā'anapali** on this route leaves Whaler's Village at 9.55am, the last at 9.55pm. The other route connects the two malls with the Lahaina and Pu'ukoli'i train stations (see below), with seven trips each day. Buses leave the Wharf Cinema Center between 9.25am and 4.30pm; buses from Kā'anapali operate between 8.45am and 4.10pm.

Boat trips and other Lahaina-based activities are detailed on p.49 onward.

The Sugar Cane Train

The **Sugar Cane Train** (adults $11.50 one-way, $15.75 round-trip, under-13s $6.75/$8.75; ℡ 667-6851 or, in the US only, 1-800/499-2307) is a train with a restored locomotive (complete with "singing conductor") that runs six-mile, half-hour excursions through the cane fields along the tracks of the old Lahaina & Kā'anapali Railroad. It travels from Lahaina to Kā'anapali and then a half-mile beyond to turn around at Pu'ukoli'i. For anyone other than a small child, it's not an exciting trip. The first departure from Lahaina is at 9.45am daily and the last at 4.50pm; from Kā'anapali, the first is at 9.05am daily, the last at 4.10pm. Free shuttle buses connect the Lahaina and Kā'anapali stations with the Wharf Cinema Center and the Whaler's Village, respectively.

Ferries

In addition to its many excursion vessels, Lahaina Harbor is home to the only scheduled **inter-island ferry services** in Hawaii. *Expeditions* (☎661-3756 or, off Maui, 1-800/695-2624) sails from in front of the *Pioneer Inn* to Mānele Bay on **Lanai** daily at 6.45am, 9.15am, 12.45pm, 3.15pm and 5.45pm. Departures from Lanai are at 8am, 10.30am, 2pm, 4.30pm and 6.45pm; the adult fare is $25 each way, while under-12s go for $20. The trip takes about 50 minutes.

It's also possible to make a 1hr 15min ferry crossing between Maui and Molokai on the *Molokai Princess* (adults $40 one way, children $20; ☎667-6165 or 1-800/275-6969; ⓦwww.mauiprincess.com). On Monday through Saturday, the boat brings commuters over from Molokai to their jobs on Maui, leaving Kaunakakai Harbor at 6am and setting off on the return trip from Lahaina at 5.15pm. On Sundays, it runs day-trips in the other direction, leaving Lahaina at 7.30am and Kaunakakai at 3.30pm. The *Molokai Princess* also offers commercial sightseeing cruises.

ACCOMMODATION

In terms of **accommodation**, Lahaina has nothing to rival the opulence of Kā'anapali and Kapalua, further up the coast. However, the *Pioneer Inn* harks back romantically to the old days of Hawaiian tourism, and there are also a couple of classy B&B inns, plus a few central but quiet hotel-cum-condos.

Aloha Lani Inn

13 Kaua'ula Rd ☎661-8040, ⓕ661-8045; ⓦwww.maui.net/~tony. Two small, simple rooms in a welcoming private house, a stone's throw from the beach, roughly half a mile south of central Lahaina. Guests share a bathroom plus use of the kitchen (no breakfast is served); laundry facilities are

ACCOMMODATION PRICE CODES

All accommodation prices in this book have been graded with the following symbols; for a full explanation, see p.29.

❶ up to $40   **❹** $100–150   **❼** $250–300

❷ $40–70   **❺** $150–200   **❽** $300–400

❸ $70–100   **❻** $200–250   **❾** over $400

available. The resident owner can advise on activities. Two-night minimum stay. **❸**.

Aston Maui Islander

660 Waine'e St ☏ 667-9766, 1-800/922-7866 (US & Can) or 1-800/321-2558 (HI), ℻ 661-3733; ⓦ www.aston-hotels.com. Low-key but attractively refurbished and good-value complex a couple of blocks from the sea in central Lahaina. Options range from hotel rooms to two-bedroom condos; the buildings are connected by a rambling system of walkways through colorful gardens. Free use of a swimming pool and tennis courts is included. Rooms **❹**, suites **❺**.

Best Western Pioneer Inn

658 Wharf St ☏ 661-3636 or 1-800/457-5457, ℻ 667-5708; ⓦ www.pioneerinnmaui.com. Historic and highly atmospheric wooden hotel on the seafront in the very center of Lahaina (described on p.106), now associated with the Best Western chain. The tastefully furnished rooms, all with private bath and air-conditioning, open onto a lovely *lānai* overlooking Banyan Tree Square, and there are also some luxurious two-bedroom suites. Rooms **❹**, suites **❺**.

Lahaina Inn

127 Lahainaluna Rd ☏ 661-0577 or 1-800/669-3444, ℻ 667-9480; ⓦ www.lahainainn.com. Luxurious, antique-furnished re-creation of how a century-old inn ought to look, set

The telephone area code for all Hawaii is ☏ 808.

slightly back from Front Street above *David Paul's Lahaina Grill* (see p.115). Twelve air-conditioned rooms of varying sizes, equipped with private baths and phones, but no TV. Two-night minimum Friday and Saturday. No children under 15. ❹–❺.

Lahaina Shores Beach Resort

475 Front St ⓣ661-3339 or 1-800/642-6284 (US & Can), ⓕ667-1145; ⓦwww.lahaina-shores.com. Large, light-filled shorefront hotel building, facing a pretty little beach a few hundred yards south of central Lahaina, next door to the 505 Front Street mall. Two-, three- and four-person rooms and suites, all with kitchens and *lānais*; an ocean view costs around $30 more than a mountain view. Rooms ❺, suites ❼.

Old Lahaina House

PO Box 10355, ⓣ667-4663 or 1-800/847-0761, ⓕ667-5615; ⓦwww.oldlahaina.com. Good-quality B&B accommodation in friendly private home complete with pool, a few hundred yards south of downtown Lahaina. One guest room is in the house, and four more are in a separate garden wing; all are en-suite, with refrigerators, TVs, and air-conditioning. Rates include breakfast on the *lānai*. ❸.

Plantation Inn

174 Lahainaluna Rd ⓣ667-9225 or 1-800/433-6815, ⓕ667-9293; ⓦwww.theplantationinn.com. Luxury B&B hotel, not far back from the sea and styled to resemble a Southern plantation home, with columns and verandahs. All rooms have bathrooms and *lānais*, some also have kitchenettes, and there's a twelve-foot-deep pool. Guests get a discount at the downstairs restaurant, *Gerard's* (see p.116). Rooms ❹–❺, suites ❻.

All properties listed here share the zip code Lahaina HI 96761.

ACCOMMODATION

DOWNTOWN LAHAINA

Almost all the activity of modern Lahaina is concentrated along **Front Street**, where a few historic buildings such as the Baldwin Home and Wo Hing Temple hang on amid an awful lot of shopping malls, souvenir stores and fast-food outlets. The very heart of town is **Banyan Tree Square**, an attractive public space kept too busy for comfort by coachloads of tourists.

For respite, locals and visitors alike gravitate toward the **waterfront**. The views are superb, whether you look straight across to the island of Lanai, where you'll probably be able to make out the crest of Norfolk pines along its topmost ridge, or north toward Molokai, where the west-end mountain of Mauna Loa is visible on a clear day. Closer at hand, fishermen angle for sandfish in the inshore waters, boats and yachts bob beyond the placid roll of white surf fifty yards out, and parasailers peer down upon all this activity from on high.

If you're looking for **shops**, the two largest malls are the modern **Lahaina Center** – three blocks north of downtown and home to a reproduction Hawaiian village, the **Hale Kahiko**, which offers *hula* shows and explanatory tours (daily 11am–4pm) – and the **Lahaina Cannery**, a long walk further north near Māla Wharf.

Banyan Tree Square

Map 4, E6.

A magnificent banyan tree, planted on April 24, 1873, to commemorate the fiftieth anniversary of the arrival of Maui's first missionaries, almost completely fills **Banyan Tree Square**. It consists of at least twenty major trunks, plus any number of intertwined tendrils pushing back down into the ground. A phenomenal number of chirruping birds congregate in the branches, while portrait artists tout for customers in the shade below.

Here and there on the surrounding lawns, a few outlines mark the former extent of **Lahaina Fort**. This was built by Governor Hoapili in 1832, in response to several incidents in which unruly whalemen had bombarded the town. Its walls once held as many as 47 cannons, salvaged from assorted shipwrecks throughout Hawaii; a drum was beaten on its ramparts at nightfall as a signal for all foreign seamen to return to their ships. The fort was demolished in 1854, but one small corner has been reconstructed, at the south-west end of the square.

The **Court House**, on the harbor side of Banyan Tree Square, was constructed in 1859, after a storm had destroyed most of Lahaina's previous official buildings. It now holds the small local visitor center (see p.100), as well as the Banyan Tree Gallery, which hosts interesting, free **art exhibitions** (daily 9am–5pm).

Across Canal Street from the Court House, the **Pioneer Inn** has since 1901 been the main social center of Lahaina. Its original owner was a Canadian "Mountie." Having pursued a criminal all the way to Maui, he decided to stay on and go into the hotel business, catering to passengers on the Inter-Island Steamship line. It makes an atmospheric spot to stop in for a beer, though it's hardly very peaceful.

The Brick Palace and the Hauola Stone

Map 4, D5.

Lahaina Public Library, immediately north of the *Pioneer Inn*, stands on the site of the former **royal *taro* patch**, personally tended by the first three Kamehamehas. A line of bricks set into the grass on its seaward side traces the foundations of the **Brick Palace**, the first Western-style building in Hawaii. Two stories high and measuring 20ft by 40ft, it was built for Kamehameha the Great in 1798 by an English convict who had managed to escape from Australia; the palace survived until the 1860s.

Poking out from the waves beyond the seawall to the north, the approximately chair-shaped **Hauola Stone** was a "healing rock" where Hawaiian women would give birth. In thanks for a trouble-free labor, the umbilical cord (*piko*) of the infant would be left under the rock.

The Carthaginian

Map 4, D5. Daily 10am–5pm, last admission 4pm; $3 per person, $5 per couple or family.

The square-rigged sailing brig *Carthaginian* may look like a superb relic of Lahaina's whaling days, gently swaying at its permanent moorings in front of the *Pioneer Inn*, but in fact it's a rather pointless fake. Even the original *Carthaginian*, which was moored here until it sank in 1972, was only a replica of a nineteenth-century whaling vessel, refitted for use in the movie version of James Michener's *Hawaii*. This one started life in 1920 as a two-masted German schooner, then plied the Baltic for several decades as a diesel-powered cement carrier, and only took on its present shape after being brought from Europe in 1973 to replace the previous version.

Paying the steep admission charge entitles you to cross the gangplank and descend into its interior. As a whaling museum, it's not a patch on the free displays at Kāʻanapali (see p.128): half the space within is taken up by a plain nineteenth-century whaleboat from Alaska, and half by benches facing a TV screen showing endless video commercials for local whale-watching trips. The highlight is the chance to pick up a phone and hear recorded whale songs "for education or entertainment."

THE CARTHAGINIAN

Lahaina Harbor

Map 4, D6.

Alongside the *Carthaginian*, a simple and modern white structure has replaced what was said to be the oldest **lighthouse** in the entire Pacific Ocean, built to serve the whaling fleet in 1840. Shielded by a breakwater of boulders, **Lahaina Harbor** now serves as a pleasure-boat marina, despite becoming ever less able to cope with the scale of West Maui's tourist activity. The harbor wall holds kiosks for most local **boat operators**, but it's not much of an area to stroll around. You can, in any case, usually get better prices from the activity centers along Front Street.

Lahaina Beach

Map 4, D7.

Immediately south of the marina, **Lahaina Beach**, with its shallow water, sandy bottom and gentle breaks, is where companies such as the Goofy Foot Surf School (☎244-9283) and Soul Surfing Maui (☎870-7873) teach their clients the rudiments of **surfing**, and beginners and old-timers alike swoop back and forth – the latter with rather more panache. The beach itself is too narrow for long days of family fun, but it's fine for a stroll.

Baldwin Home

Map 4, D5. Daily 10am–4.15pm; $3 per person, $5 per couple or family; ☎661-3262.

The **Baldwin Home**, on Front Street just north of Banyan Tree Square, is the oldest surviving building in Lahaina. Dating from the days when this was Hawaii's royal capital, it was built as the Maui base of the Sandwich Islands Mission and is now a reasonably interesting museum of missionary and local history. The price of admission includes a brief narrated tour, after which visitors are free to take a closer look around.

Although its 24-inch-thick walls of plastered lava and coral were constructed in 1834 by Reverend Ephraim Spaulding, the house bears the name of Reverend Dwight Baldwin, who took it over when Spaulding fell sick three years later. Baldwin remained as pastor of Lahaina's Waine'e Church until 1871, and much of his original furniture is still in place. Oddly frivolous touches among the chairs, quilts and gifts to and from whaling captains include an inlaid *koa* gaming table, and a table-top croquet set. On one wall hangs a "Native Doctor's License" from 1865, with a scale of charges ranging from $50 down to $10, according to whether the patient had a "Very great sickness," "Less than that," "A Good Deal Less," a "Small sickness" or a "Very Small."

The **Masters' Reading Room**, next door to the Baldwin Home and of similar vintage, is the headquarters of the Lahaina Restoration Foundation, which manages most of Lahaina's historic sites. It's not open to the public.

Wo Hing Temple

Map 4, C3. Mon–Fri 10am–4.30pm; free.

The distinguished-looking building with an unmistake-ably Oriental facade, a short walk north of downtown Lahaina on Front Street, is now known as the **Wo Hing Temple**. It was built in 1912 as the meeting place for the Wo Hing Society, a mutual-aid organization established in China during the seventeenth century. Until the 1970s it housed elderly members of the society, but it's now an interesting little museum devoted to the subject of Chinese immigration to Hawaii, with a small Taoist altar on its second story.

WO HING TEMPLE

Amid the faded signs and battered pots and pans in the decrepit adjacent **cookhouse**, there are continuous showings of scratchy film footage shot by Thomas Edison in Hawaii in 1898.

Hale Pa'ahao

Map 4, F5.

At the corner of Prison and Waine'e streets, the plain one-story **Hale Pa'ahao** ("Stuck-in-Irons House") replaced the fort as Lahaina's prison during the 1850s; in fact, as the fort came down, the prison went up, using the same stones. Now a public hall, it's usually left open, and you're free to wander into the former cells, which hold a few exhibits about the days when they were filled to bursting with drunken sailors.

Waine'e Church

Map 4, G7.

The first church on Maui, built in 1828 after five years of open-air services, was **Waine'e Church**, one block back from the sea. Twice destroyed by hurricanes, and burned down in 1894 in protests against the overthrow of the Hawaiian monarchy, this less-than-enthralling edifice has been known as Waiola Church since it was last rebuilt in 1953.

Tombs in the sun-scorched graveyard alongside, however, include some of the greatest names in early Hawaiian history. A simple monument commemorates the last king of Kauai, **Kaumuali'i**, who was buried here in 1825 after being kidnapped by Liholiho and forced to live in exile. Nearby are **Queen Keopuolani**, one of the many wives of Kamehameha the Great, who was of such distinguished *ali'i* blood that her husband could only enter her presence naked on all fours; the governor of Maui, **Hoapili Kāne**, who died in 1840; and his widow and successor **Hoapili Wahine**, who died two years later.

Lahainaluna

High above Lahaina town, reached by a winding two-mile climb up Lahainaluna Road past the Pioneer Sugar Mill, **Lahainaluna Seminary** was founded by American missionaries in 1831. Its goal was to teach Hawaiians to read and write, in the hope of producing future teachers and ministers. In 1850, however, the seminary passed into government control, and eventually became Hawaii's most prestigious public **high school**. Although not originally on US soil, it's regarded as being the first American educational institution west of the Rockies, and in the Gold Rush years many Californians sent their children here rather than risk the long journey to the East.

Visitors are welcome to take a quick look around the high school grounds: pause to identify yourself at the gate first. The only building you can enter is the seminary's small printing house, **Hale Pa'i** (Mon–Fri 10am–3pm; free). Dating from 1837, it holds some of Hawaii's first printed books, as well as a replica of the press that produced them.

Among Lahainaluna Seminary's earliest pupils were Hawaii's most famous native historians, **Samuel Kamakau** and **David Malo**. Malo had been brought up at the court of Kamehameha the Great on the Big Island, and was 38 when he first came here. Although he became a Christian, and was a minister at the old village of Kalepolepo in what's now Kīhei, he was also a passionate defender of the rights of the Hawaiian people. At the time of the Great Mahele – the disastrous 1848 land division that made the American takeover of Hawaii possible (see

Contexts, p.235) – Malo was regarded as the firebrand behind native Hawaiian resistance. Before he died in 1853, he asked to be buried "beyond the rising tide of the foreign invasion." His gravesite is above Lahainaluna at **Puʻu Paʻupaʻu**; it is marked with a huge letter "L" (for Lahainaluna) etched into the hillside and visible from all over Lahaina.

RESTAURANTS

Literally dozens of places to **eat** line the waterfront in Lahaina, with sophisticated gourmet **restaurants** mingling with national and local chain outlets and takeout places. Not all are good by any means, but you should find something to suit you within a few minutes' wandering.

For a quick snack, the best local **fast-food court** is in the Lahaina Cannery mall, a mile north of downtown. There's also a *Starbucks* next to the *Foodland* supermarket in the Old Lahaina Center.

INEXPENSIVE

- -

Aliʻi Mocha

505 Front St ☎ 661-7800.
Small café in oceanfront mall, with indoor and outdoor seating, offering espresso coffees and smoothies, bagels and pastries, and Internet access. Daily 6am–11pm.

Buns of Maui

878 Front St ☎ 661-4877.
Appealing little bakery, tucked away in a mall just behind Front Street, that serves fresh pastries and muffins along with its coffees in the morning, and graduates to sandwiches later on. Mon–Sat 6am–6pm.

- -
Full listings of all Maui's *lū ʻaus* appear on p.35
- -

Cheeseburger in Paradise

811 Front St ☎ 661-4855.
Busy, crowded seafront restaurant, perched on stilts above the water, with great views and seafaring bric-a-brac. Very much what the name suggests, though in addition to meaty $7–8 cheeseburgers they have fish sandwiches and spinach-nut-burgers at similar prices. There's live music nightly. Daily 8am–midnight.

Hapa's Café

Lahaina Center, 900 Front St ☎ 661-8988.
Owned by Maui's most popular musicians, this late-night smoothie and espresso bar also sells sandwiches and snacks. Sun–Tues 8am–7pm, Wed–Sat 8am–2am.

Moose McGillycuddy's

844 Front St ☎ 667-7758.
Hectic restaurant-cum-nightclub that starts the day with very cheap breakfasts (twenty different omelets at $4–5, plus $2 specials); follows up with standard lunches and dinners of burgers, sandwiches, pastas and steak; and tops things off with live music and/or dancing nightly. 9.30pm–2am ($2 cover charge). Restaurant open daily 7.30am–10pm.

Penne Pasta

180 Dickenson St ☎ 661-6633.
Cheerful Italian café, with sidewalk and indoor seating, serving straightforward but tasty pastas, salads and pizzas for under $10. The flatbread topped with olives, capers, basil, oregano and roasted peppers is particularly good. Mon–Fri 11am–9pm, Sat & Sun 5–9pm.

Sunrise Café

693A Front St at Market St ☎ 661-8558.
Small, laid-back and very central café, with outdoor seating beside its own tiny patch of beach. Coffees, smoothies and full cooked breakfasts from dawn onward, plus $6–9 salads, sandwiches and plate lunches later on. Daily 6am–6pm.

RESTAURANTS

●

WARREN AND ANNABELLE'S MAGIC SHOW

Apart from eating and drinking, Lahaina is very short on evening entertainment. Well worth recommending, therefore, is **Warren and Annabelle's Magic Show**, presented in a purpose-built theater in the oceanfront Lahaina Center (Mon–Sat 5.30pm; adults only, $36; 900 Front St; ⓣ 667-6244; ⓦ www.warrenandannabelles.com). The whole experience has been very thoughtfully designed. Each group of guests has to solve a puzzle to gain admission to the pre-show bar, where cocktails and a substantial selection of appetizers and desserts are served while an invisible pianist (the ghostly "Annabelle") plays show tunes. The whole audience then moves to the intimate showroom, where they're treated to a wonderful display of sleight-of-hand magic by Warren Gibson, originally from South Carolina. Gibson works very hard to keep his audience entertained – he manages to know almost everyone by name after the first few minutes – and many of his tricks are truly mind-boggling. It's a shame that the show bears no relevance to Hawaii whatsoever, but for a fun night out it's unbeatable.

MODERATE

- - - - - - - - - - - - - - - - - - -

Bubba Gump Shrimp Co
889 Front St ⓣ 661-3111. Lahaina didn't exactly need another themed diner, but this outlet of a burgeoning national chain of *Forrest Gump* restaurants, styled to resemble a tumbledown shrimp shack, does at least serve reasonably tasty food in an attractive waterfront setting. Shrimp entrees, priced at $13–18, are prepared in every imaginable way, from steamed-in-beer or flash-fried with ginger and garlic to New Orleans blackened. You can also get $4 smoothies and $8–9 sandwiches, and there's live music nightly. Daily 11am–10.30pm.

Lahaina Coolers

180 Dickenson St ⊤ 661-7082.
Central bistro restaurant
serving eggy breakfasts, then
an extensive menu of salads,
pastas, pizzas, tortillas, steaks
and fresh Hawaiian fish,
priced at $10–16 for lunch
and dinner. A couple of
blocks from the sea, but it's
open and breezy, with a
pleasant atmosphere. Daily
8am–2am.

Lahaina Fish Co

831 Front St ⊤ 661-3472.
High-quality seafood
restaurant, poised on a
beautiful *lānai* that juts out
over the ocean. Hawaiian fish
entrees ($20-24) are available
broiled, grilled or blackened
Cajun-style, while a raw bar
serves clams and oysters on
the half-shell for around $10
and fresh sashimi for $13.
Devout carnivores can stick
to chicken or ribs. Daily
11am–midnight.

Lemongrass

930 Waine'e St ⊤ 667-6888.
Bright little Vietnamese/Thai
restaurant, behind the
Lahaina Center. In addition

to soup and noodle dishes
such as beef *phô* ($7), and pad
thai with shrimp or chicken
(under $10), they have a full
menu of meat and seafood
entrees, including plenty of
curries, almost all under $12.
Daily 10am–9pm.

Maui Brews

Lahaina Center, 900 Front St
⊤ 667-7794.
Busy, loud and popular
bistro-cum-nightclub, serving
snacks and sandwiches plus a
full menu of pasta, meat and
seafood entrees at well under
$20. It's not a brewpub, but
there is a copious selection of
beers. Restaurant daily
11.30am–10pm, nightclub
9pm until late.

EXPENSIVE

David Paul's Lahaina Grill

Lahaina Inn, 127 Lahainaluna
Rd ⊤ 667-5117.
Upmarket restaurant serving
some of Maui's finest Pacific
Rim cuisine, set a few yards
back from Front Street in
northern downtown Lahaina.

RESTAURANTS

The setting is slightly cramped and unatmospheric, but the food is great. Of the appetizers, the terrine of salmon and scallop is superb, and the deep-fried oysters succulent; entrees include rack of lamb flavored with coffee ($38), *kālua* duck ($29), and various fish dishes; the fruity desserts are wonderful. A five-course tasting menu costs $67. Daily 6–10pm.

The Feast at Lele

505 Front St ⊤ 667-5353.
An inspired cross between a lu'au and a gourmet restaurant, which, for once, lavishes as much care on the food as on the entertainment. Chef James McDonald, of the adjoining restaurants *'Io* and *Pacific 'O*, prepares a feast of Polynesian specialties, including *kālua* pork from Hawaii, *fafa* (steamed chicken) and *e'iota* (marinated raw fish) from Tahiti, and grilled fish in banana leaves from Samoa. Each of the five courses consists of at least two dishes – it really is a colossal amount of food, but it's both excellent and unusual. The beachfront setting is also superb and very romantic, with individual white-clothed tables set out facing the ocean at sunset, and dance, music, and *hula* performances between each burst of gluttony. The one drawback is the cost, though at least the $89 adult charge includes unlimited cocktails and other beverages; for children, it's $59. Reservations are essential. Tues–Sat: April–Sept 6pm, Oct–March 5.30pm; schedules may vary.

Gerard's

Plantation Inn, 174 Lahainaluna Rd ⊤ 661-8939.
Adding a Hawaiian twist to traditional French cuisine results in a menu of $10–25 appetizers such as snails with wild mushrooms or foie gras with truffles, and entrees like stuffed quails, veal sweetbreads and roasted *'ōpakapaka* priced at up to $40. Desserts include profiteroles and other classic patisserie. Nightly 6–9.30pm.

Pacific 'O

505 Front St ☎ 667-4341.
Really nice oceanfront mall
restaurant, serving Pacific
Rim cuisine on a beach-level
terrace with indoor dining
above. Typical, relatively
simple lunch specials for
$10–15 include satay, shrimp
pasta and chicken sandwich.
In the evening, try $9–12
appetizers such as fish tartare
with raw *'ahi*, or shrimp won
tons in Hawaiian salsa, and
$20 entrees like fish tempura
or fish grilled in a banana
leaf. The Shrimp Nui is
utterly amazing; *nui* means
"big," and for $28 you get
four lobster-sized shrimp in a
delicious lemongrass pesto
broth. The delicious
chocolate desserts are
similarly huge. Sun–Thurs
11am–4pm & 5.30–10pm,
Fri & Sat 11am–4pm &
5.30–10.30pm; live jazz Fri &
Sat from 9pm.

SOUTH OF LAHAINA

Few people live along the parched coastline to the **south of
Lahaina**, though ditches in the hillside still irrigate extensive green cane fields. There are no significant settlements,
but the only road, Honoapi'ilani Highway, is prone to
hideous traffic congestion, especially as it narrows to climb
around McGregor Point in the far south and head back to
Māʻalaea (see p.88).

Launiupoko County Wayside Park

Map 1, B5.
While always scenic enough, the beaches that lie immediately south of Lahaina are not nearly as appealing as those to
the north, consisting as a rule of narrow strips of sand
deposited atop sharp black rocks. The first one you come
to, **Puamana Beach County Park**, offers no visitor facilities, but **Launiupoko County Wayside Park**, three miles
out, makes an attractive picnic spot. Coconut palms lean

THE OLOWALU MASSACRE

Olowalu was the site of the worst **massacre** in Hawaiian history, perpetrated by **Captain Simon Metcalfe** of the American merchant ship *Eleanora* in 1790. Metcalfe had been told that the Hawaiians who stole a ship's boat off East Maui, and killed a member of his crew, came from Olowalu. Mooring offshore, he lured more than two hundred canoes out to the *Eleanora*, many filled with children coming to see the strange ship. After asking them to gather on the starboard side, Metcalfe bombarded them with his seven cannons. More than a hundred Hawaiians died.

Metcalfe's 18-year-old son **Thomas** was to pay for his father's sins. Metcalfe had previously antagonized a Big Island chief, Kame'eiamoku, who vowed to kill the next white man he met. Ignorant of events at Olowalu, Thomas Metcalfe landed his tiny six-man schooner *Fair American* at Kawaihae on the Big Island a few days later and was killed when it was stormed by Kame'eiamoku. Of its crew, only **Isaac Davis** was spared, for putting up valiant resistance.

When the *Eleanora* arrived at Kawaihae, searching for the younger Metcalfe, first mate **John Young** was sent ashore. Kamehameha the Great prevented Young from rejoining his vessel with news of the killings, so Captain Metcalfe concluded that his envoy had been killed and sailed away. He died soon afterwards, without learning of his son's death; both Davis and Young, however, remained on the islands for the rest of their lives. They were responsible for teaching the Hawaiians to fight with muskets and cannon, and personally directed Kamehameha's armies at the battle of 'Iao Valley (see p.82).

out from the shoreline, while larger trees shade the tables on the lawn; the only snag is that it's very much in earshot of the highway. From the center of the park, boulder walls curve out to enclose a shallow artificial pool, suitable for small children, with two narrow outlets to the sea. South of that is a small beach of gritty sand, while to the north the lava rocks create a sea wall, alive with scuttling black crabs. The offshore waters here are a good spot for beginners to practice their surfing skills – thus the parking lot normally holds plenty of gleaming rental cars, but few local rustbuckets. Launiupoko has showers and restrooms, but camping is forbidden.

Olowalu

There's little more to **OLOWALU**, six miles south of Lahaina, than a tiny row of stores *mauka* of the highway. The most noteworthy of these is *Chez Paul* (℡661-3843), an incongruous and very expensive French bistro set behind a pretty little brick wall. It's open for dinner only, nightly except Sunday, with two seatings, at 6.30pm and 8.30pm. Most of the appetizers cost at least $10, though there's caviar for $65, while entrees such as seafood bouillabaisse or Tahitian duck are well over $30.

Although there's no public access to the ocean on the promontory across the road, where all the land belongs to the Pioneer Mill Company, a short hike toward the mountains leads to a cluster of ancient **petroglyphs**. Start by heading round to the left behind the stores and then continue inland, following not the dirt road facing you, but the one that starts immediately left of the nearby water tower. After about ten minutes' walk through the cane fields, you'll notice that the nearest side of the cinder cone straight ahead of you has sheared off to create a flat wall of red rock.

Fresh-painted red railings a few feet up the rock mark the site of the petroglyphs, but the stairs and walkways that once enabled visitors to climb up to them have largely vanished. So too have many of the petroglyphs, and others have been vandalized. However, you should still spot several wedge-shaped human figures etched into the rock, together with a sailing canoe or two, characterized by their "crab-claw" sails. Looking back, you'll also get good views across to Lanai.

Ukemehame and Pāpalaua

South of Olowalu, the cane fields come to an end, and Hwy-30 skirts the shoreline only a few feet above sea level. It's possible to park just about anywhere, and in whale-watching season that's exactly what people do – often with very little warning.

Ukemehame Beach County Park, three miles along, consists of a very small area of lawn between the highway and the ocean, with picnic tables and a couple of portable restrooms, fringed by a small strip of sand. Lots of trees have been planted, but they remain very short so far. By now, the mountains begin to rise only just inland of the road, and are much drier and barer than further north.

Pāpalaua State Wayside Park, which leads on south from Ukemehame, is a long dirt strip used as a parking lot, separated from the sand by a thin line of scrubby trees. Local surfers and snorkelers set up tents among the trees, but there are virtually no facilities. Immediately beyond Pāpalaua, the highway starts its climb over (and through) the headland of **Papawai Point**, where a roadside look-out is one of Maui's best **whale-watching** sites. From there it's less than two miles to Mā'alaea (see p.88) and the isthmus.

The Lahaina Pali Trail

Map 1, C5.

Until the hard labor of convicts constructed the first road around the southern coast of West Maui in 1900, the only way to reach Lahaina via dry land was to follow the centuries-old *alaloa*, or "long road," across the mountains. A five-mile stretch of this has recently been reopened as the **Lahaina Pali Trail**. The grueling trail climbs 1600 feet above sea level, and, being at the dry, exposed southern tip of the island, it's also a very hot one. Don't expect to penetrate into the mysterious green heart of the interior; your rewards instead will be the sight of some ravishing upland meadows, carpeted with magnificent purple, yellow and red flowers, and long-range views out to the islands of Lanai and Kahoolawe and down across the isthmus.

If you want to explore the West Maui mountains, the Waihe'e Ridge Trail (see p.87) is a better bet.

Both ends of the trail are a long way from the nearest town, so you'll need a car to reach either trailhead, and unless you can arrange to be picked up at the far end, hiking its full length necessitates a ten-mile round-trip. The path leaves Honoapi'ilani Highway from a parking lot near the 11-mile marker at Ukemehame and rejoins it five miles south of Wailuku, immediately south of the white bridge that lies between its intersections with Hwy-31 (to Kīhei) and Hwy-380 (to Kahului). Whichever end you start – the eastern slope is the steeper – you'll have at least a mile of stiff climbing before the trail levels out, still far below the top of the mountains. As it then meanders through successive gulches to cross Kealaloloa Ridge, almost the only – very welcome – shade is provided by the occasional native dryland sandalwood tree.

THE LAHAINA PALI TRAIL

The West Maui Resorts

O ver the eons, the older of Maui's two volcanoes has eroded away to create a long, curving ridge, whose serrated peaks are known collectively as the **West Maui mountains**. The highest point – Pu'u Kukui, barely six miles inland from Lahaina – is deluged by around 400 inches of rain per year and is almost always obscured by clouds. However, the leeward (western) slopes are consistently dry, and for eight miles north of Lahaina the sun-baked beaches are lined by a seamless succession of hotels and condos, in purpose-built resorts such as **Kā'anapali**, **Honokōwai** and **Kapalua**. While Lahaina itself is appealing and historic enough to deserve a chapter to itself – see Chapter Two – no one could accuse its neighbors to the north of being interesting in their own right. They do, however, offer superb facilities for family vacations, although room rates tend to be way too high for travelers on any kind of restricted budget.

No road crosses the mountains; parts of the all-but-impenetrable wilderness of the interior have never been explored. The main road to Lahaina from central Maui –

Honoapiʻilani Highway, named for the six northwestern bays conquered by the great Maui chief Piʻilani – is forced to loop laboriously around the south end of West Maui. Thanks to a sensible policy of only allowing development on its *makai* (oceanward) side, it's an attractive drive, with the inland hills and valleys largely untouched except by drifting rainbows; it's also a very slow one, thanks to horrendous and ever-growing traffic problems.

At the northern end of West Maui, beyond Kapalua, the weather becomes progressively wetter; the coast is more indented with bays; and driving conditions grow increasingly difficult. Honoapiʻilani Highway eventually gives up altogether around Nākālele Point. Sinuous, undulating **Kahekili Highway** beyond narrows to a single lane for several miles, and rental-car companies forbid their clients to use it. Nonetheless, it is possible to complete a full circuit of West Maui, and the extravagant beauty of the windward coast should not be missed.

KĀʻANAPALI

When American Factors (Amfac), the owners of the Pioneer Sugar Mill, decided in 1957 to transform the oceanfront cane fields of **KĀʻANAPALI** into a luxury tourist resort, they established a pattern that has been repeated throughout Hawaii ever since. There had never been a town at Kāʻanapali, just a small plantation wharf served by a short railroad from the sugar mill at Lahaina. What Kāʻanapali did have, however, was a superb white-sand **beach** – far better than anything at Lahaina – backed by a tract of land that was ripe for development and more than twice the size of Waikīkī.

Kāʻanapali's first hotel opened in 1963 and has been followed by half-a-dozen similar giants, whose four thousand rooms now welcome half-a-million visitors each year. It took a good twenty years before the resort began to feel at all lived in, however, and there's still nothing else here apart from the central, anodyne **Whaler's Village** mall. Kā'anapali is a pretty enough place, with its two rolling **golf courses** and sunset views of the island of Lanai filling the western horizon, but it's only worth staying here if you know you're happy with the same bland lifestyle you could find at a hundred tropical resorts around the world.

As for **Kā'anapali Beach**, it's divided into two separate long strands by the forbidding, 300-foot cinder cone of Pu'u Keka'a, known despite its reddish hue as the **Black Rock**. The sand shelves away abruptly from both sections, so swimmers soon find themselves in deep water, but bathing is usually safe outside periods of high winter surf. The rugged lava coastline around the Black Rock itself is one of the best **snorkeling** spots on Maui.

Nonguests of Kā'anapali's hotels are free to use the main beach, and it makes a better choice than either of the two **public beach parks** just around the headland to the south. Both **Hānaka'ō'ō** and **Wahikuli** are right alongside Hwy-30; swimming is generally safer at Wahikuli, but the facilities and general ambience are more appealing at Hānaka'ō'ō.

KĀ'ANAPALI SHUTTLE BUSES

The **West Maui Shopping Express** runs between Kā'anapali and Lahaina; see p.101 for details. The same company also offers a bus service between Whaler's Village in Kā'anapali and **Kapalua** to the north, making eleven trips each day between 9am and 8.20pm; the flat fare is $2. The free **Kā'anapali Trolley** circles the Kā'anapali resort area several times daily (9am–11pm; ☎667-0648), calling at the golf courses as well as all the hotels.

Accommodation

Kāʻanapali is very far from being a budget destination, but its consistently lavish **hotels** do at least compete in offering cut-price deals on rental cars or longer stays, and all feature activity programs for kids. For the latest offers, and general information on Kāʻanapali, call the Kāʻanapali Beach Resort Association on ☎661-3271 or 1-800/245-9229 (US & Can).

**All the Kāʻanapali properties listed
below share the zip code HI 96761.**

Hyatt Regency Maui
200 Nohea Kai Drive ☎661-1234 or 1-800/554-9288, ⓕ667-4498; ⓦwww.maui.hyatt.com. Possibly Kāʻanapali's grandest hotel, approached via an avenue lined with flaming torches at the south end of the resort area. The lobby has colossal chandeliers; the atrium is filled with coconut palms and holds a pool filled with live penguins; the gardens are opulent; there's a full-service spa; and the vast labyrinth of swimming pools includes a swinging rope bridge and bar. The main tower has ten stories, and there are subsidiary wings to either side, with a total of 815 luxurious rooms and five restaurants. Rack-rate guests

ACCOMMODATION PRICE CODES

All accommodation prices in this book have been graded with the following symbols; for a full explanation, see p.29.

❶ up to $40 ❹ $100–150 ❼ $250–300
❷ $40–70 ❺ $150–200 ❽ $300–400
❸ $70–100 ❻ $200–250 ❾ over $400

get the fifth night free, except in high season. Mountain view ❽, ocean view ❾.

Kāʻanapali Beach Hotel

2525 Kāʻanapali Parkway ☏ 661-0011 or 1-800/262-8450 (US & Can), ☏ 667-5978; Ⓦ www.kbhmaui.com.

The least expensive beachfront option in Kāʻanapali, this low-rise property, arrayed around spacious lawns, is poised between Whaler's Village and the Black Rock snorkel spot, and enjoys a fine stretch of beach plus a whale-shaped swimming pool. All its large, well-equipped rooms have balconies or patios, though some offer shower rather than bath. Garden view ❺, ocean view ❻.

Maui Eldorado Resort

2661 Kekaʻa Drive ☏ 661-0021 or 1-800/688-7444 (US & Can), ☏ 667-7039; Ⓦ www.outrigger.com.

Condo resort, run by the Outrigger company, which dominates Waikīkī's hotel scene, and consisting of several low buildings ranged up the hillside, well back from the shoreline; shuttle buses run to the resort's own reserved beach area. All units offer air-conditioning, *lānai*, washer/dryer, and a kitchenette if not a full kitchen. Garden view ❺, ocean view ❻.

Maui Marriott

100 Nohea Kai Drive ☏ 667-1200, 1-800/228-9200 (US & Can) or 1-800/763-1333 (HI), ☏ 667-8192; Ⓦ www.marriott.com.

Imposing, luxurious resort hotel at the south end of Kāʻanapali Beach, offering extra-large rooms, two swimming pools with a waterslide and a pirate lagoon for kids, twenty on-site shops, three restaurants (including a beachside restaurant and an espresso bar), a nightly *lūʻau* (see p.35), exercise facilities, and good-value room-and-car package deals. ❽.

The telephone area code for all Hawaii is ☏ 808.

KĀʻANAPALI ACCOMMODATION

Royal Lahaina Resort

2780 Keka'a Drive ⓣ 661-3611
or 1-800/44-ROYAL, ⓕ 661-
6150; ⓦ www.2maui.com.
One of Kā'anapali's two
original resorts, commanding
a long stretch of perfect
sands at the north end of the
beach. The hotel has 600
rooms, with a central
twelve-story tower of plush
suites, another smaller hotel
building, and a couple of
dozen "cottages" of condo-
style apartments on the
grounds. It has four
restaurants, a nightly *lū'au*,
and a 3500-seat tennis
stadium that's occasionally
used for concerts. ❻.

Sheraton Maui

2605 Kā'anapali Parkway
ⓣ 661-0031 or 1-800/782-9488,
ⓕ 661-0458;
ⓦ www.sheraton-hawaii.com.
This luxury resort was the
first to open at Kā'anapali, in
1963, and has since been
almost entirely rebuilt, with
five tiers of rooms dropping
down the crag of Black Rock
and separate oceanfront
wings, all at the broadest end
of Kā'anapali Beach. Garden-
view rooms ❽, ocean-view
rooms and suites ❾.

The Westin Maui

2365 Kā'anapali Parkway
ⓣ 667-2525 or 1-800/937-8461
(US & Can), ⓕ 661-5831;
ⓦ www.westin.com.
High-rise hotel in the center
of Kā'anapali Beach,
immediately south of
Whaler's Village, with five
swimming pools (including
Maui's largest) fed by artificial
waterfalls, a lagoon of live
flamingos to match the
predominantly pink decor,
and even its own *Starbucks*.
Bright, modern, luxurious if
somewhat characterless hotel
rooms, all with private *lānais*.
Mountain view ❽, ocean
view ❾.

The Whaler on Kā'ana-
pali Beach

2481 Kā'anapali Parkway
ⓣ 661-4861, ⓕ 922-8785,
reserve through Aston Hotels &
Resorts, 1-800/922-7866 (US &
Can) or 1-800/321-2558 (HI);
ⓦ www.aston-hotels.com.
Just north of Whaler's Village,
this condo complex holds
comfortable one- and two-

KĀ'ANAPALI ACCOMMODATION

bedroom units, each with bathroom, *lānai* and full kitchen. Unfortunately, the narrowest side of each of the two separate wings faces the ocean, so most of the rooms do not. As a condo property, it features much less in the way of services than the neighboring hotels, but the accommodation itself is good, and there is a small pool. **❻**.

Whale Center of the Pacific

Map 5, G4. Daily 9.30am–10pm; free.

A pavilion at the main (inland) entrance to the Whaler's Village mall shelters the articulated skeleton of a sperm whale; note the vestigial "fingers" in its flippers. Nearby, a mock-up of a small nineteenth-century whaleboat is fully labeled with its various esoteric components and gadgets. Both serve by way of introduction to the grandly named and grisly **Whale Center of the Pacific**, which takes up half the mall's uppermost floor.

This free **museum** is devoted to Maui's long-lost heyday as a whaling center, illustrating the tedium and the terror of the seamen's daily routine through scrimshaw, shellwork valentines, log books, tools, equipment, letters and bills. The largest single exhibit is a cast-iron "try pot," used for reducing whale blubber at sea; such pots gave rise to the stereotyped but not entirely untrue image of cannibals cooking missionaries in big black cauldrons. Contrary to what you might imagine, no actual killing of whales took place in Hawaiian waters. Hawaii was simply the place where the whaling ships came to recuperate after hunting much further north in the Pacific. What's more, the humpback – the whale most commonly found in Hawaiian waters – was not hunted at all during the nineteenth century; the target for the fleets was instead the right whale, so named, logically enough, because it was deemed the "right" whale to kill.

Restaurants

All of Kāʻanapali's hotels have at least one flagship **restaurant**, though catering on such a large scale makes it hard for staff to pay much attention to detail. Away from the hotels, the only alternative is to eat at the **Whaler's Village** mall. In addition to its more formal oceanfront restaurants, it holds a **food court**, set back on the lower level, featuring Korean, Japanese and Italian outlets, plus an espresso bar and a *McDonald's*.

Cascades

Hyatt Regency Maui
200 Nohea Kai Drive ☎ 667-4420.
Open-sided yet intimate resort restaurant, just off the *Hyatt's* main lobby, with large ocean views. The Asian-influenced menu includes crab-cake sandwiches among the $10–15 lunchtime burgers, salads and pastas. In the evening you can get sushi and sashimi platters for $17–34 as well as steaks, ribs and ginger chicken from $20. Daily 11.30am–2pm & 5.45–10pm.

Hula Grill

Whaler's Village ☎ 667-6636.
Large, long oceanfront restaurant, open to the sea breezes, featuring live, gentle Hawaiian music nightly. Chef Peter Merriman prepares some interesting appetizers, such as a Tahitian *poisson cru*, marinated in lime and coconut milk ($8), and plenty of dim sum and sashimi, but the entrees tend to be less imaginative, presumably to suit the family-dining atmosphere. The basic choice is fish or steak, for $20–25. Daily 11am–11pm.

Rusty Harpoon

Whaler's Village ☎ 661-3123.
Beachfront mall restaurant, with terrace and covered seating. Simple, inexpensive lunch menu with a few inventive touches, such as a $13 seafood curry casserole, and more traditional dinner entrees – steaks, ribs, fresh

KAʻANAPALI RESTAURANTS

fish – for $20–30. A limited "Happy Hour" menu is served 2–6pm and 10.30pm–1am. Daily 8am–1.30am.

Swan Court

Hyatt Regency Maui, 200 Nohea Kai Drive ⓣ 667-4420.
Romantic, enchanting resort restaurant, laid out around a lagoon populated by live swans, with tableside *hula* performances. The food is expensive but exquisite, with appetizers at around $15 including a seafood Napoleon made with papadum (an Indian crispbread), and entrees such as a distinctly un-Hawaiian pepper-seared bison, in a combo with basil-scented prawns for $36. Tues–Sat 6–10pm.

Va Bene

Maui Marriott, 100 Nohea Kai Drive ⓣ 667-1200.
The *Marriott's* principal dining room enjoys a gorgeous oceanfront setting, facing the beach across a brief expanse of lawns. Breakfasts are conventional enough, with a healthy $13 buffet and a cholesterol-packed $18 version, while for the rest of the day they serve fresh, zestful Italian dishes. At lunchtime, salads, pizzas and pastas cost around $10, and there's a great $12 oyster sandwich. Most pasta dishes are also $10 at dinner, but the full range of meat and seafood entrees cost $18–28. A $25 four-course Sunset Dinner is served nightly 5–6.30pm. Daily 6.30am–2pm & 5–10pm.

NORTH OF KĀ'ANAPALI: FROM HONOKŌWAI TO KAPALUA

If you found Kā'anapali dull, just wait until you see the coastline further north. A mile or so out of Kā'anapali, Lower Honoapi'ilani Road branches down toward the ocean from the main highway, to undulate its way through **Honokōwai**, **Kahāna** and **Nāpili**.

None of these barely distinguishable, purpose-built communities holds an ounce of interest for casual visitors. They do have some great **beaches** – especially around Nāpili Bay – but you'll hardly get a glimpse of them unless you're staying at one of the innumerable identikit condo buildings that line the entire road. Few shops or restaurants are nearby, which is why the highway is always busy with traffic heading south to the hot spots of Lahaina and beyond.

KAPALUA, at the end of Lower Honoapi'ilani Road in Maui's far northwest corner, is the West Maui equivalent of the exclusive resort of Wailea, at the southwest tip of East Maui (see p.152). Few ordinary mortals stray into this pristine enclave, whose two luxurious hotels were sited here mainly because of the proximity of **Kapalua Beach**. Previously known as Fleming Beach, this perfect little arc of white sand, set between two rocky headlands, is one of Maui's safest and prettiest beaches, and good for snorkeling and diving.

Kapalua Airport

Map 6, E7.

Tiny **Kapalua Airport** – a short distance above Hwy-30, halfway between Kapalua and Kā'anapali – is too small to be served by anything other than commuter flights, principally Island Air services from Honolulu, and Pacific Wings connections with Honolulu, Kahului, and Lanai. For details of flight frequencies and fares, see p.16. All the major car-rental chains have outlets at the airport – see p.24 – but there's no public transport.

Accommodation

The condo properties along Lower Honoapi'ilani Road make reasonable cut-price alternatives to the Kā'anapali and Kapalua resort hotels, though if you don't rent a car you could feel very stuck indeed.

CHAPTER THREE

Aston Kā'anapali Shores

3445 Lower Honoapi'ilani Rd
ⓣ667-2211, ⓕ661-8036,
reserve through Aston Hotels &
Resorts, ⓣ1-800/922-7866 (US
& Can) or 1-800/321-2558 (HI);
ⓦwww.kaanapalishores.com.
Grand oceanfront condo
development, right on the
beach at the south end of
Honokōwai, with a nice pool
and air-conditioning
throughout, and some large
good-value family suites.
Rooms ❺, suites ❻.

Aston Paki Maui

3615 Lower Honoapi'ilani Rd
ⓣ669-8235, reserve through
Aston Hotels & Resorts, ⓣ1-
800/922-7866 (US & Can) or 1-
800/321-2558 (HI);
ⓦwww.pakimaui.com.
Long, low, curving building,
beside the sea but fronted by
lawns rather than a beach, in
the center of KaHāna. Non-
air-conditioned apartments,
ranging from studios to two-
bedroom units, with kitchens
and *lānais*. Rooms ❺, suites ❻.

Aston at Papakea Resort

3543 Lower Honoapi'ilani Rd
ⓣ669-4848, ⓕ665-0662,
reserve through Aston Hotels &
Resorts, ⓣ1-800/922-7866 (US
& Can) or 1-800/321-2558 (HI);
ⓦwww.aston-hotels.com.
Oceanfront Honokōwai
complex of condo suites of all
sizes, housed in eleven
separate structures arranged
around two matching
gardens, each of which holds
a pool, spa, lagoon and
putting course. Garden-view
rooms and suites ❺, ocean-
view rooms ❻, suites ❼.

Embassy Vacation Resort

104 Kā'anapali Shores Place
ⓣ661-2000 or 1-800/669-3155
(US & Can), ⓕ667-5821, or
reserve through Marc Resorts
ⓣ922-9700 or 1-800/535-0085
(US & Can);
ⓦwww.marcresorts.com.
Giant pink ziggurat at the
south end of Honokōwai,
right on the ocean just
beyond Kā'anapali Beach, and

All the properties listed here share the zip code Lahaina, HI 96761.

complete with one-acre pool, a 24ft waterslide and a twelfth-floor rooftop miniature golf course reached by glass-walled elevators. All the one- and two-bedroom units have separate living rooms, shower and bath facilities and kitchenettes. ❽.

Hale Maui

3711 Lower Honoapi'ilani Rd ⓣ 669-6312, ⓕ 669-1302; ⓦ www.maui.net/~halemaui. Small family-run "apartment hotel" in Honokōwai, offering one-bedroom suites that sleep up to five guests, with kitchens and *lānais*. ❸.

Kahāna Reef

4471 Lower Honoapi'ilani Rd ⓣ 669-6491 or 1-800/253-3773 (US & Can), ⓕ 669-2192; ⓦ www.mauicondo.com. Four-story row of well-furnished – if characterless – oceanfront non-air-conditioned studios and one-bedroom units, all at relatively low rates. They're right next to the sea, though there's little beach here. Discounted car rental available. ❹.

Kahāna Sunset

4909 Lower Honoapi'ilani Rd ⓣ 669-8011 or 1-800/669-1488, ⓕ 669-9170; ⓦ www.kaHānasunset.com. Luxury condos, spacious inside but squeezed close together, in lush gardens by a lovely sandy beach. Only the larger two-bedroom units have ocean views. Garden view ❹, ocean view ❺.

Kapalua Bay Hotel

1 Bay Drive ⓣ 669-5656 or 1-800/325-3589 (US & Can), ⓕ 669-4649; ⓦ www.luxury collectionhawaii.com. The older of Kapalua's two resorts still epitomizes luxury. Beautifully landscaped, it features an intimate white-sand beach, an irresistible pool, three championship-standard golf courses and twenty tennis courts. All the rooms are huge and offer private *lānais*. Sixth night free. Garden view ❽, ocean view ❾.

The Mauian

5441 Lower Honoapi'ilani Rd ⓣ 669-6205 or 1-800/367-5034 (US & Can), ⓕ 669-0129; ⓦ www.mauian.com.

ACCOMMODATION

Very friendly, old-fashioned little resort on ravishing, sandy little Nāpili Beach. Three two-story rows of tastefully furnished studio apartments with kitchenettes but no phones or TVs. Garden view ❹, ocean view ❺.

Noelani

4095 Lower Honoapi'ilani Rd
Ⓣ 669-8374 or 1-800/367-6030 (US & Can), Ⓕ 669-7904;
Ⓦ www.noelani-condo-resort .com.
Condo apartments of all sizes, set on a promontory so all units enjoy views across to Molokai. Amenities include cable TV and video, plus use of pool, Jacuzzi, and laundry. ❹.

Polynesian Shores

3975 Lower Honoapi'ilani Rd
Ⓣ 669-6065, Ⓕ 669-0909.
Friendly, fifty-room KaHāna condo property, with shared pool, oceanfront lawns and good snorkeling. Units of all sizes, all with kitchens and *lānais*. ❹.

Ritz-Carlton, Kapalua

1 Ritz-Carlton Drive Ⓣ 669-6200 or 1-800/262-8440,

Ⓕ 665-0026;
Ⓦ www.ritzcarlton.com.
Modern, opulent, marble-fitted resort hotel that had to be relocated slightly back from the beach after its intended site turned out to be an ancient Hawaiian burial ground. The sheer elegance can make it feel a bit formal for Maui, but there's no disputing the level of comfort, with three swimming pools, a nine-hole putting green to complement the three nearby golf courses, a spa and a croquet lawn. ❽.

Royal Kahāna Resort

4365 Lower Honoapi'ilani Rd
Ⓣ 669-5911 or 1-800/447-7783 (US & Can), Ⓕ 669-5950,
reserve through Marc Resorts,
Ⓣ 922-9700 or 1-800/535-0085 (US & Can), Ⓕ 922-2421;
Ⓦ www.marcresorts.com.
Twelve-story oceanfront condo building in central KaHāna, with views of Molokai and Lanai. All the air-conditioned units, which include studios as well as one- and two-bedroom suites, have kitchens, washer-dryers and private *lānais*. ❺.

Restaurants

Considering its vast number of visitors, the Honokōwai to Kapalua stretch has traditionally been short of places to **eat**. That's starting to change, however, as clusters of restaurants appear in each of the three highway-side **malls**. The southernmost, the **Honokōwai Marketplace**, is home to *A Pacific Café* and some smaller snack places. Next comes the **Kahāna Gateway**, which holds two *Roy's* and the *Fish & Game* as well as an *Outback Steakhouse*, a *McDonald's* and an ice-cream parlor, while the **Nāpili Plaza** further on has *Maui Tacos* and the *Coffee Store,* an espresso bar that also offers Internet access (daily 6.30am–6pm; ☎669-4170).

Erik's Seafood Grotto

4242 Lower Honoapi'ilani Rd
☎669-4806.
Traditional Continental fish dishes, served just across from the ocean on the lower of the two coastal highways, alongside the Kahāna Villas condos. A full dinner, such as baked stuffed prawns or a seafood curry, costs around $20, a *cioppino* or bouillabaisse is more like $26, and you can also get sashimi or pick from the raw bar. Daily 5–10pm.

Fish & Game Brewing Company & Rotisserie

Kahāna Gateway, 4405
Honoapi'ilani Hwy ☎669-3474.
Large mall location consisting of several different parts, including a pub serving pilsners, stouts and wheat beers brewed on the premises; an open restaurant area dominated by a *kiawe* grill; an oyster bar; and some more private dining rooms. The food is surprisingly good, with grilled ribs or chicken for under $20, a truly colossal steak for $24, and fresh fish prepared in various styles for $28. A lighter, limited menu is served 3–5.30pm & 10.30pm–2am. Daily 11am–2am.

Java Jazz

Honokōwai Marketplace, 3350
Lower Honoapi'ilani Rd ☎667-0787.

Trendy juice and espresso bar, with lots of comfy seating. Breakfast eggs and omelets go for $7–8, falafel and other lunchtime sandwiches are under $10; and assorted evening specials cost just a little more. Daily 6am–8pm.

A Pacific Café

Honokōwai Marketplace, 3350 Lower Honoapiʻilani Rd ☏ 667-2800.

This stylish "Hawaii Regional" joint is very much a classy resort restaurant, even if it is between a supermarket and a main road rather than beside the ocean. The delicious stacked, seared and drizzled goodies that pour from its curving central "display kitchen" include appetizers such as sushi tempura for $13 or barbecue ribs for $7, and $20–30 entrees like wok-charred *mahimahi* and coffee-smoked pork chops. Daily 5.30–9.30pm.

Roy's Kahāna Bar & Grill,

Kahāna Gateway, 4405 Honoapiʻilani Hwy ☏ 669-6999.
Celebrity chef Roy

Yamaguchi's Maui showcase is open for dinner only – which is just as well, given its lack of views. The scents of its superb "Euro-Asian" food waft from its open kitchen as soon as you walk in. A set three-course dinner costs $34, or you can choose from a menu on which signature dishes such as hibachi salmon and "Roy's 'Original' Blackened Rare Ahi" appear both as appetizers (around $10) and entrees (more like $25). Daily 5.30–10pm.

Roy's Nicolina Restaurant

Kahāna Gateway, 4405 Honoapiʻilani Hwy ☏ 669-5000.
Sister restaurant to *Roy's KaHāna Bar & Grill*; the two entrances face each other atop the staircase in this small mall, and although each has its own kitchen, *Nicolina*'s Pacific Rim menu is all but identical to that of its senior neighbor. Appetizers include "butterfish" (black cod) steamed with *miso*, and seared sea scallops at $8–11; entrees like herb-rubbed rack of

lamb with baby bok choy cost $20–30. Daily 5.30–9.30pm.

Sansei Seafood Restaurant

The Shops at Kapalua, 115 Bay Drive, Kapalua ⓣ 669-6286. Top-quality, dinner-only seafood specialist, adjoining the *Kapalua Bay Hotel*. Both decor and menu are fundamentally Japanese, though there's a strong Pacific Rim element as well. The extensive list of fresh sushi includes a wonderful mango crab salad roll at $8, while among the entrees are seared salmon and seafood pasta at $20, and daily fish specials at around $25. Certain items, like the $5 crispy fried *onaga* (snapper) head and the Korean-spiced raw octopus are labeled "for locals only." There's also karaoke until 2am on Thursday and Friday nights. Mon–Wed, Sat & Sun 5.30–11pm, Thurs & Fri 5.30pm–2am.

BEACHES BEYOND KAPALUA

Honoapi'ilani Highway sweeps down beyond Kapalua to rejoin the ocean at **DT Fleming Beach Park**, in Honokahua Bay. The dunes here, knitted together with ironwood trees, drop sharply into the sea, and swimming can be dangerous – though surfers love the big waves.

From here, the highway climbs again to cross a rocky headland. You can't see it from the road, but **Mokulē'ia Bay** lies at the foot of the cliffs. The landowners, Maui Pineapple, have erected fences along the highway at this point, in an attempt to preclude access to shaded, sandy **Slaughterhouse Beach**. If it is still possible to reach it, you should see cars parked on the verge, next to breaks in the vegetation that mark the start of steep footpaths down. Winter conditions usually preclude bathing, but the nude sunbathing carries on year-round.

Honolua Bay

Map 1, B2.

Both Mokulē'ia Bay and **Honolua Bay**, just past the point, have been set aside as a Marine Life Conservation District, and in summer offer some of the island's best **snorkeling**. Honolua's major claim to fame, however, is as Maui's most famous **surfing** spot. Between September and April, the waters regularly swarm with surfers. So long as the swell remains below five feet, intermediate surfers can enjoy some of the longest-lasting and most predictable waves in all Hawaii. By the time they exceed ten feet, however, only absolute experts can hope to survive, with perils including not only a fearsome cave that seems to suck in every passing stray, but cutthroat competition from other surfers. Parking for surfers is at several ad-hoc lots along the rough dirt roads that line the pineapple fields covering the headland on the far side of the bay. Large galleries of spectators assemble on the clifftop to watch the action, while the surfers themselves slither down to the ocean by means of treacherous trails.

To reach the **beach** at Honolua, park instead beside the road at the inland end of the bay and walk down. The access path is the width of a road, but the surface is terrible and driving on it is illegal. It leads through a weird, lush forest with the feel of a Louisiana bayou; every tree, and even the barbed-wire fence, has been throttled by creeping vines. Across a (usually dry) stream bed lies the neat, rocky curve of the beach itself, with the eastern end of Molokai framed in the mouth of the bay.

Honokōhau Bay

Map 1, C2.

Honoapi'ilani Highway runs past one final beach, at **Honokōhau Bay**. You're still only five miles out of

Kapalua here, but it feels like another world. The entire valley is swamped by a dense canopy of flowering trees; there's a hidden village in there, but it's hard to spot a single building. The beach itself is a small crescent of gray pebbles, used only by fishermen.

KAHEKILI HIGHWAY

The warnings of the rental-car companies concerning the **Kahekili Highway**, which looks on the map like a potential route around northwest Maui and back to Wailuku, are worth taking seriously: it's undeniably a dangerous drive. What's more, it's certainly not a short cut; Wailuku is little more than twenty miles beyond Honokōhau Valley, but you have to allow well over an hour for the journey.

While not quite on a par with the road to Hāna – see p.197 – the Kahekili Highway can be exhilaratingly beautiful, and it provides a rare glimpse of how Maui must have looked before the advent of tourism. Often very narrow, but always smoothly surfaced, it winds endlessly along the extravagantly indented coastline, alternating between scrubby exposed promontories, occasionally capable of supporting a pale meadow, and densely green, wet valleys.

Nākālele Point

Map 1, C2.

Kahekili Highway begins at Maui's northernmost limit, **Nākālele Point**, 6.5 miles out of Kapalua, at milepost 38. This rolling expanse of bare, grassy heathland fell victim some years ago to a bizarre craze that swept most of Hawaii. In remote spots all over the islands, people suddenly started erecting miniature stone cairns, possibly under the impression that they were maintaining an ancient tradition. Stacks of perhaps a dozen small rocks are dotted all over the landscape, and many visitors have also used pebbles to spell out their names or other messages – much to the displeasure of Maui Pineapple, which still owns the land.

Various deeply rutted dirt roads drop away from the highway toward the sea in this area, starting both from the parking lot at milepost 38 and from another more makeshift lot half a mile further on. Hiking in that direction enables you to inspect the small **light beacon** that warns passing ships of the rocky headland, and an impressive natural **blowhole** in the oceanfront shelf.

Kahakuloa

Map 1, D2.

A few miles after Nākālele Point, the huge and very un-Hawaiian crag of **Kahakuloa Head** towers 636 feet above the eastern entrance to Kahakuloa Bay. The succulent valley behind it once ranked among the most populous on Maui and still looks like a classic *ahupua'a* – the fundamental ancient land division, reaching from the sea to the mountain via low-lying *taro* terraces and groves of fruit trees.

The perfect little village of **KAHAKULOA** ("tall lord," for the nearby crag) stands just behind its beach of black and gray boulders and centers on the St Francis Xavier Mission, built in 1846. The stream bed is lined with trees, while dirt roads crisscross the valley between the fields and the ramshackle houses.

For an account of the exhilarating Waihe'e Ridge Trail, which leads off from Kahekili Highway closer to Wailuku, see p.87.

South Maui

The area generally referred to as **South Maui** is in fact the western shoreline of eastern Maui, stretching south of Māʻalaea Bay. Until well after World War II, this was one of the island's least populated districts, a scrubby, exposed and worthless wasteland. Since then, an unattractive and almost unchecked ribbon of resort development has snaked down the coast, with the mass-market hotels and condos of **Kīhei** in the north being joined in recent years by far more exclusive luxury properties at **Wailea** and **Mākena**.

Almost all the way down, narrow strips of clean, white sand fill each successive bay, so every hotel is within easy walking distance of a good stretch of **beach**. So far, the development stops just short of the best beach of all, **Oneloa** or **Big Beach**, while the coastal highway peters out not far beyond. This final stretch, and the oceanfront trail to secluded **La Pérouse Bay**, is the only part of South Maui worth visiting on a sightseeing tour of the island; none of the resort communities holds any interest in itself.

Kīhei

If you've always thought of Hawaii as Condo Hell, then **KĪHEI** probably comes closer to matching that image than anywhere else in the state. Stretching for seven miles south from Māʻalaea Bay, it's a totally formless sprawl of a place, whose only landmarks consist of one dull mall or condo building after another. That said, it can be a perfectly pleasant place to spend your vacation, with abundant inexpensive lodging and dining options and plentiful beaches. Just don't come to Kīhei expecting a town in any sense of the word.

In the 1960s, Kīhei spread for just a hundred yards to either side of the point where Mokulele Highway (Hwy-50) reaches Māʻalaea Bay. **North Kīhei Road** is still a hundred yards long, but **South Kīhei Road** now keeps on going for around five miles. It's not totally built up, but the occasional half-mile gaps are simply derelict land, left empty while the developers await their moment. Those moments are now arriving thick and fast; according to the 2000 census, Kīhei had the second-highest percentage increase in population of any community in the United States. Traffic congestion is so rife that for all journeys of any length, you'd do better to follow the parallel **Piʻilani Highway**, half-a-mile or so up the hillside. There's even talk of building another highway even further up the slope.

The largest of Kīhei's shopping malls are the matching pair of **Azeka Place 1**, *makai* at 1280 S Kīhei Rd, and **Azeka Place 2** opposite. Between them they hold the local **post office**, a large Bank of Hawaii with ATM machines, and lots of fast-food places. Otherwise, the new **Piʻilani Village Shopping Center**, not far away on the upper highway, is expanding rapidly and holds a huge Safeway, while **Kukui Mall**, opposite Kalama Park, has a four-screen movie theater and more takeout eateries.

Café society in Old Lahaina

Palauea Beach, Wailea

Windsurfing on Ho'okipa Beach

Fishing in Olowalu

Molokini Crater

Haleakalā Crater

GREG WARD

Big Beach

EDMUND NAGELE

Wailua Falls, on the road to Hāna

ACCOMMODATION

There's little difference between Kīhei's countless **condos** and **hotels**, with standards in even the cheapest options tending to be perfectly adequate. Very few visitors simply pass through for a single night; there are no rock-bottom budget alternatives or B&Bs, and most places insist on a minimum stay of at least three nights. Rates on the whole are low, but Kīhei is more seasonally sensitive than most destinations, and in peak season (mid-Dec to March) you can expect to pay a premium of at least $25 over the prices coded below.

Aloha Pualani Beach Resort

15 Wailana Place ⓣ 874-9265 or 1-800/PUA-LANI (US & Can), ⓕ 874-9127; ⓦ www.alohapualani.com.
Five homely two-story condo units across from Māʻalaea Bay at the north end of Kīhei. Each has a living room, kitchen and bedroom and shared use of a pool and garden. On-site owners provide breakfast and advice, and there's a three-night minimum stay. ❸.

Hale Kai O'Kīhei

1310 Uluniu Rd ⓣ 879-2757 or 1-800/457-7014 (US & Can), ⓕ 875-8242, also available through Condominium Rentals Hawaii (see box on p.145). Three stories of straightforward one- and two-bedroom condos in an absolutely stunning and very quiet beachfront location near Kīhei's best malls and restaurants. Private coconut grove, spacious *lānais*, and discounted car rental. Four-night minimum stay. ❹.

Kamaʻole Nalu Resort

2450 S Kīhei Rd ⓣ 879-1006 or 1-800/767-1497, ⓕ 879-8693; ⓦ www.mauigateway.com /~kamaole.
Large beachfront complex set on neat lawns at the south end of Kamaʻole Park 2. Two-bedroom, two-bath condos, all with kitchen and

ACCOMMODATION PRICE CODES

All accommodation prices in this book have been graded with
the following symbols; for a full explanation, see p.29.

❶ up to $40   ❹ $100–150   ❼ $250–300
❷ $40–70   ❺ $150–200   ❽ $300–400
❸ $70–100   ❻ $200–250   ❾ over $400

laundry facilities; the long private *lānais* offer spectacular sunset views. Discounts on car rental; five-night minimum stay. ❹.

Kama'ole Sands

2695 S Kīhei Rd ⓣ874-8700, 1-800/367-5004 (US & Can) or 1-800/272-5257 (HI), ⓕ879-3273; ⓦwww.castleresorts.com.
Sprawling condo complex just across the street from Kama'ole Park 3, with units of all sizes plus free tennis and swimming. Studio and garden-view suite ❺, ocean-view suite ❻.

Kīhei Akahi

2531 S Kīhei Rd, available through Condominium Rentals (see box opposite)

The ascending rows of good-value, well-furnished condos in this garden property across from Kama'ole Park 2 have use of two swimming pools and a tennis court. Those with air-conditioning cost $5 extra per night. Studios ❸, suites ❹.

Mana Kai Maui

2960 S Kīhei Rd, available through Condominium Rentals (see box opposite)
Large building beside lovely Keawakapu Beach at the grander south end of Kīhei, with plush hotel rooms and fully-fledged condo apartments, plus a pool and the excellent *Five Palms* grill restaurant (see

KĪHEI ACCOMMODATION

All the properties listed here share the zip code HI 96753.

CONDO RENTALS

Individual apartments in virtually all the properties listed here, and a great many more besides, can also be booked through various specialist agencies. As a rule, prices start around $80 per night in low season, rising to $100 between Christmas and March; be sure to check whether you're expected to pay an additional one-time "cleaning fee," which is typically around the $50 mark.

Condominium Rentals Hawaii, 362 Huku Liʻi Place, #204, Kīhei, HI 96753; ☎ 879-2778, 1-800/367-5242 (US) or 1-800/663-2101 (Can), ⓕ 879-7825; ⓦ www.crhmaui.com.
Kīhei Maui Vacations, PO Box 1055, Kīhei, HI 96753; ☎ 879-7581 or 1-800/541-6284 (US & Can), ⓕ 879-2000; ⓦ www.kmvmaui.com.
Maui Condominium and Home Realty, 2511 S Kīhei Rd, #H, PO Box 18400, Kīhei, HI 96753; ☎ 879-5445 or 1-800/822-4409 (US & Can), ⓕ 874-6144.

p.151). Rates include rental car. ❹.

Maui Coast Hotel

2259 S Kīhei Rd ☎ 874-628 or 1-800/426-0670 (US & Can) or 1-800/895-6284 (US & Can), ⓕ 875-4731; ⓦ www.westcoasthotels .com/mauicoast.
Tasteful, luxurious, and good-value modern hotel, set slightly back from the highway opposite Kamaʻole Park 1. Standard hotel rooms as well as one- and two-bedroom suites, plus an attractive pool and on-site restaurants. ❺.

Maui Vista

2191 S Kīhei Rd ☎ 879-7966, reserve through Marc Resorts, ☎ 922-9700 or 1-800/535-0085 (US & Can), ⓕ 922-2421 or 1-800/633-5085 (US & Can); ⓦ www.marcresorts.com.
Comfortable, well-equipped condos of all sizes, on the hillside across from Kamaʻole

KĪHEI ACCOMMODATION

●

145

Park 1. Not the best views, but three pools and six tennis courts. ❹.

Royal Mauian Resort

2430 S Kīhei Rd ⓣ 879-1263 or 1-800/367-8009 (US & Can), ⓕ 874-7639; ⓦ www.royalmauianresort.com. Huge, luxurious, but non-air-conditioned oceanfront condo complex, beyond the south end of Kama'ole Park 1. Lovely views, especially from the roof terrace, and a nice pool. Discounts on car rental; five-night minimum stay. ❺.

Shores of Maui

2075 S Kīhei Rd ⓣ 879-9140 or 1-800/367-8002, ⓕ 879-6221. Long, low complex of good-value one- and two-bedroom air-con condos, screened behind coconut palms across from Cove Park. Three-night minimum stay, or one-week minimum stay at Christmas/January. ❸.

Sunseeker Resort

551 S Kīhei Rd ⓣ 879-1261 or 1-800/532-MAUI (US & Can), ⓕ 874-3877; ⓦ www.maui.net/~sunseekr. Pretty little hotel-cum-condo building, resembling an old-fashioned motel, very close to Mā'alaea Bay beach (and, unfortunately, also the main road) at the north end of Kīhei. All the inexpensive rooms and suites have kitchen facilities and ocean views. Three-night minimum stay. Room ❷, suite ❸.

Wailana Inn

14 Wailana Place ⓣ 874-3131 or 1-800/399-3885 (US & Can); ⓦ www.wailanabeach.com. Motel-like structure set just back from the road, near Mā'alaea Bay beach in northern Kīhei. The rooms inside are much nicer than the exterior might suggest. All have kitchens or kitchenettes, TV and phone, and share use of a rooftop hot tub. ❸.

The telephone area code for all Hawaii is ⓣ 808.

BEACHES

The first easy point of access to the ocean along South
Kīhei Road comes within a few hundred yards, at **Mai
Poina 'Oe Ia'u Beach County Park**. This narrow,
shadeless beach is not somewhere you'd choose to spend
a day, but it's a good launching point for surfers, kayakers
and especially windsurfers. The park was established in
1952 as a war memorial: its name means "forget me
not."

To the naked eye, and especially to guests staying at
oceanfront properties such as the *Hale Kai O'Kīhei* and its
neighbors (see p.143), the beaches of northern Kīhei look
attractive enough, if rather narrow. However, thanks to the
output of a **sewage treatment facility** above the next formal roadside beach park, at **Kalama Beach**, three miles
south of Mai Poina, this entire stretch is best admired from
dry land. Swimming is not recommended. Nonetheless, the
large lawns and sports fields on the promontory at **Kalama**
remain popular with locals, especially in the evenings, and
there's a pretty coconut grove.

Much the busiest of the Kīhei beaches – and for good
reason – are the three separate, numbered segments of
Kama'ole Beach County Park, immediately beyond. All
boast clean white sand and are generally safe for swimming,
with lovely views across the bay to West Maui, and all are
constantly supervised by lifeguards. Most of the beautifully
soft **Kama'ole 1** beach is very close to the road, but it also
curves away out of sight to the north. Sweet little **Kama'ole
2**, cradled between two headlands, is a bit short on shade,
and very near a large concentration of condos, so the pick of
the bunch is long, broad **Kama'ole 3**. Families gather
under the giant trees on its wide lawns, while the beach
itself is shielded from the road at the bottom of a ten-foot
grassy slope.

KIHEI BEACHES

In high season, **Keawakapu Beach Park**, at the far south end of South Kīhei Road, makes a less crowded alternative. Swimming is best in the center, while there's good snorkeling off the rocks to the south, thanks to an artificial offshore reef, made up mostly of old automobile parts that were submerged in the hope of boosting the local fish population.

Hawaiian Islands Humpback Whale National Marine Sanctuary

At the northern end of Kīhei, squeezed onto a minor headland not far south of Mai Poina 'Oe Ia'u Beach, a small compound serves as the headquarters of the **Hawaiian Islands Humpback Whale National Marine Sanctuary** (☎1-800/831-4888; ⓦwww.hihwnms.nos.noaa.gov). The organization was created to protect and study the estimated three thousand humpback whales that annually winter in Hawaiian waters. Enthusiastic volunteers can explain its work and talk you through the displays in the garage-like **Education Center** (Mon–Sat 9.30am–3pm; free; ☎1-800/831-4888; ⓦwww.hihwhms.nos.noaa.gov). The organization's offices are in the larger blue house on the seafront, whose interior is not open to the public. Its spacious verandah, however, is equipped with free binoculars and makes an ideal spot for watching any whales there may be in Mā'alaea Bay.

A six-acre tract of ocean immediately offshore from the sanctuary headquarters is still enclosed by the ancient lava walls of the **Kō'ie'ie Fishpond**, which dates originally from the sixteenth century. This area was then the site of the village of **Kalepolepo**, whose inhabitants left after the fishpond became silted up during the 1860s thanks to runoff caused by the expansion of agriculture further up the slopes.

RESTAURANTS

The **restaurants** listed below represent just a small selection of what's available in Kīhei. Virtually all the malls also hold at least one budget diner or takeout, and most have an espresso bar, too. The best places for **food shopping** are the Safeway supermarket at Pi'ilani Village Shopping Center on the upper highway (where there's also a *Starbucks*), and the Hawaiian Moons wholefood store at the Kama'ole Beach Center, 2411 S Kīhei Rd.

INEXPENSIVE

Azeka's

Azeka Place 1, 1280 S Kīhei Rd
ⓣ 879-0611.
Small snack shop and takeout, with a few tables, serving *saimin* for under $3, plus sushi and the Hawaiian favorite *loco moco*, an egg-topped hamburger. Marinated ribs ($6 for a pound) are also served; in fact, from 3pm to 5pm they're the only things available here. Main counter open daily 7.30am–2pm; ribs daily 7.30am–5pm.

Canton Chef

Kama'ole Shopping Center, 2463 S Kīhei Rd ⓣ 879-1988.
Roomy Chinese restaurant, with $6 lunch specials and a dinner menu bursting with chicken, shrimp, scallop and fish entrees ($7–12), including several served in black-bean sauce. With advance notice, they'll prepare a whole Peking duck for $35. Daily 11am–1.45pm & 5–9pm.

The Coffee Store

Azeka Place 2, 1279 S Kīhei Rd
ⓣ 875-4244.
Cheery mall café serving espressos of all kinds and flavors, as well as breakfast pastries, lunch salads, pizzas and sandwiches. Daily 6am–10pm.

Kīhei Caffe

1945 S Kīhei Rd ⓣ 879-2230.
Friendly café, offering espressos, flavored lattes and

smoothies, plus breakfast fry-ups and $6 lunchtime sandwiches or burgers to take out or eat at a shaded roadside gazebo that's perfect for people-watching. Mon–Sat 5am–3pm, Sun 6am–3pm.

Royal Thai

Azeka Place 1, 1280 S Kīhei Rd ⊤ 874-0813.
Small place, tucked away at the back of the mall, serving Kīhei's best Thai food. Red, yellow and green curries in vegetarian, meat and fish versions; *tom yum* and long rice soups; and mussels in black-bean sauce; all for $7–10. Mon–Fri 11am–3pm & 4.45–9.30pm, Sat & Sun 4.45–9.30pm.

South Beach Smoothies

1455 S Kīhei Rd ⊤ 875-0594.
Small kiosk in a parking lot beside the main highway, which prepares superb $4 smoothies using your choice of mango, coconut, banana, papaya or other fresh fruits, and also offers bagels and ice cream. Mon–Sat 9am–5pm.

MODERATE

Hapa's Brew Haus

41 E Lipoa St ⊤ 879-9001.
Large and very popular brewpub, whose success as a music venue – Maui stars like Hapa themselves and Willie K play 9pm–1.30am nightly – has resulted in ever less space being devoted to its basic restaurant, where predictable rib or chicken dinners cost around $10. Daily 5.30pm–1.30am.

Pizazz Café

Azeka Place 2, 1279 S Kīhei Rd ⊤ 891-2123.
Mall bistro where the lagely conventional menu of $10-15 meat and fish entrees includes an (un)healthy smattering of Deep South specialties such as catfish and okra. But the real draw is the live jazz performed from 7.30pm nightly. Sun & Mon 11am–11pm, Tues–Sat 11am–midnight.

Stella Blues Café & Deli

Longs Center, 1215 S Kīhei Rd ⊤ 874-3779.
California-style café with big

plate-glass windows, a few tables outside, and Grateful Dead posters and ponytailed waiters within. Continental and cooked breakfasts $7–9; $7–10 burger, salad and sandwich lunches (try the special of grilled and roasted vegetables on herb bread); dinners like fettuccine Alfredo, Cajun chicken, crab cakes and ribs for $14–20; and all-day smoothies and espressos. Daily 8am–9pm.

Ziziki's

2511 S Kīhei Rd ☏ 879-9330. Friendly Greek place on a garden terrace set back from the road and crammed with coconut palms and a banyan tree. Authentic appetizers like a feta and olive salad, or stuffed grape leaves for $6–8; entrees include moussaka and souvlaki for under $20, and a full "Greek Gods Platter" for $30 per person. Daily 5–10pm.

EXPENSIVE

- - - - - - - - - - - - - - - - - - - -

Five Palms Beach Grill

Mana Kai Maui, 2960 S Kīhei Rd ☏ 879-2607.

Beachfront restaurant on ground floor of condo building, with open terraces within earshot of the waves, and live music nightly. Egg breakfasts, including smoked-salmon Benedict for $11, and salad or daily special lunches for $10–15. The food at dinner – mostly Pacific Rim, along with standard ribs and steaks – is beautifully presented and tastes delicious. Appetizers such as soft-shell crab cakes in ginger rémoulade cost around $12; entrees like fresh *opah* (moonfish), and grilled chicken fettuccine with wild mushroom couscous, are more like $25–30. Mon–Fri 8am–2.30pm & 5–9pm, Sat & Sun 8am–2.30pm & 5–10pm.

Pacific Café Maui

Azeka Place 2, 1279 S Kīhei Rd ☏ 879-0069.

Maui's finest gourmet restaurant, part of an upmarket chain that originated on Kauai, the *Pacific Café* serves the "Hawaii Regional" cuisine of Jean-Pierre Josselin and is focused on a huge wood-burning grill. The food is superb, with an amazing "*ahi* tower" appetizer for $13 that includes a raw-tuna *poke*, oysters with tuna, and a tuna carpaccio. Entrees (around $30) feature grilled meats and fish with roasted vegetables. Decadent desserts include mac-nut profiteroles and a bittersweet chocolate soufflé. With the cheapest bottle of wine costing around $25, a meal for two will probably top $100. Reservations essential; daily 5.30–9.30pm.

Roy's Kīhei Bar and Grill

Pi'ilani Village, 303 Pi'ikea Ave ⓣ 891-1120.

Large new mall outlet of the upmarket island chain, on the upper highway half a mile up from Kīhei Road. Signature *Roy's* dishes such as lemongrass-crusted *shutome* (swordfish) and blackened rare *ahi* stream from the open kitchen, at around $10 for an appetizer or $25 for an entree. The steamed fresh catch ($27) is irresistible. Daily 5.30–10pm.

Wailea and Mākena

Both South Kīhei Road and Pi'ilani Highway end on the southern fringes of Kīhei. The only road south, branching off Okolani Drive halfway between the two, is **Wailea Alanui Drive**, which becomes **Mākena Alanui Drive** after a couple of miles. It's forced to run several hundred yards inland by a sequence of half a dozen colossal resort hotels, constructed on a scale to rival any in Hawaii. Neither **WAILEA** nor **MĀKENA** is a town as such; were it not for the resorts, the names would not even appear on island maps. The only **shops** in the area are congregated in the very upmarket new **Shops at Wailea** mall, whose target audience can be assessed from the presence of Louis Vuitton, Cartier, and Dolce & Gabbana stores.

Until the 1950s, what is now Wailea was just barren oceanfront acreage belonging to the 'Ulupalakua Ranch (see p.175). It was then bought by Matson Cruise Lines, who planned to turn it into the "City of Roses," but nothing happened until control of Matson passed to Alexander & Baldwin in the 1970s.

Mākena, which segues imperceptibly into the south end of Wailea, was developed even more recently: its first hotel appeared at the end of the 1980s. For a period in the late nineteenth century, however, it ranked as Maui's second port after Lahaina, thanks to the comings and goings at 'Ulupalakua Ranch, just two miles higher up the gentle slope of Haleakalā. These days, in the absence of any direct road, getting to the ranch requires a forty-mile drive.

Wailea and Mākena together constitute a luxurious enclave of velvet golf courses and pristine beaches, where nonguests can feel distinctly unwelcome. In theory, outsiders are free to use any of the beaches, but with magnificent Oneloa Beach (see p.161) lying just beyond Mākena, few bother.

ACCOMMODATION.

The moment you see the manicured lawns of Wailea, let alone its gleaming resorts, it will become clear that you need a *lot* of money to **stay** at this end of South Maui. There is one small B&B nearby, but otherwise rooms can rarely be found for under $200 a night.

Ann & Bob Babson's B&B

3371 Keha Drive, Wailea ⓣ874-1166 or 1-800/824-6409, ⓕ879-7906; ⓦwww.mauibnb.com. Lovely garden B&B on the slopes above Wailea, with three en-suite units in the main family home and a separate guest cottage. Ocean-view *lānais* and lavish breakfasts are highlights. Five-night minimum stay. ❸–❹.

Four Seasons Resort

3900 Wailea Alanui Drive, Wailea ⓣ874-8000 or 1-800/334-6284, ⓕ874-2222; ⓦwww.fshr.com.

KAHOOLAWE

The uninhabited island of **Kahoolawe**, eight miles offshore, is visible from all along Maui's south and west coasts. Measuring just eleven miles by six, it's the eighth-largest Hawaiian island, and looks from a distance like a barren hillock. Trapped in the rainshadow of Haleakalā, it gets a mere thirty inches of rain a year.

Whether Kahoolawe ever held much of a population is hotly debated, thanks to the campaign by **native Hawaiians** to claim the island back from the **US Navy**. The Navy used it for target practice for almost fifty years, arguing that it was of no value to humans; the Hawaiians claimed that it held great spiritual significance to their ancestors, and that access to it remained their inalienable birthright.

Both sides marshaled archeologists and anthropologists, so Kahoolawe has been more thoroughly probed and excavated than anywhere else in Hawaii. The consensus seems to be that, although it was principally a seasonal base for fishermen, it also held permanent agricultural settlements, at least perhaps until its scanty resources were used up. In addition, Kealaikahiki Point at its southwest corner – the name means "the way to foreign lands" – was a marker for navigators voyaging to and from Tahiti. A "navigator's chair" of shaped boulders still stands atop the island's second-highest peak, the 1444-foot Moa'ulaiki, which is thought to have served as a school and observatory for apprentice navigators.

Captain Cook described Kahoolawe as "altogether a poor Island" in 1779, and what little vegetation it held was eaten away by sheep and goats during the nineteenth century. The last of the few ranchers who attempted to eke out a living here was evicted after the attack on Pearl Harbor.

After World War II, the military declined to hand Kahoolawe back, claiming the ability to practice island landings there had been a major factor in its defeat of Japan. In 1953, President Eisenhower granted the Navy control over the island, with the proviso that it should be cleaned up at Federal expense and returned when no longer needed. For forty more years, Kahoolawe was blasted by thunderous explosions that could be seen and heard from Maui.

Hawaiian efforts to reclaim Kahoolawe crystallized in 1975 with the formation of the **Protect Kahoolawe ʻOHāna** (PKO). This group of young activists saw Kahoolawe as a unifying cause for all native Hawaiians, symbolizing the desecration of Hawaiian lands by the United States. The PKO organized illegal occupations of the island from January 1976 onward. In 1977, members George Helm and Kimo Mitchell were lost at sea as they attempted to return to Maui after one such venture, a martyrdom that attracted huge publicity.

The PKO then turned to the courts. Accusing the Navy on several fronts – water, noise and air pollution; the threat to endangered marine mammals and historic sites; and the infringement of religious freedoms – they won restrictions on bombing and gained "visiting rights" of up to ten days per month. President George H.W. Bush finally called a halt to the bombing in 1990, and Kahoolawe was handed back to the state of Hawaii in May 1994. The Navy was scheduled to control access until the year 2003, or until all unexploded ordnance has been removed. Because the $400 million originally budgeted as the cost of the cleanup now seems inadequate for the job, it looks as though Hawaiians are in for a very long wait. Hawaiian groups nonetheless regularly visit Kahoolawe, and a program of reforestation has begun.

KAHOOLAWE

Lavish resort property at the south end of Wailea, with a large, beautiful, white-sand beach on view beyond the open lobby, and a gorgeous, palm-ringed pool. Private *lānais,* bamboo furnishings, 24-hour room service and several restaurants, including the superb *Seasons.* Mountain-view room ❽, ocean-view room or suite ❾.

Grand Wailea Resort

3850 Wailea Alanui Drive, Wailea ⊤ 875-1234 or 1-800/888-6100, ⓕ 874-2442; ⓦ www.grandwailea.com. Large and very ostentatious resort hotel, with a five-level swimming pool ("Wailea Canyon") that's linked by waterslides and features a swim-up bar, hot-tub grottoes, and even a water elevator back to the top. There's also a luxurious spa and half a dozen restaurants, and tropical flowers are everywhere. The *Tsunami* is Maui's hottest, flashiest nightclub. ❾.

Kea Lani Hotel

4100 Wailea Alanui Drive, Wailea ⊤ 875-4100 or 1-800/882-4100, ⓕ 875-1200; ⓦ www.kealani.com. Locals call it the Taj Mahal, but this dazzling white resort is more like something from the *Arabian Nights.* Despite its flamboyant silhouette, the interior is characterized by smooth curves, and you can see through the lobby to lily ponds and the lagoon-cum-pool, crossed by little footbridges. Two huge wings of plush rooms (each equipped with TVs, a VCR and a CD player) plus 37 garden villas, and some excellent restaurants, all focused on lovely Polo Beach (see p.158). Garden view ❽, ocean view ❾.

Maui Prince

5400 Mākena Alanui Drive, Mākena ⊤ 874-1111 or 1-800/321-6284, ⓕ 879-8763 or 1-800/338-8763. South Maui's southernmost resort is a secluded and stylish low-rise facing a pretty sandy cove, within walking distance of wonderful Big Beach (see p.161). A strong Japanese influence means that the main building focuses inwards and around a central courtyard, rather than outwards. Top-quality Japanese and Pacific Rim restaurants, golf packages and early-morning snorkel cruises to Molokini. **❽**.

Outrigger Wailea Resort

3700 Wailea Alanui Drive, Wailea ⓣ 879-1922, 1-800/688-7444 (US & Can) or 001-800/688-74443 (UK & Ireland), ⓕ 875-4878; ⓦ www.outrigger.com. Wailea's first resort hotel, previously the *Maui Inter-Continental Resort* and the *Aston Wailea*, has been upgraded by *Outrigger* to match its neighbors. It comprises several small buildings in the landscaped gardens and a larger

central tower, all with spacious, comfortable rooms. Three pools, two restaurants, plus Hawaiiana lectures and four weekly *lū'aus* (see p.35). Garden view **❽**, ocean view **❾**.

Renaissance Wailea Beach Resort

3550 Wailea Alanui Drive, Wailea ⓣ 879-4900 or 1-800/992-4532, ⓕ 874-5370; ⓦ www.renaissancehotels.com. Relatively low-profile but highly luxurious resort (formerly the *Stouffer*), stacked in seven tiers above twin crescent beaches. The gardens hold swimming pools, and a statue of the god Maui. Very luxurious rooms, with VCRs, and *lānais* angled toward the ocean. The *Hāna Gion* serves good Japanese food. Mountain view **❽**, ocean view **❾**.

BEACHES

Five separate little bays indent the coastline of Wailea, with two more at Mākena. All hold crescent beaches of white sand that in all but the worst winter conditions are ideal for swimming.

A short access road just past the *Renaissance Wailea* leads down to **Ulua Beach**. This usually has the highest surf along this stretch of coast, so it's popular with body-surfers and boogie-boarders. There's also great snorkeling around the rocky point that separates it from **Mōkapu Beach**, a short walk to the north.

By Wailea's high standards, **Wailea Beach** itself, reached by a spur road between the *Grand Wailea* and the *Four Seasons*, is perhaps not exceptional, though anywhere else in the US it would rank as a beauty. **Polo Beach**, the next along, is the best of the lot for good old-fashioned swimming. There's public access along the path from the south side of the *Kea Lani Hotel*, with plenty of parking just off Kaukahi Street. The footpath hits the sand at Polo Beach's northern end which, being right beneath the hotel, can be rather a goldfish bowl, crammed with loungers and short on shade. Double back south, however, and you'll come to two much less crowded stretches, which in winter become distinct beaches.

Ten minutes' walk south from Polo Beach, **Palauea Beach** is the quietest of the Wailea beaches. For the moment, it remains well removed from the built-up areas, though not surprisingly there's talk of imminent development. Surfers and boogie-boarders predominate, but it's also a good spot for a family day by the sea. In 1994, Palauea Beach was chosen as the site of the ceremony in which the US Navy formally handed control of the island of Kahoolawe back to the people of Hawaii.

Mākena Road, which leaves Mākena Alanui Drive a little over a mile south of the *Kea Lani*, skirts the shoreline of **Mākena Bay**. This was once the site of busy **Mākena Landing** harbor, which was superseded by the creation of Kahului's new docks in the 1920s. The jetty has now gone, to leave a sleepy black-lava bay with little sand.

A little further on, the **Keawala'i Congregational Church** stands on an oceanfront patch of lawn that doubles as a graveyard, surrounded by trees with multicolored blossoms. It's a plain cement structure, topped by a pretty, wood-shingled belfry, and painted with a neat green trim; the coconut palms beyond front a tiny beach. Visitors are welcome to the 9.30am Sunday services, which incorporate Hawaiian language and music.

Keawala'i Church is opposite the parking lot for **Mākena Beach Park**, a hundred yards down the road. Somewhat overshadowed by the *Maui Prince*, it's still an attractive little half-moon beach, with reasonable snorkeling.

RESTAURANTS

Neither Wailea nor Mākena holds many alternatives to the resort hotels' own **restaurants**, but there are enough excellent ones to choose from that, provided you don't mind paying $40 for dinner each night, there isn't a problem. For cheaper meals, you'll just have to head back to Kīhei.

Joe's Bar & Grill
131 Wailea Iki Place ☎ 875-7767.

One of Maui's most fashionable restaurants, owned by the same top-notch team as the *Hāli'imaile General Store* (see p.168) and located just off Wailea Iki Drive as it drops down into Wailea proper. Neither the tennis-club setting nor the decor – dull rock-music memorabilia – is at all inspiring, but the food is heavenly, a fusion of cutting-edge Pacific Rim cuisine

with down-home local favorites. Appetizers ($6–18) include 'ahi tartare with *wasabi* aioli, while entrees ($20 and up) range from meatloaf with garlic mashed potatoes to a smoky, applewood-grilled salmon. Daily 5.30–9.30pm.

Prince Court,
Maui Prince, 5400 Mākena Alanui Drive, Wailea ☎ 875-5888.
Relatively formal, somewhat solemn resort restaurant. Appetizers include oysters at $11 and a $12 Napoleon of

Hawaiian tuna. Apart from the steamed *moi* (threadfish) for $22, the steak and fish entrees tend to be rather predictable. Sunday morning sees a buffet brunch for $38. Mon–Sat 5.30–9.30pm, Sun 9am–1pm & 5.30–9.30pm.

SeaWatch Restaurant at Wailea

100 Wailea Golf Club Drive, Wailea ☎ 875-8080.
Grand terrace restaurant a few hundred yards uphill from the ocean, with sea views and a player piano. Daytime menus feature griddled breakfasts and lunchtime deli sandwiches and salads; at night the cuisine is Pacific Rim, with $7–12 appetizers such as five-spice crab cakes, and $25 entrees including fish, grilled chicken, and lamb with

onion torte. A light menu is served 3–5.30pm. Daily 8am–10pm.

Tommy Bahama's Tropical Café

The Shops at Wailea, 3750 Wailea Alanui Drive, Wailea ☎ 875-9983.
Bar and restaurant, adjoining the clothes store of the same name, also a "Purveyor of Island Lifestyles." Lunch is good value, with huge fishy sandwiches or pasta specials for around $10, along with sweeping (if distant) ocean views from the elevated terrace. The dinner entrees are more overtly Caribbean, including Jamaican spiced pork in rum sauce for $23 and Trinidad tuna with cilantro and lemongrass for $25. Sun–Thurs 11am–11pm, Fri & Sat 11am–midnight.

Beyond Mākena

Once past the *Maui Prince*, you're finally clear of South Maui's resorts and can enjoy some of the island's finest beaches and most unspoilt scenery. The road gives out altogether before long, but it's possible to hike on beyond the end.

ONELOA BEACH — "BIG BEACH"

Maui's most spectacular sweep of golden sand stretches for more than half a mile south of the landmark cinder cone of Puʻu ʻŌlaʻi, just south of Mākena. There's not a building in sight at **Oneloa Beach** (literally "long sand," and widely known as **Big Beach**), just perfect sands and mighty surf, backed by a dry forest of *kiawe* and cacti. During the 1970s, it was home to a short-lived hippy commune; recently it has become **Mākena State Park**, with two paved access roads.

The very first turning off the main road south of Mākena, though labeled "Mākena State Park," is a dirt track that leads via an orange gate to a scrubby gray-sand beach. Keep going on the main road instead until you reach the paved turnoff to Oneloa, half a mile beyond the *Maui Prince*. A footpath from the parking lot here leads through the trees to a small cluster of portable toilets and picnic tables, and then emerges at the north end of Big Beach. The sand is so deep and coarse that walking can be difficult, but the clear blue ocean is irresistible. The major drawback with Big Beach is that it faces straight out to sea and lacks a reef to protect it, so it's extremely **dangerous**. Huge waves crash right onto the shoreline, while a few feet out fearsome rip currents tear along the coast. Despite many drownings, all lifeguards were controversially withdrawn in 1995 to cut costs.

Most visitors to Big Beach can't resist strolling its full length southwards, before heading for the red-brown cliffs at its northern end. A natural cleft appears as if by magic to reveal the "stairway" across the rocks that enables you to reach the much smaller, and much safer, **Little Beach**. Sheltered by the rocky headland, and shaded by the adjacent trees, this is perhaps the most idyllic swimming spot on Maui, with views of Molokini and Lanai. One relic of the hippy days is that it's still widely known as an (illegal) **nudist** beach; even if you don't go naked yourself, some of your fellow beachgoers certainly will.

Pu'u 'Ōla'i

Halfway along the easy trail between Big and Little Beaches, where the ground levels off at the top of the first cliff, another trail doubles back to climb **Pu'u 'Ōla'i** itself. This crumbling cinder cone was produced by one of Maui's very last volcanic eruptions, perhaps two centuries ago, and is barely held together by scrubby grass and thorns. The ascent is so steep that strongly worded signs warn against making the attempt. If you do try, you may find you have to advance on all fours. Scrambling over the raw red, – and very sharp – cinders is extremely painful in anything other than proper hiking boots.

The summit of Pu'u 'Ōla'i – which is not the peak you see at the start of the climb – is a wonderful vantage point for watching humpback whales in winter. It commands views all the way up the flat coast to Wailea and Kīhei, down the full length of Big Beach, inland to the green uplands of Haleakalā, across the ocean to the low ridge of Molokini – circled by cruise boats from dawn onward – and beyond to glowing red Kahoolawe, the West Maui mountains and Lanai.

LA PÉROUSE BAY

Mākena Road continues for another three miles south from Big Beach, clinging to the coastline of **'Āhihi Bay** around several small, clinkery (very rough jagged lava) coves, and then crossing a wide, bare field of chunky *'a'ā* lava. **La Pérouse Bay** lies beyond the parking lot at the far end, where a cairn bearing a bronze plaque commemorates the voyages of the French Admiral Jean François de Galaup, Comte de la Pérouse.

**Both the operators listed on p.50
run kayak excursions in La Pérouse Bay.**

By spending three hours ashore here on May 30, 1786, La Pérouse became the first foreigner to set foot on Maui. He was under orders to claim the island for the king of France but, unusually for a European, considered that he had no right to do so. His ships, the *Astrolabe* and the *Boussole,* sailed away and were lost with all hands in the Solomon Islands two years later.

La Pérouse encountered a handful of coastal villages at this spot. Its inhabitants knew it as *Keone'ō'io,* or "bonefish beach," and still told of how chief Kalani'ōpu'u of the Big Island had landed a fleet of canoes there during an attempted invasion of Maui a few years earlier. However, the villages were largely destroyed just four years after the visit of La Pérouse by the last-known eruption of Haleakalā. A river of lava two miles wide flowed into the sea in the center of what had been one long bay, to create the two separate bays seen today.

The waters around the headland are set aside as the **'Āhihi–Kīna'u Natural Area Reserve**, notable for its large numbers of dolphins. All fishing is forbidden; **snorkeling** is allowed, but it's easier to enter the water in the inlets around La Pérouse Bay itself than to go in off the headland. The trail from the road meanders alternately across the sands and among the scrubby *kiawe* trees to follow the whole curve of the bay. The lichen-covered walls of ancient dwellings can often be glimpsed in the undergrowth.

**Proposals have recently been submitted to
make this entire area a national park; watch
the press for the latest developments.**

LA PÉROUSE BAY

KANAIO BEACH

At the far end of La Pérouse Bay, you come to another field of crumbled, reddish-brown lava. A separate trail – not the obvious coastal path, which soon ends, but one further inland – heads onward from here. While it has some historic interest, as it traces the route of the King's Highway footpath that once ringed the entire island, it's extremely rugged, hot and exposed. **Kanaio Beach**, a pretty cove of turquoise water two miles along, is as far as it makes any sense to go, and even that's not a hike to undertake lightly.

Upcountry Maui

The lower western slopes of Haleakalā, which enjoy a deliciously temperate climate a couple thousand feet above the isthmus, are known as Upcountry Maui. While most visitors simply race through on their way up the mountain, the Upcountry is among the most attractive regions in the state. A narrow strip that stretches for at most twenty miles, it varies from the wet, lush orchards and rainforests around Makawao in the north to the parched cattle country of the venerable 'Ulupalakua Ranch in the south. There are few significant towns and even fewer tourist attractions, but the whole region is laced with quiet rural lanes that make for relaxing explorations. Although commuter traffic up and down Haleakalā Highway attests to its status as one of the most popular residential districts on the island, accommodation for visitors is limited to a handful of pretty, small-scale B&Bs.

At this altitude, the pineapple and sugar plantations of the isthmus give way to smaller private farms. In the past these grew the white potatoes that first lured the whaling fleet to Maui, as well as coffee, cotton and Maui onions, but the most conspicuous crop now is flowering plants, especially dazzling **protea blossoms**.

If you expect a nonstop riot of greenery and color, however, you may be disappointed to find that much of the

Upcountry is dry and desolate. It takes irrigation to render this land fertile, and the many gulches that corrugate the flanks of Haleakalā only manage to support sparse grass, dry stunted trees, and cacti. This becomes ever more true as you head further south. Clumps of high, old trees mark the sites of ranch buildings, but otherwise the slopes are bare, scattered with the rounded knolls of ancient cinder cones.

Within the next few years, a new stretch of highway, or even a whole new road, will probably be constructed to connect Kīhei directly with Upcountry Maui. For the moment, however, the only route up from the island's south or west coasts is via Kahului.

MAKAWAO

The small town of **MAKAWAO**, seven miles up from coastal Pā'ia (see p.91), represents Maui at its best. Still recognizable as the village built by plantation workers and *paniolo* cowboys in the nineteenth century, it's now home to an active artistic community dominated by 1970s exiles from California. When they're not giving each other classes in yoga, feng shui, belly dancing and Hawaiian healing, they make its galleries, crafts stores and coffee bars some of the liveliest hangouts on the island.

Makawao – "edge of the forest" – barely existed before Kamehameha III chose it as the site of Hawaii's first experiment in private land ownership in 1845, when almost a hundred Hawaiians acquired small homesites. Their enterprising tradition has endured, although most of the area was grabbed by outsiders when they were permitted to buy land by the Great Mahele of 1848 (see p.235). Local timberyards, harvesting the rainforest to the east of town, provided the dark *koa* wood used in Honolulu's 'Iolani Palace, while Portuguese immigrants arrived to work on the neighboring cattle ranches toward the end of the nineteenth century.

The moment when Makawao's lawless cowboy past gave way to the outlaw chic of today can be pinned down to July 30, 1970, when **Jimi Hendrix** played one of his last concerts, barely a month before he died, to eight hundred people gathered in a field above Seabury Hall private school – an occasion that was immortalized in the turgid movie *Rainbow Bridge*.

Although Makawao extends for well over a mile, only its central intersection – where **Baldwin Avenue**, climbing from Pāʻia, meets **Makawao Avenue** from Pukalani – holds any great interest. Baldwin Avenue here points straight up Haleakalā, framing the lush green meadows on the slopes above town. Its timber-frame buildings, painted in fading pastel hues, are connected by a rudimentary boardwalk and hold half a dozen quirky art galleries. The real artistic epicenter of town, however, is the **Hui Noʻeau Visual Arts Center**, a country estate a mile south at 2841 Baldwin Ave (Tues–Sun 10am–4pm; ☎572-6560). As well as offering classes in practical arts and crafts, it houses its own small store (Mon–Sat 10am–4pm) and a gallery for temporary exhibitions.

Makawao's *paniolo* days are commemorated on July 4 each year by the **Makawao Rodeo**, which includes a parade through town as well as competitive events at the Oskie Rice Arena.

There's no accommodation in Makawao;
see "Accommodation" in the Pāʻia section
(p.93) for B&Bs within a few minutes' drive.

Restaurants

Makawao has an excellent selection of friendly local **restaurants**, good for inexpensive lunch stops, and a lively night-time scene focused on *Casanova's*. If you're buying your own supplies, head for Down to Earth Natural Foods at 1169 Makawao Ave, a wholefood store with a deli counter.

Casanova's

1188 Makawao Ave ☎ 572-0220.

The 1970s-style Art Nouveau lettering and faded exterior of this single-story wooden building in the heart of Makawao belies its status as one of Maui's hottest nightspots (Willie Nelson and Kris Kristofferson are among stars to have played here). There's a dance floor and bar just inside the door, a romantic Italian restaurant further back and a breakfast deli/espresso bar alongside. Lunchtime salads, pastas and sandwiches range from $5 to $14, while in the evening, wood-fired pizzas cost $10–15, pasta entrees are $10–18, and specials are $20–25. Portions are huge. The cover charge of $5 on dance nights (unless you dine) can rise to $10 when there's live music (typically Friday and Saturday). Mon & Tues 5.30am–12.30am, Wed–Sun 5.30am–1am.

Courtyard Café

3620 Baldwin Ave ☎ 572-4877. Off-street café in the Courtyard Mall, serving espressos, pastries and sandwiches at shaded garden seating. Mon–Sat 8am–5pm, Sun 8am–3pm.

Duncan's Coffee Co

3647 Baldwin Ave ☎ 573-9075. Smart little coffee place on the main drag, serving panini, espressos and smoothies. Mon–Sat 7am–5pm.

Hāli'imaile General Store

900 Hāli'imaile Rd ☎ 572-2666. Gourmet Hawaiian food in a converted store in the village of Hāli'imaile, which is two miles down Baldwin Avenue, and then a mile west toward Haleakalā Highway. Appetizers (up to $18) include an Asian pear and duck taco, and fresh island fish cakes, while entrees, like Szechuan barbecued salmon or rack of lamb Hunan-style, can cost more than $30. Mon–Sat

side
MAKAWAO RESTAURANTS

11am–2.30pm &
5.30–9.30pm, Sun 10am–
2.30pm & 5.30–9.30pm.

Polli's
1202 Makawao Ave ☎ 572-7808.
Busy, good-value Mexican

restaurant at Makawao's
central crossroads. Individual
dishes cost under $10, while
a full chimichanga dinner is
$13, and a fajita plate is $16.
Mon–Sat 7am–10pm, Sun
8am–10pm.

PUKALANI

Now that a bypass carries traffic on the busy Haleakalā
Highway (Hwy-37) around, instead of through,
PUKALANI, seven miles up from Kahului, there's no reason for tourists ever to see the town at all. This shapeless
sprawl is home to six thousand people, but has no apprecia-
ble downtown area.

The run-down **Pukalani Terrace Center** mall holds
the closest gas station to the summit of Haleakalā, as well as
a big Foodland supermarket, a *Subway* sandwich shop and a
KFC, the *Mixed Plate* budget diner (Mon–Wed, Sat & Sun
6am–1pm, Thurs & Fri 6am–1pm & 4–8pm), and the
Chinese *Royal King's Garden* (Mon–Sat 11am–2pm &
4–9pm, Sun 4–9pm; ☎ 572-7027).

KULA AND THE HEART OF THE UPCOUNTRY

Immediately beyond Pukalani, Hwy-37 changes its name to
Kula Highway, while **Haleakalā Highway**, now Hwy-
377, branches off up the mountain. It meets the route to
the summit, **Haleakalā Crater Road**, after six miles, and
then as **Kekaulike Highway** swings back to rejoin Kula
Highway.

This general region is known as **Kula**. None of the four
separate communities – from north to south, **Ōma'opio**,
Pūlehu, **Waiakoa** and **Kula** itself – amounts to very much,

but the views they afford are superb. Far below, the curve of the ocean bites into either side of the flat, green isthmus, while on the horizon clouds squat on the West Maui mountains. In the morning sun, you can make out the condo buildings lining the Kīhei coast, but by afternoon, apart from the odd glint of a car or window, the long gentle slopes seem predominantly rural.

For details of the few restaurants in the Kula district, see p.175.

Accommodation

Driving across the Kula district, you probably won't notice any **accommodation** apart from the *Kula Lodge*. Tucked away on the backroads, however, are some lovely little B&Bs. All require advance reservations, and some can only be booked through specialist B&B agencies.

Halemanu B&B

221 Kaweihi Place, Kula, HI 96790 ⊤878-2729; Ⓔcarolaus@maui.net.
B&B in private home with peaceful gardens, near the foot of Waipoli Road as it climbs to Polipoli (see p.173). Just one guest room, packed with oddments from around the world, with en-suite bath and amazing views. Two-night minimum stay. ❸.

Kili's Cottage

Kula; ⊤885-4550 or 1-800/262-9912, Ⓕ885-0559, reserve through Hawaii's Best B&B, PO Box 563, Kamuela, HI 96743; ⓌWwww.bestbnb.com.
A real bargain: a comfortable three-bedroom, two-bathroom house, set in beautiful upland gardens and equipped with TV, VCR and full kitchen, rented for less than the price of most Maui hotel rooms. Two-night minimum stay. ❹.

ACCOMMODATION

The telephone area code for all Hawaii is ⊤808.

ACCOMMODATION PRICE CODES

All accommodation prices in this book have been graded with
the following symbols; for a full explanation, see p.29.

1 up to $40   **4** $100–150   **7** $250–300

2 $40–70   **5** $150–200   **8** $300–400

3 $70–100   **6** $200–250   **9** over $400

Kula Lodge

RR1, Box 475, Kula, HI 96790
℡878-1535 or 1-800/233-
1535, ℻878-2518;
ⓦ www.kulalodge.com.
Upmarket board and lodging
in Hawaiian approximation of
an Alpine inn, *makai* of
Haleakalā Highway, just before
the Haleakalā Crater Road
turnoff. Accommodation is in
five chalets, four of which can
sleep family parties: all are
comfortably furnished, though
they don't have phones or TV.
4–**5**.

Silver Cloud Guest Ranch

Old Thompson Rd, PO Box
201, Kula, HI 96790 ℡878-
6101 or 1-800/532-1111,
℻878-2132;
ⓦ www.silvercloudranch.com.
Relaxing ranch-style B&B,
just over a mile southeast of
Kēōkea, along the one-lane
road (signed for Kula San)
that branches off opposite
Grandma's (see p.175). Twelve
comfortable and well-
furnished en-suite rooms –
the six in the main house
have gorgeous long wooden
lānais facing down the
mountain and into the sunset,
while the others are in
outbuildings nearby. Horses,
cats and pigs roam the
surrounding meadows, and
the owners can arrange trail
rides in the hills. **3**–**5**.

Holy Ghost Church

Map 9, D7.

The lower Upcountry road, the Kula Highway, passes just
below the white octagonal **Holy Ghost Church**. Portuguese

Catholics came to Maui from 1878 onward, and by 1894 were prosperous enough to construct their own church, shipping the hand-carved high-relief gilt altar from Austria, and capping the structure with a gleaming silver-roofed belfry. The interior is very light, with pink-painted walls, and features the Stations of the Cross labeled in Portuguese.

Not surprisingly, this was the only octagonal structure built in nineteenth-century Hawaii. Depending on who you believe, it is eight-sided either because the crown of the Portuguese Queen Isabella was octagonal, or because the German parish priest came from near Aachen, the site of the octagonal palace chapel of Charlemagne.

Kula Botanical Gardens

Map 9, D7. Daily 9am–4pm; adults $5, children aged 6–12 $1.

A couple of miles beyond the foot of Haleakalā Crater Road, on Kekaulike Highway, the **Kula Botanical Gardens** offer self-guided tours through large and colorful landscaped gardens. Among its broad range of plants are proteas, hydrangeas, lurid yellow and red canna, and spectacular purple and yellow birds of paradise from South Africa. Many of its species betray their Pacific origins by bearing the Latin name *banksia*, in honor of Sir Joseph Banks, the pioneering botanist who sailed with Captain Cook; perhaps the finest is the red and white "Raspberry Frost" from Australia.

Polipoli State Park

Map 9, D9.

Maui residents rave about thickly wooded **Polipoli State Park**, set high above the Upcountry, but visitors from beyond Hawaii may feel it has little they can't see at home. The drive up is fun, though, taking you off the beaten track into Maui's remoter reaches.

Polipoli Park stands at the top of the ten-mile Waipoli Road – not the further south Polipoli Road, oddly enough – which climbs away from Kekaulike Highway just south of the Kula Botanical Gardens. The first six miles, in which you do all the climbing, are paved, passing through tough springy ranchland where cattle graze on the open range. This is Maui's best launching spot for **hang-gliders**, which you may see sharing the winds with circling Hawaiian owls (unique in that they fly by day, rather than by night).

It shouldn't be too difficult to coax a rental car along the rough but level dirt road that meanders along the hillside above the ranch. After three miles, the road surface improves; drop right at the fork half a mile further along, and after another half-mile you'll come to Polipoli's **campground** in a grassy clearing. Tent camping here ($5), and overnight stays in the simple cabin nearby ($45 for four people), can be arranged through the state parks office in Wailuku (see p.54).

The Redwood Trail
The entire Polipoli area was planted with Californian redwood trees by the Civilian Conservation Corps during the 1930s. The **Redwood Trail**, which leads down from a hundred yards before the campground, burrows through such thick forest that the persistent rain can barely penetrate it, and very little light does either. The forest floor is too gloomy even to support a light scattering of moss, and many of the tightly packed trees are dead. It comes as a huge relief when the trail emerges from the bottom-most strip of eucalyptus after a mile and a half to show expansive views across the ranchlands.

The Skyline Trail
Various other trails crisscross throughout Polipoli, including some to lava caves hidden in the woods, but the only one

likely to interest visitors from outside Hawaii is the **Skyline Trail**. This epic thirteen-mile trek follows the southwest rift zone of Haleakalā right the way up to Science City, at the summit (see p.188). It climbs a dirt track that heads off to the left two miles along the left fork from the junction 9.5 miles up Waipoli Road, described above. Unless you arrange a pickup at the far end, it's too far for a day-hike, and the higher you get the more exposed to the biting winds you'll be. **Mountain-biking** is permitted.

Kēōkea

A couple of miles south of the intersection of the Kekaulike and Kula highways, the village of **KĒŌKEA** consists of a small cluster of roadside stores, together with the green and white **St John's Episcopal Church**. All were built at the end of the nineteenth century to serve the local Chinese community, which also supported three Chinese-language schools and, allegedly, a number of opium dens. Alongside *Grandma's Coffee Store* (see opposite), one room of Henry Fong's general store houses the **Kēōkea Gallery** (Tues–Sat 9am–5pm, Sun 9am–3pm), an appealing little gallery of arts and crafts.

The wife and children of Sun Yat-sen, the first president of China, stayed on his brother's ranch here during 1911 and 1912, while Sun was away fomenting revolution. Hence the statue of Sun, flanked by two Chinese dragons, that looks out over Wailea and Kahoolawe from the some-what neglected **Dr Sun Yat-Sen Memorial Park**, which lies at the intersection of Hwy-37 and Kealakapu Road, just under two miles beyond Kēōkea.

Thanks to its healthy elevation, Kēōkea was also the site of **Kula Sanatorium**, a facility for treating tuberculosis sufferers that opened in 1910, and was soon joined by a "Preventorium" that set out to reduce the incidence of the disease. The signposts for "Kula San" are not in Chinese, but simply refer to the popular abbreviation.

Kula district restaurants

The few **eating options** in the Kula district include the wood-furnished dining room of *Kula Lodge* (see p.171; ☏878-1535), open daily from 6.30am until around 9pm; it's busiest at the start of the day, when most of the customers are already on their way back *down* Haleakalā. The food is American, with a definite Pacific Rim tinge; the lunch menu consists of sandwiches, burgers and a few selections from the dinner menu, priced at $10–13, while evening offerings include crab-cake appetizers ($12), and seared '*ahi* or large steaks for just under $30. Protea blossoms adorn the tables, and the views are immense. A couple hundred yards higher up, *mauka* of the highway, *Kula Sandalwoods* (☏878-3523) offers a similar menu for breakfast and lunch only.

For smaller snacks, or an espresso fix, call in at *Grandma's Coffee Store* in Kēōkea (daily 7am–5pm; ☏878-2140). You're unlikely to see "Grandma," but there's plenty of fresh Maui-grown coffee, plus sandwiches, salads, *saimin* and killer homemade desserts such as blueberry cobbler.

'ULUPALAKUA RANCH

Map 1, F8.

Six miles on from Kēōkea, the six tin-roofed, single-story wooden buildings of the **'Ulupalakua Ranch** headquarters nestle into a shady bend in the road. Comings and goings are carefully monitored by the three carved wooden cowboys stationed permanently on the porch of the 'Ulupalakua Ranch Store (daily 9am–4.30pm); inside, you can buy sodas and snacks, *paniolo* hats, T-shirts and limited basic supplies.

'Ulupalakua Ranch started out in the middle of the nineteenth century as **Rose Ranch**, owned by an ex-whaling captain, **James McKee**. Originally its main business was sugar, but the focus soon shifted to cattle, and it employed expert *paniolo* cowboys such as Ike Purdy, a former world rodeo champion. In his huge mansion, the site of Hawaii's first-ever swimming pool, McKee played host to Robert Louis Stevenson and King David Kalākaua among others. Spotting ships arriving at Mākena Landing (see p 158), he'd fire a cannon to signal that he was sending a carriage down to meet his guests. The mansion burned down during the 1970s, but the ranch itself is still going, raising elk and sheep as well as cattle.

TEDESCHI WINERY

Map 1, G8. Store and museum daily 9am–5pm; free tours, every hour on the half-hour, daily 9.30am–2.30pm; ☏ 878-6058.

Around the corner, beyond 'Ulupalakua Ranch, one of the ranch's co-owners has established the **Tedeschi Winery** as a successful sideline on the site of James McKee's original Rose Ranch. It uses two annual grape harvests from a small vineyard in a fold below the highway, a mile to the north, to produce 30,000 cases a year of white, red, and rosé wines, as well as Maui Brut champagne and a "sparkling pineapple" wine. They're on sale in the new **King's Cottage**, which also houses an entertaining little museum of ranch and cowboy history and serves as the assembly point for fifteen-minute **guided tours**. The converted and imitation ranch buildings used for processing and bottling are less than enthralling, but you do at least get to see some amazing trees, including a pine drowning in multicolored creeping bougainvillea, and a giant camphor.

PI'ILANI HIGHWAY

South of 'Ulapalakua, Kula Highway confusingly becomes the **Pi'ilani Highway**, despite having no connection with the parallel road of the same name that runs through Wailea and Mākena down below. For all the strictures of the rental companies – see p.25 – it takes appalling weather to render it unsafe, and for most of the year it's possible to drive all the way along the south coast to Hāna, 37 miles away. A detailed description of the route, coming in the opposite direction, begins on p.221.

Haleakalā

Although the briefest glance at a map shows the extent to which mighty Haleakalā dominates Maui, it's hard to appreciate its full ten-thousand-foot majesty until you climb right to the top. With its summit often obscured by clouds, the vast volcano can often seem no more than a shallow slope rising a short distance above the rest of Maui.

By ascending more than ten thousand feet above sea level in just 38 miles from Kahului, **Haleakalā Highway** is said to climb higher, faster than any road on earth. En route, it crosses a bewildering succession of terrains, equivalent to a drive from Mexico to Alaska. Beyond the exclusive homes and white clapboard churches of Upcountry Maui, it leads through purple-blossoming jacaranda, firs and eucalyptus trees to reach open ranching land, and then sweeps in huge curves to the volcanic desert and the awe-inspiring **Haleakalā Crater** itself. Almost eight miles across, this eerie wasteland would comfortably hold Manhattan.

The record time in the annual 38-mile Run-to-the-Sun foot race up Haleakalā is an incredible 4hr 45min.

THE GEOLOGY OF HALEAKALĀ

For visitors who arrive on Maui eager for their first glimpse of "the volcano," it can be hard to accept that they're already standing on it. With its endless gentle gradient, Haleakalā fails to conform to the popular notion of a volcano as a cone-shaped mountain, topped by a neat round crater filled with bubbling lava. This is because Hawaiian volcanoes are **shield volcanoes**, which grow slowly and steadily rather than violently, adding layer upon layer as lava seeps out of fissures and vents all along the "**rift zones**" that cover their sides. The effect is to create a long, low profile, supposedly resembling a warrior's shield laid on the ground.

Similarly, the dramatic, multicolored **Haleakalā Crater**, 10,023 feet above sea level at the summit of Haleakalā, and measuring more than seven miles long, two miles wide and half a mile deep, is often hailed as the largest extinct volcanic crater in the world. As far as geologists are concerned, however, it's none of these things. They insist that not only is the "crater" not a crater at all – in shape, size, origin and location it bears no relation to any summit crater Haleakalā may once have possessed – but strictly speaking it's not even volcanic, having been created by erosion rather than eruption.

Like all the volcanoes of Hawaii, Haleakalā was fueled by a "**hot spot**" in the earth's crust, way below the sea floor, which has been channeling magma upwards for seventy million years. As the continental plates drift northwest, at around three inches per year, that magma has found its way to the surface in one volcano after another. Each island in turn has clawed its way up from the depths, emerged above the waves, and then ceased to grow as its volcanoes became ever further removed from the life-giving source. In time, erosion by rain and sea wears away the rock, and eventually the ocean washes over it once more, perhaps leaving a ring of coral – an **atoll** – to bear witness. Though Kauai is the oldest Hawaiian island of any size, the oldest of all are by now 3500 miles away, mere specks off the coast of Japan.

Haleakalā originally thrust its way from the ocean around 800,000 years ago. In the 400,000 years that followed, it first fused with, and eventually came to dominate, the West Maui mountains. At its highest, it may have stood 15,000 feet tall, which is higher than Mauna Kea and Mauna Loa on the Big Island today. It towered over the land mass geologists call "**Maui Nui**," or Big Maui, which also incorporated the present-day islands of Kahoolawe, Molokai and Lanai.

DOWNHILL BIKING

One of Maui's most popular tourist activities is to be taken by minivan to see the dawn on top of Haleakalā and then to ride back down the mountain on a **bike**. It's not an exaggeration to say that it's possible to make it back down to the ocean at Pā'ia, a 39-mile ride, without pedaling; even Dan Quayle managed it, accompanied by six Secret Service men, also on mountain bikes. Approaching 100,000 people now make the descent each year, with several companies taking twenty or more customers every morning. It can be great fun, although serious cyclists tend to find it a bit pointless, especially as most operators make their groups ride together, at the pace of the slowest member. Plenty of activities desks offer discount rates on biking trips: it normally costs around $60 for a daytime ride, up to $120 to go at sunrise. Unguided trips, or shorter routes, cost about $20 less. All riders must have at least some experience, and be aged 12 or over.

The volcano then slumbered for several hundred thousand years, during which time torrential rainfall eroded away its topmost 6000 feet, and sculptured vast canyons into its flanks. Two of these valleys, **Keanae** to the north and **Kaupō** to the east, cut so deeply into the mountain that they met in the middle, to create a huge central depression. When the "hot spot" beneath Haleakalā finally reawakened, a series of smaller eruptions poured another 3000 feet of lava into that cavity, and gushed out of the Koʻolau and Kaupō gaps to refill the valleys. Peppering the summit with raw, red cones of cindery ash, it made it look to the untrained eye like the sort of crater you might expect to find at the top of a volcano.

Although the "hot spot" today directs most of its energy into Kīlauea volcano on the Big Island, Haleakalā is not extinct, but **dormant**, which is in fact a reassuring

Aloha Bicycle Tours ☎ 249-0911, ⓦ www.maui.net/~bikemaui. Small-group tours, ending at Tedeschi Winery rather than the sea.

Haleakalā Bike Co ☎ 575-9575, ⓦ www.bikemaui.com. Unguided tours; they provide the bikes and a van service to the top, and you descend at your own pace.

Hawaii Downhill ☎ 893-2332. Sunrise and morning guided rides down to Pāʻia.

Maui Downhill ☎ 871-2155; ⓦ www.mauidownhill.net. Long tours, mostly including lunch, to Pāʻia or Kula.

Maui Mountain Cruisers ☎ 871-6014; ⓦ www.mauimountain cruisers.com. Sunrise or morning downhill rides to Pāʻia with hotel pickup included.

Mountain Riders Bike Tours ☎ 242-9739; ⓦ www.mountain riders.com. Sunrise and morning tours down Haleakalā, ending at Pāʻia, Kula, or Tedeschi Winery. Hotel pickup included.

Upcountry Cycles ☎ 573-2888; ⓦ www.maui.net/~wayner. Unguided rides, at sunrise or in the morning.

THE GEOLOGY OF HALEAKALĀ

STAYING AT HALEAKALĀ: CAMPGROUNDS AND CABINS

Hosmer Grove (see p.184) is the only Haleakalā campground accessible by car, and the only one for which campers do not need to obtain permits.

Wilderness camping is not permitted anywhere in the park. There are, however, three rudimentary but sound **backcountry cabins** within Haleakalā Crater, which can only be reached on foot. All are on the grassy fringes of the crater, sheltered by the high surrounding cliffs, and are padlocked to deter casual backpackers from wandering in. Each is rented to one group only per night, and has twelve bunk beds, with no bedding, plus a kitchen, a stove for heating, and an outhouse. **Hōlua** and **Palikū** cabins offer **tent camping** in the adjacent meadows – the 25 daily permits are issued on a first-come, first-served basis at the park headquarters – but **Kapalaoa Cabin** does not. Water is normally available, but it's up to you to purify it before you drink it.

Permits to stay in the cabins are heavily over-subscribed, and limited to three days in total, with no more than two days at any one cabin. In a system that effectively prioritizes island residents and their guests over ordinary tourists, you have to apply in writing at least three months in advance, stating the exact dates you want, to Haleakalā National Park, PO Box 369, Makawao, HI 96768 (call ☏ 572-9306 for more information). A lottery at the start of each month decides the schedule for the month ahead; at that point successful applicants are requested to pay $40 per night for groups of one to six people, or $80 for groups of seven to twelve.

euphemism for **active**. It has erupted at least ten times in the last thousand years, with the most recent volcanic activity in the area being in 1790 (see p.163). That it's been peaceful for two hundred years doesn't mean it always will be – in 1979, for example, it was thought more likely to explode than Mount St Helens. Meanwhile, the rains have set to work again, wearing away the mountaintop.

INTO THE NATIONAL PARK

To the ancient Hawaiians, Haleakalā was "the House of the Sun." They told of how at one time the sun crossed the sky much faster than it does today, until the demi-god Maui captured it here in a web of ropes, and only released it on the condition that it travel slowly enough to give his mother time to dry her tapa (bark-cloth). These early Hawaiians trekked to the summit in search of basalt for adzes, to hunt birds, for religious ceremonies and to bury their dead; traces have even been found of a paved trail that crossed the crater and led down through the Kaupō Gap (see p.195).

The higher reaches of the mountain joined with the volcanoes of the Big Island to form Hawaii Volcanoes National Park in 1921, and became the independent **Haleakalā National Park** in 1961. It now ranks as the tenth most visited national park in the US, with around a million people a year reaching the summit. The most popular time to come is for sunrise – described by Mark Twain as "the sublimest spectacle I ever witnessed" – but don't let that give you the impression that it's not worth coming later in the day. The views of the crater itself are at their best in mid-afternoon, while you can enjoy superb views from the roadside lookouts along the way up whatever time you arrive. It's also possible to hike into the crater, and even to spend the night there.

Haleakalā National Park also includes Kipahulu Valley and ʻOheʻo Gulch, on Maui's southeast coast. However, no hiking trail, let alone direct road, connects those areas with Haleakalā Crater.

Haleakalā Crater Road

From all the major accommodation centers on Maui, the quickest route to the top of Haleakalā is from Kahului; follow **Haleakalā Highway** into the Upcountry. From there, only **Haleakalā Crater Road** continues all the way to the summit, entering the park after a twisting twelve-mile climb through the meadows, and reaching the park headquarters shortly after that. With another ten miles to go before the summit, you should allow two full hours to get to the top from Lahaina, Kāʻanapali or Kīhei, and an hour and a half from Kahului or Wailuku.

The last gas station before the summit of Haleakala is at Pukalani, 28 miles below; the last food and lodging is at Kula Lodge (see p.171), 22 miles short.

Assuming you join the majority in attempting to drive up to Haleakalā Crater in time for the sunrise – which varies between 5.50am in summer and 6.50am in winter – you'll need to make a very early start and a long hard drive in the dark. If you end up late for the sunrise, be warned that you'll be driving straight into the dazzling sun, and watch out for the endless posses of downhill bikers coming the other way.

Hosmer Grove

Map 10, B2.

Just beyond the **park entrance** – the gates never close, though there's not always a ranger on duty – a short road off to the left leads to the park's main **campground**, at **Hosmer Grove**. Set almost exactly at the mountain's tree line, this may look like a pleasant wooded copse, but in fact it marks the failure of an early-twentieth-century experiment to assess Maui's suitability for timber farming. Out of almost a hundred different tree species planted by Ralph Hosmer, only twenty survived, though that's enough to provide a nice thirty-minute **nature trail**.

By way of contrast, **Waikamoi Preserve**, adjoining Hosmer Grove, is a five-thousand-acre tract of upland rainforest that's home to a wide assortment of indigenous Hawaiian **birds**. You can only hike through it with an authorized guide, so the best time to come is for the Park Service's free **Waikamoi Cloud Forest Hike**, which sets off from Hosmer Grove on Mondays and Thursdays at 9am.

There's **tent camping** at Hosmer Grove in a soft sloping meadow surrounded by tall pines; a small open pavilion holds basic washing facilities. No permit is required, but there's a three-night maximum stay.

It's possible to walk all the way into Haleakalā Crater from Hosmer Grove; a supply trail up the mountain meets the Halemau'u Trail after 2.5 miles, just short of the crater rim (see p.192).

The park headquarters

Map 10, A2. Daily 8am–4pm; ☏ 572-4400; ⓦ www.nps.gov/hale.
The **park headquarters** – as opposed to the main visitor center, ten miles further up – looks out across central Maui from the left of the highway, three-quarters of a mile up from the park entrance. Inquire here about the day's quota of camping places (see p.182), or register if you've managed to reserve a cabin. The HQ holds little by way of exhibits or printed information, but you can get a basic park brochure and buy detailed hiking maps.

THE PARK HEADQUARTERS

**Haleakalā National Park remains open around
the clock; $10 per vehicle, or $20 annual fee;
national passes are valid and on sale.**

The roadside lookouts

Beyond the park headquarters, Haleakalā Crater Road zigzags for another ten miles up the mountain, repeatedly sweeping toward the lip of the crater and then doubling back. Each of its final three closest approaches is marked by a roadside parking lot.

The first of these, 2.5 miles up from the park headquarters, is the **Halemauʻu Trailhead**. One of the park's two main hiking trails begins its long descent into the crater from here, as described on p.192, but the edge of the *pali* is almost a mile away; there's nothing to see at the parking lot.

Another 4.5 miles up the road, **Leleiwi Overlook** is set a couple of hundred yards beyond its parking lot. It offers views across the isthmus to West Maui, as well as a first glimpse into Haleakalā Crater, but you'll probably have seen enough of West Maui from the Crater Road, and better vantage points over the crater lie ahead.

Don't "ride your brakes" as you drive back down
Haleakalā; it's much safer to use a low gear.

It's only legal to stop at the **Kalahaku** or **"Silversword" Overlook**, a couple of miles short of the visitor center, as you drive down rather than up the mountain; in fact it's easy to pass by without noticing it all. That's a shame, because this sheltered viewpoint provides perhaps the best overall prospect of Haleakalā Crater, especially in the afternoon when the sun is behind you. Mauna Kea on the Big Island is often visible through the Kaupō Gap in the ridge to the right, and when the clouds clear you can also see down to the north coast of Maui. Unless you hike into the crater, this may be the only place you see any **silverswords** (see p.190). In theory, there are a few in the small enclosure below the parking lot, across from the overlook, though they tend to be pretty scrawny.

Haleakalā Visitor Center

Map 10, A6. Daily from dawn until 3pm; information ⊤ 572-4400;
weather ⊤ 871-5054; Ⓦ www.nps.gov/hale.

Although the highway continues beyond it, most visitors
regard themselves as having reached the top of Haleakalā
when they get to the **Visitor Center**, eleven miles up from
the park entrance. The railed open-air viewing area beside
the parking lot commands great views of Haleakalā Crater. In
the pre-sunrise chill, however, many people prefer to admire
the procession of red-brown cinder cones, marching across
the moonscape far below, through the panoramic windows
of the small Visitor Center itself. If you're feeling more energetic, follow the short paved trail to the right instead, which
leads up **Pā Kaʻoao**, or White Hill, for 360° views.

The exhibits inside the Visitor Center are pretty minimal,
though there's a good 3-D model of Haleakalā to help you
get oriented. Park rangers also provide hiking tips and lead
free **guided hikes**. Their **Cinder Desert** walk sets off
from here along the Sliding Sands Trail (see p.190) on
Tuesdays and Fridays at 9am, while the **Waikamoi Cloud
Forest Hike** (see p.185) leaves Hosmer Grove on Mondays
and Thursdays at 9am.

Puʻu Ulaʻula (Red Hill)

Map 10, A6.

A few hundred yards farther up the highway, a smaller parking lot at a final loop in the road stands just below **Puʻu
Ulaʻula**, or **Red Hill** – at 10,023 feet, the highest spot on
Maui. A circular shelter at the top of a short stairway offers
what feel like aerial views of Haleakalā Crater. In clear conditions – soon after dawn is the best bet – you may be able
to see not only the 80 miles to Mauna Loa on the Big
Island, but even the 130 miles to Oahu.

PUʻU ULAʻULA (RED HILL)

'A'Ā AND PĀHOEHOE

'A'ā and pāhoehoe, the terms used by geologists throughout the world to distinguish the two main kinds of lava, are among the very few Hawaiian words to have been adopted into other languages. Chemically the two forms are exactly the same, but they differ due to the temperature at which they are ejected from the volcano. Hotter, runnier pāhoehoe is wrinkled and ropey, like the sludgy skin of custard pushed with your finger, but still with a sandpaper finish; cooler 'a'ā does not flow so much as spatter, creating a sharp, jagged clinker.

Confusingly, the peak that officially bears the name of Haleakalā is five miles east, above Kapalaoa Cabin (see p.195), and a couple of thousand feet lower.

Science City

Map 10, A7.

The road beyond Pu'u Ula'ula is closed to the public, but leads in a few more yards to **Kolekole** or **Science City**. This multinational astronomic research facility, perched at the top of the House of the Sun, monitors the earth's distance from the moon by bouncing laser signals off a prism left there by the Apollo astronauts.

For details of the 13-mile Skyline Trail, connecting Science City with Polipoli State Park, see p.172.

HIKES IN HALEAKALĀ CRATER

The only way to get a real sense of the beauty and diversity of **Haleakalā Crater** is to get down into it. Although there are just two principal trails – the **Sliding Sands** and **Halemau'u** trails – the terrain varies far more than you could ever tell from the crater-edge viewpoints, ranging from forbidding desert to lush mountain meadows.

The obvious problem is that, once you've descended into the crater, you'll have to climb back out again, which at an altitude of 10,000 feet is never less than grueling. That said, reasonably fit hikers should be able to manage a **day-hike** that takes them down one trail and back up the other – a minimum distance of eleven miles. More ambitiously, you could aim to take in Kapalaoa Cabin along the way, for a total of thirteen miles, but heading any further east would be unrealistic. The easier route is to go down Sliding Sands and back on Halemau'u, though since the trailheads are several miles apart you'll need to arrange a pickup or hitch a ride between the two; the prospects of getting a lift *down* the mountain in the afternoon are marginally better.

For details of companies that organize horse-riding expeditions in Haleakalā Crater, see p.55.

If you've arranged to stay overnight in the crater – see p.182 – you could see the whole thing in two days, although most hikers spend longer. It takes a hardy and very well-prepared backpacker, however, to trek out via the **Kaupō Trail** to the south.

Don't underestimate the effects of the **altitude**. Allow an hour or so in the summit area to acclimatize before you set off on the trails; not only will that prepare you for the effort ahead, but it will also mean that you're still close to the road if you start to feel ill. By far the most effective treatment for altitude sickness is to descend a few thousand feet. **Scuba divers** should not go up Haleakalā within 24 hours of a dive; ask your dive operator for detailed advice.

In addition, Haleakalā is such an ecologically delicate area that it's essential to practice **minimum-impact hiking**. Carry out everything you carry in, take all the water you need (reckon on six pints a person a day), and stick to established trails. Above all, never walk on the cinder soil surrounding a silversword plant (see box below).

Route 1: The Sliding Sands Trail

Map 10, A6.

From the Visitor Center parking lot, the **Sliding Sands Trail** briefly parallels the road to skirt White Hill. It then starts its leisurely switchback sweep into the crater, down a

SILVERSWORDS

Not far from the ragged edge of the crater, we came upon what we were searching for; not, however, one or two, but thousands of silverswords, their cold, frosted silver gleam making the hill-side look like winter or moonlight. They exactly resemble the finest work in frosted silver, the curve of their globular mass of leaves is perfect, and one thinks of them rather as the base of an épergne for an imperial table, or as a prize at Ascot or Goodwood, than anything organic.

– Isabella Bird, May 1873

Haleakalā is a treasure-trove of unique plants, birds and animals, but the most distinctive of all its species is the **silversword**. A distant relative of the sunflower, presumably descended from a lone seed that wafted across the Pacific from America, this extraordinary plant has adapted perfectly to the forbidding conditions of Haleakalā Crater.

Known by the ancient Hawaiians as the '*āhinahina*, or "silvery-gray," it consists of a gourd-shaped bowl of curving gray long scree slope of soft red ash. While the *pali* to the north of the Visitor Center is scattered with buttresses of rock and patches of green vegetation, this side is almost completely barren, the smooth crumbling hillside only interrupted by an occasional bush. Far ahead, mists and clouds stream into the crater through the Koʻolau Gap.

For most of the way down, a close look at the ground beneath your feet reveals that it's made of tiny fragments of rock with different colors, textures and characteristics; hard-baked pink clay is interspersed with tiny brown gravel and little chunks of black basalt. It takes a while to appreciate the immensity of the crater; for the first mile, you expect to arrive at the crater floor at a group of multicolored rocks in

leaves, a couple of feet across, and cupped to collect what little moisture is available. Slender roots burrow in all directions just below the surface of the low-quality cinder soil; merely walking nearby can crush the roots and kill the plant. Each silversword takes between three and twenty years to grow to full size, and then blossoms only once. Between May and June of the crucial year, a central shaft rises like a rocket from the desiccated silver leaves, reaching a height of three to eight feet, and erupting with hundreds of reddish-purple flowers. These peak in July and August, releasing their precious cargo of seeds, and the entire plant then withers and dies.

The slopes of Haleakalā no longer glow with the sheer abundance of silverswords, thanks to the attentions of wild goats from the late nineteenth century onward. In recent years a new threat has been posed by the appearance of Argentinian ants, which prey on the Hawaiian yellow-faced bee responsible for pollinating the silversword. However, the park authorities have so far managed to reverse the decline, and clusters of silverswords can be seen at many places along the crater trails.

ROUTE 1: THE SLIDING SANDS TRAIL

the middle distance, but when you reach them you find a longer descent ahead.

Two miles down, the trail passes between a clump of twenty-foot-high 'a'ā rock outcroppings. A spur trail from here leads 0.4 miles, by way of a miniature "garden" of silverswords, to the smooth lip of the **Ka Lu'u O Ka 'Ō'ō Crater**. This full round cinder cone, glinting with pink, red, yellow and ochre highlights in the bright sun, cradles a hollow core filled with tumbled boulders. From the trail above, you can see long clinker flows extending for two miles north of it, eating away at the neighboring Kamaoli'i Crater.

Continuing on the main trail, you wind down through a rough field of 'a'ā lava. In season, the silverswords that almost line the path shoot up above head height. For the final stretch of the total 3.8-mile descent, the desolate crater floor spreads out broad and flat ahead of you, punctuated by heaped mounds of ash.

Route 2: The Halemau'u Trail

Map 10, C2.

The alternative route down into the crater, the switchbacking **Halemau'u Trail**, starts at a trailhead half a dozen miles down Haleakalā Crater Road from the Visitor Center. Toward the end of the relatively featureless 0.75-mile descent from the parking lot to the crater rim, the main trail is joined by a side trail up from Hosmer Grove (see p.185). It then passes through a gate, to run parallel to the wire fence that marks the park boundary. After a few more minutes, it crosses a high, narrow ridge; provided the afternoon clouds aren't siphoning over it, you'll get staggering views down to the north Maui coastline, as well as south into the crater.

Only the first few switchbacks cross back and forth between the north and south sides of the high bluff. Here at the tip of the **Leleiwi Pali**, it's very obvious how the landscape below has simply poured down through the Koʻolau Gap, from the crater toward the ocean. Soon, however, the trail narrows to drop sharply down the south side of the *pali*; it never feels too dangerous, though the drop-offs are enormous. The tiny shape of the overnight Hōlua Cabin comes into view a couple of miles ahead, a speck at the foot of the mighty cliff.

**For details of how to stay overnight at Hōlua,
Kapalaoa or Palikū cabins, see p.182.**

The trail eventually levels out beyond a gate at the bottom of the final switchback, then undulates its way through a meadow filled with misshapen and overgrown spatter cones toward **Hōlua Cabin**, just under four miles from the trailhead. A slight detour is required to reach the cabin itself, where the lawns are often filled with honking *nēnē* geese. Beyond it, the trail climbs on to a much more rugged *aʻā* lava flow, the youngest in the crater area. Indentations in the rocky outcrops are scattered with red-berried *ʻōhelo* bushes, thanks to the wet clouds that drift in through the Koʻolau Gap.

As you climb slowly toward the heart of Haleakalā Crater, you can branch away to the left to follow the brief **Silversword Loop**, which holds the park's greatest concentration of silversword plants.

The crater floor

At the point where the **Halemauʻu Trail** reaches the floor of the crater, almost six miles from the start, a bench enables weary hikers to catch their breath while contemplating the onward haul around the north side of the **Halāliʻi** cinder cone. If you continue south, and turn right

THE CRATER FLOOR

after 0.3 miles, you'll come to the foot of the Sliding Sands Trail 1.3 miles after that.

Keep going to the left, however, and within a couple hundred yards the Halemau'u Trail follows the crest of a low ridge to make a serpentine twist between Halāli'i and the nameless cinder cone to the north. Known as **Pele's Paint Pot**, this gorgeous stretch is the most spectacular part of Haleakalā Crater, the trail standing out as a lurid red streak of sand against the brown and yellow mounds to either side. You can tell that Halāli'i is of relatively recent origin by the fact that its rim has not yet worn smooth; look back to see the park Visitor Center framed far away on the crater rim.

It's possible to loop right around Halāli'i and head back along either trail, but the Halemau'u Trail continues east for another four miles. Immediately north of the junction where you're forced to decide, you'll see the fenced-off hole of **Kawilinau**, also known, misleadingly, as the **Bottomless Pit**; in fact, this small volcanic vent is just 65 feet deep. Spatters of bright-red rock cling to its edges, but it doesn't look especially remarkable. Ancient Hawaiians are said to have thrown the bones of important chiefs into it, to ensure their remains would never be disturbed. Half a mile further east, you have the further option of cutting south across the crater, between Pu'u Naue and Pu'u Nole, to meet the Sliding Sands Trail near Kapalaoa Cabin (see below).

Those hikers who choose on the other hand to take the **Sliding Sands Trail** down from the Visitor Center know they've reached the crater floor when they get to the south end of the clearly marked spur trail that connects the two main trails. Turning left toward the Halemau'u Trail involves a fairly stiff climb across the flanks of the ruddy **Ka Moa O Pele** cinder cone; over to the right, the triangular mountain peak of **Hānakauhi** can be seen rising beyond Pu'u Naue.

If instead you continue east along the Sliding Sands Trail, you enter a landscape that resembles the high mountain valleys of the western United States. The trail runs at the foot of a steep *pali*, on the edge of a delightful alpine meadow carpeted with yellow flowers, including the primitive native *moa*. Two miles along, shortly after two successive turnoffs to the left – one is an official trail, one a "trail of use" (it's impossible to tell which is which, and in any case they soon join to cut across to the Halemau'u Trail) – you come to **Kapalaoa Cabin**. This small, wooden-framed, green-roofed cabin, tucked in on a slight mound beneath the peak that's officially named Haleakalā, is the only overnight shelter in the crater that doesn't have its own campground.

East of Kapalaoa, the Sliding Sands Trail has two more miles to run before it finally merges with the Halemau'u Trail, and the two then run together a further 1.4 miles to **Palikū Cabin**. The hike all the way here from the crater rim and back up again is too far to attempt from the crater rim in a single day; only press on if you've arranged to stay overnight. The last three miles along either trail involve a gentle descent through sparsely vegetated terrain that turns progressively greener as you approach Palikū. There are actually two cabins at Palikū, one for public use and one for the rangers; both nestle beneath a sheer cliff, where an attractive but generally dry meadow gives way to a well-watered strip of forest.

Kaupō Trail

Map 10, I6.

The very demanding nine-mile **Kaupō Trail** heads south from Palikū Cabin, first through the Kaupō Gap to the edge of the park, and beyond that all the way down to meet the Pi'ilani Highway on Maui's remote south coast. It takes a couple of miles to escape the pervasive cindery dryness of the crater floor, but beyond that you find you've crossed to the rain-drenched eastern side of the island.

As the walls of the Kaupō Gap rise to either side, the trail drops through dense forest, then once out of the park descends steeply through lush grazing land. Now that you're on Kaupō Ranch land, be scrupulous about staying on the correct trail; free-ranging bulls roam at will on the other side of many of the fences. After several hours of extravagant switchbacks, you finally reach the highway 200 yards east of the Kaupō Store (see p.222). Unless you've arranged to be picked up, your problems may just be beginning – little traffic passes this way.

The Road to Hāna

Exposed to the full force of the trade winds, and sculptured by endless streams of rainwater cascading back down the windward slopes of Haleakalā, the northeast coast holds Maui's most inspiring scenery. Nonetheless, being devoid of safe beaches, and too wet to build resorts, the region has very little overnight accommodation, and remains the least spoiled part of the island.

Ancient Hawaiians allowed up to two days for the canoe trip from the isthmus round to the time-forgotten hamlet of **Hāna** at the easternmost tip. Now the **Hāna Highway**, hacked into the coastal cliffs by convicts during the 1920s, has become a major attraction in its own right, twisting tortuously in and out of gorges, past innumerable waterfalls and over more than fifty tiny one-lane bridges. All year round, and especially in June, the route is ablaze with color, from orchids, rainbow eucalyptus and orange-blossomed African tulip trees.

Driving the memorable **road to Hāna** forms an essential part of most Maui itineraries, but is almost always done as a day-trip. The usual excursion is roughly fifty miles each way, from Pā'ia to 'Ohe'o Gulch beyond Hāna. While not as hair-raising as popular legend would have it, driving is slow going, taking around three hours each way, and demands serious concentration. If you'd prefer to keep your eyes on the scenery rather than on the road, consider taking an **organized tour**, available from around $75 per person with the operators detailed on p.27.

Note that although the **coastal road** around East Maui is called Hāna Highway from the moment it leaves Kahului, it changes from Hwy-36 to Hwy-360 eleven miles east of Pā'ia, at the foot of Hwy-365 from Makawao, and that's where you'll find mile marker 0.

TWIN FALLS

The first potential distraction on the drive to Hāna is the short hiking trail up to Twin Falls, which leads from an unmarked parking lot immediately after the 2-mile marker and just before a bridge. The only reason to mention it here is that there are usually several vehicles parked nearby, and you may be tempted to investigate. In years gone by, this tranquil stroll was one of Maui's most popular hikes, and visitors using old editions of island hiking guides still turn up hoping to set off along the trail. As that now involves crossing private property in defiance of angry "KEEP OUT" signs, and the trail is in any case not all that special, it's best not to bother.

HUELO

Another unmarked turnoff, at a bend in the highway roughly 3.5 miles along that's marked by a double row of mailboxes, leads down to the village of **HUELO**. The dirt road soon passes the plain **Kaulanapueo** ("resting-place of the owl") **church**, built of coral cement on a black lava base and usually kept locked. It continues for a couple of miles, but neither it nor its many side roads offer access to the sea. Like many local communities, Huelo has become an uncertain mixture of Hawaiians and wealthy *haoles*.

The clifftop *Huelo Point B&B* (reserve through Hawaii's Best B&Bs, PO Box 563, Kamuela, HI 96743; ☎885-4550 or 1-800/262-9912, ⓕ885-0559; ⓦwww.bestbnb.com; ❹) offers luxury **accommodation** with spectacular views over Waipi'o Bay, plus an on-site waterfall and open-air Jacuzzi. There's one suite in the main house, with panoramic windows and a long *lānai*, and a separate self-contained cottage.

WAIKAMOI NATURE TRAIL

Map 1, J4.

Your one opportunity to explore the forested ridges above the Hāna Highway comes just over half a mile beyond the **9-mile marker**, where a short but enjoyable hike up the Waikamoi Ridge – officially designated as the **Waikamoi Nature Trail** – sets off from an obvious roadside pull-out. The one-mile loop trail starts beyond a small picnic shelter, gently zigzagging up a muddy ridge (some hikers go barefoot). Despite the stone benches along the way, there are no views – it's barely possible to see beyond the tight-packed *hala* trees and green rustling bamboos hemming the track – but sunlight dapples down through the overhead canopy to magical effect. All the various species are identified with explanatory labels; here and there, you pass a variety of eucalyptus whose bark peels like fine tissue paper. The trail tops out at a smooth grassy clearing, with another picnic shelter, and a large mosquito population. It makes little difference whether you return by the same route, or down the adjacent jeep road that drops directly to the parking lot.

A little further along the highway, **Waikamoi Falls** tumble down toward the road at a tight hairpin bend. If you want a closer look, the only place to park is immediately before the bridge – a spot it's all too easy to overshoot.

HONOMANŪ BAY

Map 1, K4.

Shortly after **mile marker 13**, the highway drops down to sea level for the first time since Hoʻokipa Beach, and you finally start to get the long coastal views for which it's famous. The Keʻanae Peninsula appears on the horizon, but much closer at hand – where the gorgeous, uninhabited **Honomanū Valley**, lit up by tulip trees, gives way to the ocean – you'll see the black gravel beach at **Honomanū Bay**. Swimming and snorkeling here only advisable on the calmest of summer days, but it's a popular site with local **surfers**.

Two separate dirt tracks cut down to the shore from the road as it sweeps around the narrow valley. The first, at 13.5 miles, leads down to the north shore of the stream; the second, just after the **14-mile marker** on the far side of the stream, is steeper and potentially muddier, but comes out at the longer side of the beach.

KEʻANAE ARBORETUM

Map 1, K4. Daily dawn–dusk; free.

From a wooded bend in the road a few hundred yards before the **17-mile marker**, a paved, level trail heads inland to the attractive public gardens of the **Keʻanae Arboretum**. Following the course of a stream you can hear but not see, it leads into a lush, narrow valley and reaches the arboretum within a quarter of a mile.

Fifty-foot-high clumps of "male bamboo" guard the entrance, with tropical plants beyond including Hawaiian species such as torch ginger and wet and dry *taro*. Beyond the *taro* fields, a mile into the park, the trail becomes a wet scramble through the rainforest, crossing up and over the valley ridge by way of tree-root footholds. As well as lots of small waterfalls, and swarms of tiny flies feasting on fallen guava and breadfruit, there's a good chance of spotting rare forest birds and even wild boar.

THE KE'ANAE PENINSULA

Not far beyond the arboretum, a side road twists down to the flat **Ke'anae Peninsula**, the site of a small, and still predominantly Hawaiian, village. It's said that this windswept promontory consisted of bare rock until a local chief forced his followers to spend two years carrying baskets of soil down the mountainside. Thereafter it became a prime *taro*-growing region. Mashed to create the Hawaiian staple food *poi*, *taro* is a root crop cultivated in paddy-like fields known as *lo'i*, which have a consistency that has been likened to a "semi-jelled chocolate pudding".

The *taro* fields are still here, making Ke'anae one of a few places in the state where traditional agriculture is still practiced. They're now surrounded by abundant banana trees and birds of paradise, and there's also a fine old **church** among the tall palms. The edge of the ocean is as bleak as ever, with *hala* trees propped up along the shoreline watching the surf crash onto headlands of gnarled black lava; swimming here is out of the question.

Practicalities

Almost the only **food** and **lodging** along the main stretch of the Hāna Highway is in the Ke'anae area. The recently renovated *YMCA Camp Ke'anae*, on the highway shortly before the arboretum, is a former prison that now offers **cabin** accommodation and also has its own grassy **campground** (☏248-8355 or ⓔYMCACampKeanae@aol.com).

Whether you stay in your own tent or in a cabin, it costs $15 per person or $30 per family. Not surprisngly, the facilities tend to be reserved way in advance.

Simple snacks are sold at two roadside kiosks – *Halfway to Hāna* and *Uncle Harry's* – before and after the **18-mile marker**, respectively. The specialty at *Halfway to Hāna* is a tasty burger; at *Uncle Harry's*, opposite a dazzling array of flowers, try the banana and pineapple smoothie. Neither keeps very regular hours, but in theory they're both open daily for lunch.

WAILUA

Within a mile of Ke'anae, as the highway veers inland, the arrow-straight Wailua Road plunges down to another traditional village, **WAILUA**. Unlike Ke'anae, its ancient rival, Wailua has always been fertile; it still holds extensive *taro* terraces.

The lower of the two churches that stand a short way down from the turnoff is known as the **Coral Miracle**. Local legend has it that, in 1860, just as its builders were despairing of finding the stone to complete it, a freak storm washed up exactly enough coral on the beach below. It's a simple but attractive chapel, painted white, with turquoise stencils around the porch and windows. Look back across the valley as you come out for a superb view of the high **Waikani Falls**, garlanded by flowering trees at the head of the valley.

Wailua Road ends just above the tranquil mouth of Wailua Stream, which makes a sharp contrast with the ocean pummeling the beach of black pebbles beyond. Don't drive down to the stream – there's no room to turn round – and don't even consider a swim.

Wailua viewpoints

Lookouts to either side of the highway beyond the Wailua turnoff offer scenic views up and down the coastline. From the inconspicuous *mauka* parking lot of **Wailua Valley State Wayside**, steps climb through a tunnel of trees to a vantage point overlooking Wailua Valley as it reaches the sea, and also inland across Keʻanae Valley, to towering waterfalls, undulating ridges and endless trees.

A little farther on, immediately after the **19-mile marker**, Wailua Valley spreads like a little oasis beneath **Wailua Lookout**. The taller of Wailua's two churches, **St Gabriel's**, pokes its head above the sea of trees, while the thickly wooded gorge stretches away to the right. At the next bend, just around the corner, a big cascade roars beside the road; you have to react quickly to stop.

PUAʻAKAʻA STATE WAYSIDE PARK

Map 1, L5.

The spacious parking lot of **Puaʻakaʻa State Wayside Park**, 22.5 miles along Hāna Highway, is every bit as big as the park itself. Nonetheless, this is a favorite stop for bus tours, because so little effort is required to negotiate the park's few yards of paved trails. If you brave the crowds, you'll see a pretty but far from spectacular sequence of small waterfalls, with picnic tables dotted on either side of the stream.

NĀHIKU

Not far after the **25-mile marker**, a narrow unmarked road takes about three miles to wind down to the ocean. The few houses along the way constitute **NĀHIKU**, though there's no town, just a jungle of trees and vines, some of which all but submerge abandoned vehicles. The road comes out at **Ōpūhano Point**, looking back toward Wailua, with tree-covered cliffs reaching down into the water.

Early in the twentieth century, Nāhiku was the site of the first – unsuccessful – rubber plantation in the US. Ex-Beatle George Harrison has long had a home here, but he only visits occasionally, following a bitter legal dispute with his neighbors that centered on the construction of a beach-access footpath.

Just before the **29-mile marker**, the *Nāhiku Coffee Shop* (daily 6.30am–4.30pm) is a roadside shack that sells espressos, smoothies, and homemade lunches such as banana bread and fish specials. There's a small crafts gallery alongside, and an open-air grill serves smoked Hawaiian fish sticks to no discernible schedule.

'ULA'INO ROAD

Map 1, M5.
You know you're finally approaching Hāna when you pass **Hāna Gardenland**, a not very exciting commercial nursery that, assuming it has reopened after extensive renovations, has a nice lunchtime café (see p.216).

Immediately afterwards, **'Ula'ino Road** drops away to the left of the highway, leading both to the largest ancient *heiau* (temple) in all Hawaii, and to one of the best **hikes** on Maui.

Kahanu Garden

Map 1, M5. Mon–Fri 10am–2pm; $5; ⓣ 248-8912 or 332-7234; ⓦ www.ntbg.org.
Three-quarters of a mile down 'Ula'ino Road, the paved surface gives out where the road crosses a minor ford. On

the far side, you'll find the entrance to Kahanu Garden, a not-for-profit facility owned by the National Tropical Botanical Garden. This holds more than a hundred acres of tropical plants, but is of most significance as the site of **Piʻilanihale Heiau**, the largest ancient temple in Hawaii. Thought to have been enlarged and rededicated by Piʻilani in around 1570 to celebrate his recent conquest of the entire island, it covers almost three acres and consists of five separate tiers on its oceanward side.

The mile-long loop trail through Kahanu Garden begins by skirting the edge of an extensive forest of splay-footed *hala* (pandanus) trees. Beyond that, you get your first sight of the *heiau* itself, towering above the lush oceanfront lawns. Constructed from black lava boulders, intricately slotted into place, it's an impressive spectacle. As usual at such sites, however, in deference to ongoing Hawaiian religious beliefs, visitors are not allowed to set foot on the actual structure and can only admire it from a distance. As a result, you're not likely to spend more time here than the half-hour it takes to walk the trail, which winds past various labeled plants and offers some gorgeous views along the coast.

The Blue Pool

ʻUlaʻino Road continues beyond the garden as a much rougher but still mostly paved track, undulating gently through the woods for another 1.4 miles. There are no long-range views, but it's a lovely stretch of countryside. The road ends abruptly in a shady grove a hundred yards short of the ocean, just above a stream whose outlet is blocked by a natural wall of heavy black boulders.

To reach a fabulous **waterfall**, make for the shoreline, then head left for a hundred yards. Here you'll find a shimmering **Blue Pool**, less than twenty yards from the sea, and constantly replenished by water cascading from the *hala*-covered ridge above. The grotto is festooned with ferns, vines and *hala* trees, with its mossy walls bursting with tiny pinks and peonies. As you sit on the rocks, fresh water from the falls splashes your face, while you can feel the salt spray on your back. It's also possible to walk to the right along the beach, where coconuts lie among the boulders. Atop a spit of rough *'a'ā* lava, five minutes along, you can watch the surf crashing and grinding the black rocks to hollow out little coves, while a jungle of *hala* trees lies, unreachable, beyond.

WAI'ĀNAPANAPA STATE PARK

Map 1, N5.
Barely two miles short of Hāna proper, beyond the turnoff to Hāna Airport (see p.211), a clearly signed road *makai* of the highway leads through a "tunnel" of overhanging trees to the shoreline at **Wai'ānapanapa State Park**. To reach the main parking lot, perched above a tiny **black-sand beach**, turn left when you reach the park cabins at the end of the first straight stretch of road. A short and easy trail descends from the parking lot to this beautiful little cove, where the beach changes from shiny black pebbles to fine black sand as it shelves into the ocean. It looks wonderful, but barely has room to hold its daily crowd of sunbathers, but swimming is deadly, with heavy surf and deep water just a few yards out.

At the right-hand side of the beach as you face the sea, look for a hollow cave in the small cliff that you just walked down. Squeeze your way through its narrow entrance and you'll find that not only does it widen inside, but it's in fact a tunnel. The far end, where it's open to the ocean, is a truly magical spot.

By contrast, a very short loop trail to the left of the parking lot back at the top leads down and through **Wai'āna-panapa Cave**. A few yards back from the sea, this "cave" is actually a collapsed lava tube, holding two successive grotto-like pools. It's slightly stagnant and smells rather like a public restroom, but you do see some nice clinging flowers.

Coastal **hiking trails** in both directions make it easy to escape the throngs at the beach. Heading **northwest** (left), you're soon clambering over a headland of black lava through a forest of *hala* and *naupaka*. Inlets in the jagged shoreline harbor turquoise pools, while surf rages against the rocks; in places, where the sea has hollowed out caverns, you can feel the thud of the ocean beneath you. A painting of a natural "lava bridge" here, executed in 1939 by Georgia O'Keeffe, now hangs in the Honolulu Academy of Arts. A mile or so along, the trail ends at the fence of Hāna Airport.

Southeast of the beach, the footpath crosses smoother, firmer lava, passing the park campground, a cemetery and an impressive blowhole. After around a mile, it reaches the ruined **Ohala Heiau**, the walls of which remain clear despite ivy-like *naupaka* growing inside. You can continue four miles on to Hāna; the scenery is invigorating all the way, but the trail gets progressively harder to follow.

Wai'ānapanapa is by far the nicest place on Maui to **camp** beside the ocean. In addition to tent camping, at $5 per person, it has basic cabins, each holding up to four people, at $45 per cabin. Permits are available from the state parks office in Wailuku (see p.54), but the cabins are usually reserved far in advance.

HĀNA

For some visitors, the former sugar town of **HĀNA** comes as a disappointment after the splendors of the Hāna Highway. Certainly, the point of driving the road is to

KA'AHUMANU: SCENES FROM A LIFE

She is prodigiously fat, but her face is interesting . . . her legs, the palm of her left hand, and her tongue, are very elegantly tattooed.   – Jacques Arago, 1823

Returning from town, I saw Queen Ka'ahumanu in her four-wheeled cart being dragged to the top of a small hill by natives. The cart was afterwards pushed off at the top and allowed to roll down hill by itself, with her in it. This ludicrous sort of amusement was always accompanied with much shouting on the part of the natives.   – James Macrae, 1825

At the Sandwich Islands, Ka'ahumanu, the gigantic old dowager queen – a woman of nearly four hundred pounds weight, and who is said to be still living at Mowee – was accustomed, in some of her terrific gusts of temper, to snatch up an ordinary sized man who had offended her, and snap his spine across her knee. Incredible as this may seem, it is a fact. While at Lahainaluna – the residence of this monstrous Jezebel – a humpbacked wretch was pointed out to me, who, some twenty-five years previously, had had the vertebrae of his back-bone very seriously discomposed by his gentle mistress.

                          – Herman Melville, *Typee*

No figure encapsulates the dramas and paradoxes of early Hawaiian history so completely as **Queen Ka'ahumanu**, the daughter of NāmāHāna, a female chief from East Maui, and Ke'eaumoku from the Big Island. Her parents' strategic alliance presented such a threat to Kahekili, the ruling chief of Maui, that they were fleeing for their lives when Ka'ahumanu was born at Hāna, around 1777.

Chief Ke'eaumoku was one of Kamehameha the Great's closest lieutenants. His daughter may have been as young as eight when she first caught the eye of the king; soon afterwards, she became the seventeenth of his twenty-two wives.

Captain Vancouver described Ka'ahumanu in 1793 as "about sixteen... [she] undoubtedly did credit to the choice and taste of Kamehameha, being one of the finest women we had yet seen on any of the islands." According to nineteenth-century historian Samuel M. Kamakau: "Of Kamehameha's two possessions, his wife and his kingdom, she was the most beautiful."

Ka'ahumanu was Kamehameha's favorite wife. As a high-ranking *ali'i*, she possessed great spiritual power, or *mana*. She was also an expert surfer and serial adulterer. Among her paramours was the dashing Kaiana, killed commanding the armies of Oahu against Kamehameha at Nu'uanu Pali, in 1795.

It was after Kamehameha's death, in 1819, that Ka'ahumanu came into her own. Announcing to her son Liholiho that "we two shall rule over the land," she proclaimed herself Kuhina Nui, or Regent, and set about destroying the system of *kapus*. This denied women access to certain foods and, more importantly, to the real source of power in ancient Hawaii – the *luakini* (war temples). At first Ka'ahumanu's goal was to break the grip of the priesthood, but in 1825 she converted to Christianity, after being nursed through a serious illness by Sybil Gingham, the wife of Hawaii's first missionary. Meanwhile, in 1821, she had married both the last king of Kauai, Kaumuali'i, and his seven-foot-tall son, Keali'iahonui.

Ka'ahumanu outlived Liholiho, who died in England in 1824, and remained the effective ruler of Hawaii when his younger brother Kauikeaouli succeeded to the throne as Kamehameha III. Her achievements included selecting Hawaii's first jury, presiding over its first Western-style trial, and enforcing its first law on marriage and divorce. After seven years spent proselytizing for her new faith, she died on June 5, 1832; her last words were reported as "Lo, here am I, O Jesus, Grant me thy gracious smile."

KA'AHUMANU: SCENES FROM A LIFE

enjoy the scenery en route, rather than to race to Hāna itself; having said that, it's a pleasant enough little town.

Although in ancient times Hāna controlled a densely populated region, these days it is home to just a few hundred inhabitants. They proudly see themselves as one of the most staunchly traditional communities in the state and have long resisted any concept of "development" for its own sake, but there are signs that their way of life may change.

When the local sugar plantation closed in 1943, most of its land was bought by **Paul Fagan**, a California businessman. He established not only the **Hāna Ranch**, whose cowboys still work cattle herds in the fields above town, but also modern Maui's first **hotel**, the *Hotel Hāna-Maui*. Fagan died in 1959 – he's commemorated by a large white cross on the hillside – but the town remains dominated by the businesses he founded. Most of the town's central area is taken up by the *Hotel Hāna-Maui*, while the Hāna Ranch headquarters on the main highway houses its most conspicuous restaurant and other utilities.

Almost the entire town, including the Ranch and the hotel, was bought by a Japanese corporation in 1989. They published plans to turn Hāna into an exclusive resort much like Wailea (see p.152), complete with a new oceanfront hotel above Hāmoa Bay, an upscale shopping and restaurant complex, a golf course, and acres of residential properties. Without any of those schemes leaving the drawing board, Hāna has recently passed back into American ownership, and in 2001 the Ranch and the hotel officially separated. What that will mean for Hāna in the long term remains to be seen, but locals have welcomed the change, believing it puts their future on a more secure footing.

For the moment, Hāna remains one of the most relaxing places on Maui to spend a few days, short on swimmable beaches and golf, perhaps, but very long indeed on character, history and beauty.

Arrival and information

The principal user of Hāna's small **airport**, perched beside the ocean three miles north of town, is the tiny Pacific Wings airline (☎248-7700 or 1-888/575-4546; ⓦwww.pacificwings.com). It operates three or four daily round-trip flights between Kahului and Hāna – each leg takes just fifteen minutes, and is timed to connect with flights to and from Honolulu and Lanai – plus one or two nonstop flights to Honolulu. Only Dollar offers **car rental** at Hāna.

Hāna has no public transport of any kind, but the Hāna Ranch Center has a **post office** (Mon–Fri 8am–4.30pm; zip code, HI 96713) and a Bank of Hawaii (Mon–Thurs 3–4.30pm, Fri 3–6pm).

In addition, Hang Gliding Maui is a one-man operation providing **hang-gliding lessons** at $95 for 30min, $165 for 1hr (☎572-6557; ⓦwww.hangglidingmaui.com).

Accommodation

More **accommodation** is available around Hāna than is immediately apparent. As well as the *Hotel Hāna-Maui*, small-scale B&Bs are scattered all over town, and many of the houses along the shoreline are for rent. You can also **camp** at Waiʻānapanapa State Park (see p.206).

ACCOMMODATION PRICE CODES

All accommodation prices in this book have been graded with the following symbols; for a full explanation, see p.29.

❶ up to $40	❹ $100–150	❼ $250–300
❷ $40–70	❺ $150–200	❽ $300–400
❸ $70–100	❻ $200–250	❾ over $400

Hāmoa Bay Bungalow

PO Box 773, Hāna, HI 96713
Ⓣ 248-7884, Ⓕ 248-7047;
Ⓦ www.hamoabay.com.
Idyllic honeymoon hideaway,
perched on stilts in jungle-
like setting two miles south of
Hāna, with distant ocean
views and not another
building in sight. Bamboo
furnishings, small kitchenette
and wooden *lānai* with an
open-air Jacuzzi. ❻.

Hāna Aliʻi Holidays

PO Box 536, 103 Keawa Place,
Hāna, HI 96713 Ⓣ 248-7742 or
1-800/548-0478.
Choose from about twenty
apartments and cottages in and
around Hāna, many by the
ocean, and some absolutely
gorgeous. Rates range from
$65 to $300 a night, but
$110–140 should get you a
spacious and attractive cottage.
The office is situated as Keawa
Place makes its final curve
onto Hāna Bay.

Hāna Kai-Maui Resort

1533 Uaʻkea Rd, Hāna, HI 96713

Ⓣ 248-8426, 248-7506 or 1-
800/346-2772 (US), Ⓕ 248-7482;
Ⓦ www.Hanakaimaui.com.
Small condo building, set in
lovely multilevel gardens
overlooking Hāna Bay, a
short way north of the beach
park. Each well-equipped
studio and one-bedroom
unit has a kitchen and
private *lānai*; the larger ones
sleep four. Studios ❹,
apartments ❺.

Heavenly Hāna Inn

PO Box 790, Hāna Hwy, Hāna,
HI 96713 Ⓣ 248-8442;
Ⓔ hanainn@maui.net.
Lovely Japanese-style B&B,
on the highway two miles
north of central Hāna, with
three two-bedroom suites and
a large common living area,
but no kitchen. Two-night
minimum stay. ❺.

Hotel Hāna-Maui

Hāna Hwy, Hāna, HI 96713
Ⓣ 248-8211 or 1-800/321-4262,
Ⓕ 248-7202;
Ⓦ www.hotelhanamaui.com.
Secluded luxury hotel, built

The telephone area code for all Hawaii is Ⓣ 808.

in the 1940s as Hawaii's first self-contained resort and integrated into the community to create a unique atmosphere. In addition to the older rooms near the lobby, rows of plantation-style Sea Ranch cottages are arranged across the lawns that drop down to the ocean. They have no TVs, but boast every other creature comfort, with kitchenettes and private *lānais* that hold individual hot tubs and enjoy great views. As well as regular shuttles to Hāmoa Beach for activities, hotel guests have use of tennis courts and a pitch-and-putt golf course. Rooms ❻, cottages ❽.

Joe's Place

PO Box 746, 4870 Ua'kea Rd, Hāna, HI 96713 ☏ 248-7033. Eight simple rooms, sharing a kitchen, in a plain house opposite the *Hāna Kai-Maui Resort*. There are no sea views and only one room has an en-suite bath. It can be hard to get through on the phone. ❷–❸.

Downtown Hāna

None of the buildings along the main highway, which passes through Hāna a hundred yards up from the ocean, is especially worth exploring, though **Wānanalua Church**, whose square, solid tower contrasts appealingly with the flamboyant gardens surrounding it, makes a photogenic landmark. Across the road, the **Hāna Ranch Center** is a dull mall, designed to feed and water the daily influx of bus tours, but given a flash of color by the odd *paniolo* cowboy. **Hasegawa's General Store**, stocked with every item imaginable, burned down in 1990. It's been rehoused in a charmless former theater, but is still a friendly place to pick up supplies. The **Hāna Coast Gallery**, at the northern end of the lobby of the *Hotel Hāna-Maui*, sells an unusually good, if expensive, assortment of Hawaiian crafts and paintings of East Maui landscapes.

Hāna Cultural Center and Museum

Map 11, D5. Daily 10.30am–4pm; $2 suggested donation.

Local history is recalled by the low-key exhibits – gourds, calabashes, fish hooks and crude stone idols – at the **Hāna Cultural Center and Museum**, on Uaʻkea Road, down from the highway and above the bay. It also holds art exhibitions and is amassing a comprehensive collection of photos of past and present Hāna residents. Nearby stands a tiny nineteenth-century jail-cum-courthouse; on the grounds alongside it, a realistic replica living compound, of the kind used by the ancient Hawaiian *makaʻāinana* (common people), has been constructed. As well as a thatched stone dwelling and a canoe house, it features garden terraces planted with *taro* and *ti*.

Hāna Bay

Hāna's reputation for beauty relies largely on broad **Hāna Bay**, a short walk below the north end of the town center. Much the safest place to swim in East Maui, it's also the only protected harbor in the area.

The small gray-sand beach known as **Hāna Beach County Park** spreads to the right – the south – at the foot of Keawa Place, backed by lawns that hold picnic tables, restrooms and changing rooms. The park's long terraced pavilion, pressed against the curving hillside across the road, houses *Tutu's* takeout counter (see p.217).

The high cinder cone of **Kaʻuiki Head**, the bay's most prominent feature, thrusts into the ocean to the south. Now covered with trees, it was once just a bare rock, and served as a fortress for the ancient chiefs of Maui; Kahekili is said to have repelled an invasion from the Big Island here in 1780. Its far side – only seen easily from the air – collapsed into the sea long ago.

A short **hiking trail** – hard to spot at first, but soon clear enough – heads off around Kaʻuiki Head from beyond the jetty, offering excellent views across the bay and up to Hāna itself. Soon after a tiny red-sand beach, it reaches a bronze plaque, set into a slab of rock near a couple of small caves in the base of the hill. This marks the birthplace of the great Hawaiian queen, **Kaʻahumanu**, though she was probably born later than the year it says, 1768. Continuing on, you discover that the rocky point beyond is in fact an island. **Puʻu Kiʻi** was once topped by a giant *kiʻi* (wooden idol), erected by the Big Island chief, Umi; it now holds an automated lighthouse. Around the next corner, the trail is blocked by an impassable red scree slope.

Red Sand Beach

Map 11, F6.

A precarious coastal footpath, which is often closed due to dangerous weathering and should only be attempted after seeking local advice as to current conditions, leads along the south flank of Kaʻuiki Head to a lovely little cove that shelters one of Maui's prettiest beaches, **Red Sand Beach**. To find it, walk left from the south end of Uaʻkea Road, below a small, neat Japanese cemetery. Approximately a five-minute walk, the path follows, and in places fills, a narrow ledge around a hillside of loose red gravel, but at this low elevation it's not too nerve-racking.

Behind a final promontory, the beach lies angled toward the rising sun, shielded by a row of black, dragon's-teeth rocks, kept well flossed by the waves. Hawaiians knew this canoe landing as Kaihalulu Beach; swimming is only ever safe in the tiny inshore area. The origin of the beach's coarse reddish cinders – the eroded red cliffs above it – is very obvious, and it's equally obvious that you can hike no further.

Restaurants

For somewhere with so many daytime visitors and overnight guests, Hāna has a remarkably limited range of **places to eat**.

Hāna Gardenland

Hāna Hwy ⊤ 248-8975.
Assuming this small nursery, three miles north of town, has finally reopened after a lengthy closure for refurbishment, it holds a simple but tasteful open-air café. You should be able to order fresh breads, pastries or sandwiches for $6–9 at the counter, plus perhaps a $4.50 smoothie, then sit amid the plants. Daily 9am–5pm.

Hāna Ranch

Hāna Hwy ⊤ 248-8255.
Unenthralling quick-fire restaurant in the heart of Hāna, serving bland $11 lunch buffets (daily 11am–3pm), pizzas Wednesday evenings, and slightly more interesting dinners on Friday and Saturday, when $18–25 entrees, such as barbecue ribs or teriyaki chicken, include a salad bar. A cheaper takeout counter at the side, with a few tables, sells *saimin* and similar local specialties daily 6.30am–4pm. Restaurant Sun–Tues & Thurs 8–10am & 11am–3pm; Wed 8–10am, 11am–3pm & 5.30–8pm; Fri & Sat 8–10am, 11am–3pm & 6–8pm.

Hotel Hāna-Maui

Hāna Hwy ⊤ 248-8211.
The deluxe resort's high-ceilinged, open-sided, wicker-furnished dining room is among the most expensive restaurants in Hawaii, and sadly the food doesn't merit the high prices. Even a humble *loco moco*, a fried egg on a hamburger, costs $12.50, while full meals are likely to total well over $40. A typical dinner might include ceviche, salad of fern shoots, and steamed tiger shrimp with 'ōpakapaka. Daily 7.30–10.30am, 11.30am–2.30pm & 6.15–9pm.

RESTAURANTS

Tutu's
Hāna Bay ☎ 248-8244.
Beachfront takeout counter,
whose indifferent sandwiches,
burgers, plate lunches, sodas
and lemonades attract long
queues every lunchtime.
Daily 8.30am–4pm.

SOUTH OF HĀNA

South of Hāna, Hāna Highway gives way to **Pi'ilani Highway**, but the scenery is, if anything, even more gorgeous than before. In those stretches where the road is not engulfed by magnificent flowering trees, you can look up beyond the ranchlands to the high green mountains, while Mauna Kea on the Big Island heaves into view across the 'Alenuihāhā Channel.

A couple of miles out of Hāna, a 1.5-mile detour down the Haneo'o Loop Road takes you to the white-sand beach at **Hāmoa Bay**, used by *Hotel Hāna-Maui* for all its oceanfront activities, including a weekly *lū'au*. There was a small settlement here until it was destroyed by the *tsunami* of 1946; it's a good surfing spot, but unsafe for swimming.

The highway continues south through a succession of tiny villages, where, apart from the odd roadside fruit stand and countless crystal-clear waterfalls, there's no reason to stop.

'Ohe'o Gulch

Map 1, M7.

Almost all the day-trippers who reach Hāna press on to beautiful **'Ohe'o Gulch**, ten miles beyond, where a natural rock staircase of waterfalls tumbles down to the oceanfront meadows at the mouth of **Kīpahulu Valley**. This far-flung outpost of Haleakalā National Park tends to be jam-packed in the middle of the day, but as one of the few places on Maui to offer easy access to unspoiled Hawaiian rainforest, it shouldn't be missed. If you hike a mile or two into the hills, you'll soon escape the crowds to reach cool rock pools, ideal for swimming.

For details of horse riding in 'Ohe'o Gulch, see p.55.

The national park charges no fee at 'Ohe'o Gulch, which is always open to the public. A **ranger station** at the roadside parking lot (daily 9am–5pm; ☏248-7375) has up-to-date information on local roads and hiking trails. **Guided hikes** to different destinations set off daily except Saturdays at 9.30am. The rangers are forbidden to recommend that visitors continue all the way around southern Maui on the Pi'ilani Highway (see p.221), as that violates rental-car agreements, but only very rarely are they obliged by flooding to declare it formally closed.

Access to the upper reaches of the Kīpahulu Valley, regarded as one of the most pristine and environmentally significant regions in all Hawaii, is barred to the public. The park hopes to purchase large tracts in the valleys to the west, in order to open more hiking trails and remote beaches.

The lower trail

The paved footpath that leads **downhill** from the 'Ohe'o Gulch parking lot – officially, **Kūloa Point Trail** – is so busy that it's forced to operate as a one-way loop. Get here early if you want to enjoy it before the onslaught, but don't avoid it otherwise. After ambling through the meadows for five minutes, the trail winds past ancient stone walls on the low oceanfront bluff, and then down to a tiny gray-grit beach. From there, a "ladder" of stream-fed pools climbs the craggy rocks, an ascent negotiated by sucker fish in breeding season. Several pools are deep and sheltered enough for swimming, though the shark-infested ocean itself is far from tempting. It's impossible to follow the stream as far up as the high road bridge; by then, the gorge is a slippery, narrow water chute.

The higher waterfalls

Thanks to the construction of two sturdy footbridges, the longer **Pīpīwai Trail** into the mountains is no longer rendered unsafe by bad weather, and ranks as one of the very best hikes on Hawaii. It too starts beside the ranger station, but swiftly crosses the highway and heads uphill through steep fields, where thick woods line the course of the 'Ohe'o Stream. After the first half-mile, which is by far the most demanding stretch of the hike, a spur trail cuts off to the right to reach a railing that overlooks the towering 200-foot **Makahiku Falls**. A deep groove in the earth nearby leads to a series of shallow bathing pools just above the lip of the falls, where the stream emerges from a tunnel in the rock. As well as commanding magnificent views, it's an utterly idyllic spot for a swim.

Be sure to carry mosquito repellent if you hike into the rainforest at 'Ohe'o Gulch.

Continuing by means of a gate in a fence along the main trail, you emerge into an open guava orchard and soon hear the thundering of smaller waterfalls to your right. There's no way to get to the water, but you'll see it framed through the thick jungle, together with the gaping cave mouth it has hollowed out on the far side. A little farther on, you may be lured off the trail again by a pair of twin falls near a small concrete dam; they can be admired from a rocky outcrop in the streambed below.

Beyond that lies a lovely meadow, with views to the high valley walls in the distance, laced by huge waterfalls. A mile up, the trail crosses high above the stream twice in quick succession, over the newly built bridges. It then follows a

'OHE'O GULCH

dark and narrow gap through a forest of old fifty-foot-high bamboo interspersed with sections of level wooden boardwalk. Eventually, two miles up from the road, you'll spot the spindle-thin, 400-foot **Waimoku Falls** ahead. Reaching its base requires a lot of scrambling, and crisscrossing the ever-narrowing stream. Despite the obvious danger of falling rocks, many hikers choose to cool off by standing directly beneath the cascade. Allow a good two hours to complete the entire round-trip hike.

Camping

The national park **campground** at 'Ohe'o Gulch is extremely rudimentary – just a field, with pit toilets and no drinking water – but it stands in the ruins of an ancient fishing village, and enjoys superb ocean views. Permits are not required, and it's free, with a three-night maximum stay.

Kīpahulu

Within a mile of 'Ohe'o Gulch, the highway passes through the village of **KĪPAHULU**. Time seems to have stood still in this attractive little spot since the local sugar mill closed down in the 1920s. The only sign of life these days comes from the occasional lunchtime fruit stand selling the produce of the roadside orchards.

A quarter-mile beyond **milepost 41** at Kīpahulu, a paved road branches left off the highway. After a couple of hundred yards, turn left again onto a dirt road through a "tunnel" of trees, and park by the giant banyan tree at the end that guards the **Palapala Ho'omau Church**. Founded in 1864, it has whitewashed coral walls and a green timber roof, and is set in pretty clifftop gardens. The interior is utterly plain and unadorned.

Visitors make their way to this tranquil spot because the fenced-off platform of black lava stones in the churchyard holds the grave of **Charles Lindbergh** (1902–74), who won fame in 1927 as the first man to fly the Atlantic. Less appetizingly, Lindbergh was also a notorious Nazi sympathizer, who once told the *Reader's Digest* that aviation is "one of those priceless possessions which permit the White Race to live at all in a sea of Yellow, Black and Brown." President Roosevelt told a friend in May 1940, "If I should die tomorrow, I want you to know this. I am absolutely convinced that Lindbergh is a Nazi." Lindbergh retired to Maui late in life and died within a couple of years.

Leading off from the cemetery, and only accessible through it, **Kīpahulu Point Park** is a small shaded clifftop lawn, fringed with bright orange-leafed bushes, where the picnic tables command wonderful ocean views.

ALONG THE SOUTH MAUI COAST

If you've driven the Hāna Highway and have a congenital aversion to going back the same way you came, it's possible in all but the most severe weather conditions to follow the **Piʻilani Highway** right around southern Maui. All the rental-car companies forbid their clients to drive this way, but that's more because it's inaccessible if you need emergency help than because it's especially difficult. The road surface has been greatly improved in the last few years, so there's now just one unpaved stretch of less than five miles. It's a bumpy ride, no faster than the Hāna Highway, and not as spectacular, but it does offer a glorious sense of isolation.

Advice on road and weather conditions along the Piʻilani Highway – almost invariably positive – is posted daily at the ʻOheʻo Gulch ranger station; see p.218. Don't attempt to drive it after dark.

This area was once known as **Kahikinui**, or Tahiti Nui; the equivalent part of Tahiti, which has the same outline as Maui, bears the same name. The countryside immediately beyond Kīpahulu is lovely, dotted with exclusive homes whose owners are no doubt happy that this is not yet a standard tourist loop.

After less than two miles, the road returns to sea level – for the first time in several miles – and skirts the long gray pebble beach at **Lelekea Bay**. As you climb the cliffs at the far end, look back to see water spouting out of the hillside above an overhang in the rock, forceful enough to be a gushing jet rather than a waterfall.

The pavement gives out after the second of the two little coves that follow. An overlook just over two juddering miles further on looks down on the small flat promontory holding the 1859 **Huialoha Church**. A mile after that, the solitary Kaupō Store is an atmospheric general store that's normally open on weekdays only. By now, the landscape has become much drier, and you're starting to get views up to the **Kaupō Gap**, where a vast torrent of lava appears to have petrified as it poured over the smooth lip of Haleakalā Crater. To the east, you can peek into the lushness of the upper Kīpahulu Valley, but the slopes to the west are all but barren.

What looks like a caravan, in a field about a hundred yards beyond the Kaupō Store, is in fact *Auntie Jane's Kau Kau Wagon*. In theory, it sells the **best burgers** on Maui, incredible $5 giants bursting with fresh beef from the ranch above, sweet corn, seaweed, salad and other fresh ingredients, and also sodas and "homemade" ices (in that they're made on Maui). As often as not, however, Auntie Jane is nowhere to be found.

The ruined outline of **St Joseph's Church** stands below the highway a mile beyond *Auntie Jane's*, just before the pavement starts up again. From here on, the road mounts the long southern flank of Haleakalā at the gentlest of angles. There's no tree cover on the deeply furrowed hillside – where some of the cracks seem like incipient versions of Kauai's Waimea Canyon – so cattle gather beneath the occasional shade tree beside the road.

Naked russet cinder cones lie scattered to either side of the road, some bearing the traces of ancient Hawaiian stone walls, while rivers of rough black *a'ā* lava snake down to the sea. An especially vast hollow cone, near the **20-mile marker**, marks the spot where small huts and ranch buildings start to reappear. Soon Mākena becomes visible below, with Molokini and Lanai out to sea, and three miles on it's a relief to find yourself back in green woodlands. The Tedeschi Winery (see p.176) is a little over a mile further on, with another 23 miles to go before Kahului.

CONTEXTS

A brief history

U ntil less than two thousand years ago, Maui remained an unknown speck in the vast Pacific, populated only by the mutated descendants of the few organisms that had been carried here by wind or wave (see p.247). Carbon dating of sites elsewhere in the archipelago, notably on Oahu and the Big Island, suggests that Hawaii's earliest human settlers arrived during the second or third centuries AD. Maui has been less thoroughly investigated than the other islands, but early occupation seems to have been concentrated on the windward coast of West Maui, especially the Waihe'e and Waiehu valleys. Rock shelters and religious shrines within the crater of Haleakalā have been tentatively dated as far back as the seventh century.

For a full account of the daily life, traditions and culture of the ancient Hawaiians, see p.241.

These first inhabitants were **Polynesians**, probably from the Marquesas Islands. Except perhaps for their first chance landfall, they came equipped to colonize, carrying goats, dogs, pigs, coconut palms, bananas and sugar cane among other essentials. Their ancestors spread from Asia to inhabit Indonesia and the Solomon Islands 30,000 years ago. Such migrations, across coastal waters shallower than they are today, involved hopping from island to island without crossing open ocean. There then followed a 25,000-year hiatus, while the techniques were acquired to venture farther. Just over three thousand years ago, the voyagers reached Fiji; they then spread via Tahiti to populate the "Polynesian Triangle," extending from Easter Island in the east to Hawaii in the north and New Zealand in the south.

Recent archeological and scientific investigations have thrown a number of long-cherished beliefs about the ancient history of Hawaii into doubt, while confirming, thanks to DNA testing, that the Polynesians did indeed enter the Pacific from southeast Asia. Thor Heyerdahl's argument for a North American origin has thus been finally disproved. On the other hand, historians are no longer sure whether traditional accounts of Hawaii being settled by successive waves of migrants at widely spaced intervals are in fact true. According to that model, Marquesas Islanders continued to arrive until the eighth century and were followed by Tahitians between the eleventh and fourteenth centuries, with each group violently supplanting its predecessors. One piece of evidence that does point to a Tahitian influx is the name **"Hawaii"** itself, which is known previously to have been an alternative, "poetic" name for the largest of the leeward Tahitian islands, Raiatea, the home of the voyaging temple of Taputapuatea. Whether or not Tahitians did reach Hawaii in significant numbers, it remains unquestioned that by the time the Europeans appeared, no two-way voyaging between Hawaii and the South Pacific had taken place for around five hundred years.

Ancient Maui was not the fertile island it is today; both the central isthmus and the upcountry slopes were arid wastelands, and the population was crowded into scattered coastal valleys. For its first thousand years of human occupation, the island consisted of several independent regions, each constantly at war with the rest. Both the two main centers were in West Maui – one was the northwestern shoreline, the other was the region of Nā Wai 'Ēha, which stretched northwards from 'Īao Valley – while remote Hāna on the east coast was a lesser chiefdom, prone to fall under the control of Big Island invaders.

The first chief to rule over all of Maui was **Pi'ilani**, who is thought to have reigned during the fifteenth or sixteenth centuries. He conquered all the way from Hāna to the six West Maui bays that have been known ever since as the Honoapi'ilani (bays of Pi'ilani), and even extended his kingdom to include Kahoolawe, Lanai and Molokai. Pi'ilani also started work on the first road to encircle a Hawaiian island: wide enough to hold eight men abreast, it was finished by his son Kihapi'ilani. Parts of the modern Pi'ilani Highway follow the ancient route, and in places, such as beyond La Pérouse Bay, the original stones can still be seen.

With a population of around 120,000, Maui held perhaps a quarter as many people as the Big Island by the time the Europeans arrived, but its warriors' military prowess and its central position in the archipelago made it a worthy rival. The eighteenth century saw endless battles for supremacy between the two neighbors. From around 1736 onward, Maui was ruled by **Kahekili**, a ferocious *pahupu* or "cut-in-two" warrior, half of whose body was tattooed black. During his sixty-year reign, Kahekili conquered almost all the other islands, invading Oahu and establishing his half-brother on the throne of Kauai.

The coming of the foreigners

No Western ship is known for certain to have chanced upon Hawaii before that of **Captain Cook**, in January 1778; the first European to sail across the Pacific, the Portuguese Ferdinand Magellan, did so without seeing a single island.

There is, however, considerable circumstantial evidence of pre-Cook contact between Hawaiians and Europeans. Spanish vessels disappeared in the northern Pacific from the 1520s onward, while during the two centuries, starting in 1565, that the "Manila Galleons" made annual voyages across the Pacific between Mexico and the Philippines, at least nine such ships were lost. Cook observed that the first Hawaiians he encountered were familiar with iron, and even suggested that some bore European features. Hawaiian legends speak of what may have been Spanish mariners being shipwrecked on the north coast of Lanai during the sixteenth century, and again off Maui some time later, while the log of the Dutch ship *Lefda* in 1599 spoke of eight seamen deserting to an unknown island at this latitude.

Spanish influence might explain the similarity of the red and yellow feather headdresses of Hawaiian warriors – unknown elsewhere in Polynesia – to the helmets of Spanish soldiers, and account for what seemed the phenomenal speed with which syphilis spread through the islands after it was supposedly introduced by the Cook expedition. The skeleton of a young woman was recently unearthed on Oahu who appears to have died of syphilis in the mid-seventeenth century; other contemporary burials have been shown to contain small scraps of sailcloth.

When Cook first encountered Hawaii, he missed both Maui and the Big Island before stumbling upon Kauai, on his way to the north Pacific, in search of the Northwest Passage. When he returned to the "Sandwich Islands" at the end of the year, Maui was the first island he reached. The "dreadfull surf" prevented him from making a landing, but he did welcome several groups of islanders aboard the *Discovery*, including at different times both Kahekili, off Wailuku, and chief Kalaniōpu'u of the Big Island, who seems to have been waging some sort of military campaign in the vicinity of Hāna. Cook then sailed on to the Big

Island, where he met his death in a skirmish in Kealakekua Bay on February 14, 1779.

After news of Cook's discoveries reached the outside world, the Sandwich Islands swiftly became a port of call for traders of all kinds, especially those carrying furs from the Pacific Northwest to China. The first outsider known to have set foot on Maui was the French Admiral **La Pérouse**, who landed in what's now La Pérouse Bay in South Maui (see p.162) on May 30, 1786. Declining to follow orders claiming the island for the king of France – "the customs of Europeans on such occasions are completely ridiculous" – he simply sailed away a few hours later.

Kamehameha the Great

For a few brief years the Hawaiians remained masters of their own destiny, with the major beneficiary of the change in circumstances being the astute young Big Island warrior **Kamehameha**. The acquisition of European military technology made it possible for a single chief to conquer the entire archipelago for the first time, and it was Kamehameha rather than Kahekili who managed to do so. Although he remains Hawaii's greatest hero, Kamehameha to some extent played into the hands of the foreigners, in that a united Hawaiian kingdom was easier for them to manipulate and, ultimately, control.

According to some accounts, the future Kamehameha the Great, who was born in 1758, was Kahekili's own bastard son. He first proved himself in the service of Kalaniōpu'u, being present at the death of Captain Cook, and then after the high chief's death in 1782 usurped power from his son.

Kamehameha successfully invaded Maui in 1790, defeating Kalanikūpule, Kahekili's chosen heir, in a bloody battle at 'Īao Valley. Soon afterwards, he was obliged to return to face his enemies at home, and briefly lost control of the

THE HAWAIIAN MONARCHY

Kamehameha I	1758–1819
Kamehameha II (Liholiho)	1819–1824
Kamehameha III (Kauikeaouli)	1825–1854
Kamehameha IV (Alexander Liholiho)	1854–1863
Kamehameha V (Lot Kamehameha)	1863–1872
William C. Lunalilo	1873–1874
David Kalākaua	1874–1891
Liliʻuokalani	1891–1893

island. However, when Kahekili in turn launched a major fleet against the Big Island in 1791, his hopes were dashed by the "Battle of the Red-Mouthed Gun" off Waipiʻo Valley – the first time Hawaiian fleets were equipped with cannons, operated by foreign gunners. By the time Kahekili died at Waikīkī in 1794, Kamehameha was back in command on Maui. Within a year, he had taken over Lanai, Molokai, and Oahu as well, and exacted tribute from Kauai. The entire kingdom took the name of his native island, and became "Hawaii;" had Kahekili had a little more luck, the modern state might easily have been named "Maui."

During the year of 1802, Kamehameha had his capital in the fledgling port of Lahaina; thereafter he spent several years based in Waikīkī. Kamehameha himself returned to the Kona Coast of the Big Island, where he died in 1819, but his immediate heirs chose **Lahaina** as the capital of their kingdom from the 1820s until the 1840s.

The end of the old order

Kamehameha's successor, his son Liholiho – a weak figure also known as **Kamehameha II** – was dominated by the regent **Queen Kaʻahumanu**, who was born in Hāna (see p.208). As a woman, excluded from the *luakini heiaus* at the center of political power, she set out to bring down the priesthood. Liholiho was plied with drink and cajoled into dining with women in public – acts which helped to end the *kapu* system (see p.245), and precipitated a civil war in which the upholders of the ancient religion were defeated. In a mass outburst of iconoclasm, Hawaiians rejoicing at their new-found freedom destroyed altars and idols throughout the islands.

Hawaii was thrown into moral anarchy just as the first Puritan **missionaries** arrived. Their harsh strictures on the easy-going Hawaiian lifestyle might have been calculated to compound the chaos, as they set about obliging Hawaiian women to cover unseemly flesh in billowing *mu'umu'u* "Mother Hubbard" dresses, condemning the *hula* as lascivious and obscene, and discouraging surfing as a waste of time, liable to promote lewdness. Lahaina attracted such an intensive missionary effort, enthusiastically supported by the island's devoutly Christian **Governor Hoapili**, that, within a few years of opening its first school and printing press in 1831, Maui had achieved the highest rate of literacy on earth.

In general, the missionaries concentrated their attentions on the ruling class, the *ali'i*, believing that they would bring the commoners to the fold in their wake. The initial tensions between missionaries and the new breed of foreign entrepreneurs were to disappear as their offspring intermarried, acquired land and formed the backbone of a new middle class.

The foreigners take control

For ordinary Hawaiians, the sudden **advent of capitalism** was devastating. Any notion of Hawaiian self-sufficiency was abandoned in favor of selling out the islands' resources for cash returns.

Sandalwood: the first sell-out

Sandalwood logs were first picked up from Hawaii in 1791, scattered among a consignment of fuel. Traders had searched for years for a commodity that the Chinese would buy in return for tea to meet English demand. Kamehameha had a monopoly on the trade until his death, but thereafter individual chiefs out for profit forced all the commoners under their sway to abandon *taro*-farming and fishing and become wage slaves. By the end of the 1820s, the forests were almost entirely denuded, and traditional agriculture had collapsed.

Whaling

The first **whaling** ships arrived in Hawaii in 1820, the same year as the missionaries – and had an equally dramatic impact. Modern visitors often assume that it was the humpback whales seen in Hawaiian waters that attracted the whaling fleet to the islands, but humpbacks were not hunted during the nineteenth century. Instead, the whalers would chase other species in the waters around Japan in winter and in the Arctic during summer, and call at Hawaii each spring and fall, to unload oil and baleen to be shipped home in other vessels, to stock up, and to change crew.

Any Pacific port would have seemed a godsend to the whalers, who were away from New England for three years at a time, and paid so badly that most were either fugitives or plain mad. Hawaii was such a paradise that up to fifty percent of each crew would desert, to be replaced by Hawaiian sailamokus, born seafarers eager to see the world.

After Governor Hoapili died in the early 1840s, and the seat of government shifted to Honolulu, Lahaina spent twenty raucous years as the "whaling capital of the world." The need to provision whaling ships was the major spur in the development of the farms and ranches of Upcountry

Maui. The Hispanic cowboys imported to work there, known as *paniolos* (a corruption of *españoles*), became the next in a long line of ethnic groups to make their homes on the island.

The Great Mahele

By 1844, foreign-born fortune-seekers dominated the Hawaiian government. As the foreign powers jostled for position, it was by no means inevitable that the islands would become American. As late as the 1840s, New Zealand was taken by the English and Tahiti by the French.

At first, foreigners could not legally own land. In the old Hawaii there was no private land; all was held in trust by the chief, who apportioned it to individuals at his continued pleasure only. The king was requested to "clarify" the situation. A land commission was set up, under the direction of a missionary, and its deliberations resulted in 1848 in the **Great Mahele**, or "Division of Lands." In theory all land was parceled out to native Hawaiians, with sixty percent going to the crown and the government, 39 percent to just over two hundred chiefs, and less than one percent to 11,000 commoners. Within two years, however, the *huoles* (non-Hawaiians) were also able to buy and sell land. The jibe that the missionaries "came to Hawaii to do good – and they done good" stems from the speed with which they amassed vast acreages; their children became Hawaii's wealthiest and most powerful class. One of the few areas in the state where Hawaiian commoners managed to hold on to their land was Makawao in Upcountry Maui.

The sugar industry and the civil war

When the whaling trade finally died down, Maui was left high and dry, with its population reduced to a mere

12,000. However, the lands that had been used to grow food for the sailors turned toward other crops, and especially **sugar**. Chinese immigrants on both Maui and Kauai began growing sugar early in the nineteenth century, but Hawaii's first sugar plantation was started in 1835 in Kōloa on Kauai. It swiftly became clear that this was an industry where large-scale operators were the most efficient and profitable, and by 1847 the field had narrowed to five main players. These **Big Five** were Hackfield & Co (later to become Amfac), C. Brewer & Co, Theo Davies Co, Castle & Cooke (later Dole) and Alexander & Baldwin. Thereafter, they worked in close co-operation with each other, united by common interests and, often, family ties.

Hawaii was poised to take advantage when the **American Civil War** broke out, and the markets of the northern US began to cast about for an alternative source of sugar to the Confederate South. The consequent boom in the Hawaiian sugar industry, and the ever-increasing integration of Hawaii into the American economic mainstream, was the major single factor in the eventual loss of Hawaiian sovereignty. Plantations swiftly spread along Maui's shoreline east of Pā'ia, and crept across the central isthmus as fast as irrigation channels could be constructed along the flanks of Haleakalā. Intense rivalry pitted the partners Samuel Alexander and Henry Baldwin, based at Pu'unēnē, against Claus Spreckels, creator of the plantation community of "Spreckelsville"; for more details, see p.72.

The ethnic mixture of modern Hawaii is largely the product of the search for **laborers** prepared to submit to the draconian conditions on the plantations – first the Chinese, then the Portuguese, brought from Madeira and the Azores, then the Koreans, Japanese, and Filipinos.

The end of the Kingdom of Hawaii

> *Hawaii is ours. As I look back upon the first steps*
> *in this miserable business, and as I contemplate*
> *the means used to complete the outrage, I am*
> *ashamed of the whole affair.*

US President Grover Cleveland, 1893

When sugar prices dropped after the Civil War, the machinations of the sugar industry to get favorable prices on the mainland moved Hawaii inexorably toward **annexation** by the US. In 1876 all trade barriers and tariffs between the US and the Kingdom of Hawaii were abolished; within fifteen years sugar exports to the US had increased tenfold.

By now, the Kamehameha dynasty had come to an end, and the heir to the Hawaiian throne was chosen by the national legislature. The first such king, William Lunalilo, died in 1874, after a year in office. The second, **King David Kalākaua**, is now remembered as the "Merrie Monarch," who revived Hawaiian pursuits such as *hula* and surfing. However, at the time he was seen as being pro-American, and was to some extent the tool of the plantation owners. In 1887 an all-white group of "concerned businessmen" forced through the "Bayonet Constitution," in which he surrendered power to an assembly elected by property owners (of any nationality) as opposed to citizens.

Kalākaua died in San Francisco in 1891, and his sister **Liliʻuokalani** became queen. When she proclaimed her desire for a new constitution, the same group of businessmen, now known as the "**Annexation Club**," called in the US warship *Boston*, and declared a provisional government. President Grover Cleveland (a Democrat) responded that "Hawaii was taken possession of by the United States forces without the consent or wish of the government of the islands. . . . [It] was wholly without justification . . . not merely a wrong but a disgrace." With phenomenal cheek, however, the provisional government rejected his demand for the restoration of the monarchy, saying the US should not "interfere in the internal affairs of their sovereign nation." Finding defenders in the Republican US Congress, they declared themselves a **republic** on July 4, 1894.

Following an abortive coup attempt in 1895, Lili'uokalani was charged with **treason**, and placed under house arrest. Though she lived until 1917, hopes of a restoration of Hawaiian independence were dashed in 1897, when a Republican president, McKinley, came to office claiming "annexation is not a change. It is a consummation." The strategic value of Pearl Harbor was emphasized by the Spanish–American War in the Philippines, and on August 12, 1898, Hawaii was formally **annexed** as a territory of the United States.

A Territory and a State

At the moment of **annexation** there was no question of Hawaii becoming a state; the whites here were outnumbered ten to one and had no desire to afford the rest of the islanders the protection of US labor laws, let alone to give them the vote. Furthermore, as the proportion of Hawaiians of Japanese descent (*nisei*) increased, Congress feared the prospect of a state of people who might consider their primary allegiance to be to Japan. Consequently, Hawaii remained for the first half of the twentieth century the virtual fiefdom of the Big Five, who through their control of agriculture dominated transport, utilities, insurance and government.

Things began to change during World War II. Hawaii was the only part of the United States to be attacked in the war, and it demonstrated just how crucial the islands were to the rest of America. Hawaii finally became the **fiftieth of the United States** in 1959, after a plebiscite showed a 17-to-1 majority in favor, with the only opposition coming from the few remaining native Hawaiians.

The main trend in Hawaiian history since the war has been the slow **decline of agriculture**. Thanks to a series of strikes by plantation laborers, the long-term Republican domination of state politics ended, and Hawaii's agricultural workers became the highest paid in the world. Arguably, this led to the eventual disappearance of their jobs in the face of Third World competition.

Since the closure of Lahaina's Pioneer Mill in 1999, Maui has been left with just one working sugar plantation, run by Alexander & Baldwin at Pu'unēnē (see p.72), as well as the only pineapple cannery in the state. **Tourism** has come to dominate everything. In 1927, 428 tourists came to the island; even in 1951 there were just 14,000 visitors, and the *Hotel Hāna-Maui* (see p.212) was Maui's only purpose-built tourist hotel. Then came the idea of turning cane fields into luxury resorts, a process pioneered at Kā'anapali in the 1950s, extended at Kīhei in the 1960s and still continuing to this day. Modern Maui, with 100,000 residents, now welcomes more than two million tourists a year.

The sovereignty movement

Since the late 1980s, support has mushroomed for the concept of **Hawaiian sovereignty**, meaning some form of restoration of the rights of native Hawaiians. Everyone now seems sure that sovereignty is coming, but no one knows what form it will take. Of the three most commonly advanced models, one sees Hawaii as an independent nation once again, with full citizenship perhaps restricted either to those born in Hawaii or prepared to pledge sole allegiance to Hawaii. Another possibility would be the granting to native Hawaiians of nation-within-a-nation status, as with

Native American groups on the mainland. Others argue that it would be more realistic to preserve the existing political framework within the context of full economic reparations to native Hawaiians.

Even the US government has formally acknowledged the illegality of the US overthrow of the Hawaiian monarchy with an official **Apology to Native Hawaiians**, signed by President Clinton in November 1993. A separate but related problem, indicative of the difficulties faced in resolving this issue, is the failure by both federal and state government to manage 200,000 acres set aside for the benefit of native Hawaiians in 1921. The state has now agreed to pay Hawaiians more than $100 million compensation, though disputes remain over where the money will come from and to whom it will go.

The sovereignty issue attained such a high profile in 1998, thanks to the centenary of annexation, as to provoke something of a backlash among elements of the state's non-native (and particular Caucasian) population. The Office of Hawaiian Affairs, the body responsible for looking after the interests of native Hawaiians and, potentially, distributing compensation, had long been run by a board whose members were elected by voting among native Hawaiians only. In a landmark ruling in February 2000, the US Supreme Court declared such race-based elections to be unconstitutional; new elections later that year were open to all state residents and produced one new non-native board member. Hawaiian activists fear that their movement is in jeopardy, with state programs liable to be dismantled by the courts. Nonetheless political support appears to remain strong for, at the very least, federal recognition of the status of native Hawaiians as being equivalent to that of native peoples elsewhere in the country, and US Senator Daniel Akaka of Hawaii has repeatedly introduced drafts of a bill to that end in Washington.

Ancient culture and society

No written record exists of the centuries between the arrival of the Polynesians and the first contact with Europeans. However, sacred chants, passed down through the generations, show a history packed with feuds and forays between the islands, and oral traditions provide a detailed picture of the day-to-day life of ordinary Hawaiians.

Developing a civilization on the most isolated islands in the world, without metals and workable clays, presented many challenges. Nevertheless, by the late eighteenth century, Hawaii was home to around a million people. Two hundred years later, the population has climbed back to a similar level. Now, however, virtually no pure-blooded Hawaiians remain, and the islands are not even close to being self-sufficient in terms of food. Maui's population was probably significantly larger than the 100,000 it is today, and Oahu's population smaller, but no precise figures are known.

Daily life

In a sense, ancient Hawaii had no economy, not even barter. Although then as now most people lived close to the coast, each island was organized into wedge-shaped land divisions called *ahupua‘a*, stretching from the ocean to the mountains. The abundant fruits of the earth and sea were simply shared out among the inhabitants within each *ahupua‘a*.

There's some truth in the idea of pre-contact Hawaii as a leisured paradise, but it had taken a lot of work to make it that way. Coconut palms had to be planted along the seashore to provide food, clothing and shade for coastal villages, and bananas and other food plants distributed inland. Crops such as sugar cane were cultivated with the aid of complex systems of terraces and irrigation channels. *Taro*, whose leaves were eaten as "greens" and whose roots were mashed to produce *poi*, was grown in the windward valleys.

Most **fishing** took place in shallow inshore waters. Fishhooks made from human bone were believed to be especially effective; the most prized hooks of all were made from the bones of chiefs who had no body hair, so those unfortunate individuals were renowned for their low life expectancy. Nets were never cast from boats, but shallow bays might be dragged by communal groups of wading men drawing in *hukilau* nets (Elvis did it in *Blue Hawaii*, and you occasionally see people doing it today). In addition, the art of **aquaculture** – fish-farming – was more highly developed in Hawaii than anywhere in Polynesia, though Maui appears to have had fewer fishponds than the other islands.

Few people lived in the higher forested slopes, but these served as the source of vital raw materials such as *koa* wood for canoes and weapons. The ancients even ventured into the crater of Haleakalā. In addition to quarrying hard basalt for their basic tools, and hunting petrels for food, they also built religious shrines and cairns, and buried what were presumably their most honored dead.

Ordinary commoners – the **maka'āinana** – lived in simple windowless huts known as *hales*. Most of these were thatched with *pili* grass, though in the driest areas they didn't bother with roofs. Buildings of all kinds were usually raised on platforms of stone, using rounded boulders taken from river beds. Matting covered the floor, while the pounded tree bark called *kapa* (known as tapa elsewhere in the Pacific, and decorated with patterns) served as clothing and bedding. Lacking pottery, households made abundant use of gourds, wooden dishes and woven baskets.

The ruling class, the **ali'i**, stood at the apex of Hawaiian society. In theory, heredity counted for everything, and great chiefs demonstrated their fitness to rule by the length of their genealogies. In fact the *ali'i* were educated as equals, and chiefs won the very highest rank largely through physical prowess and force of personality. To hang on to power, the king had to be seen to be devoutly religious and to treat his people fairly.

The most popular pastime was **surfing**. Ordinary people surfed on five- to seven-foot boards known as *alaia*, and also had *paipus*, the equivalent of the modern boogie-board; only the *ali'i* used the thick sixteen-foot *olo* boards, made of dark oiled *wiliwili* wood. On land the *ali'i* raced narrow sleds on purpose-built, grass-covered *hōlua* slides and staged boxing tournaments.

Religion

It's all but impossible now to grasp the subtleties of ancient Hawaiian **religion**. So much depends on how the chants and texts are translated; if the word *akua* is interpreted as meaning "god," for example, historians can draw analogies with Greek or Hindu legends by speaking of a pantheon of

RELIGION

battling, squabbling "gods" and "goddesses" with magic powers. Some scholars, however, prefer to translate *akua* as "spirit consciousness" – which might correspond to the soul of an ancestor – and argue that the antics of such figures are peripheral to a more fundamental set of attitudes regarding the relationship of humans to the natural world.

The **Kumulipo**, Hawaii's principal creation chant, has been preserved in full. It tells how after the emergence of the earth "from the source in the slime . . . [in] the depths of the darkness," more complicated life forms developed, from coral to pigs, until finally men, women and "gods" appeared. Not only was there no creator-god, but the gods were much of a kind with humans. It took a hundred generations for Wākea, the god of the sky, and Papa, an earth goddess, to be born; they were the divine ancestors of the Hawaiian people.

Not all Hawaiians necessarily shared the same beliefs; different groups sought differing ways of augmenting their *mana*, or spiritual power. Only the elite *aliʻi* may have paid much attention to the bloodthirsty warrior god Kū, while ordinary families, and by extension villages and regions, owed their primary allegiance to their personal *ʻaumākua* – a sort of clan symbol, possibly a totem animal such as a shark or owl, or a more abstract force, such as that embodied by Pele, the volcano goddess.

Spiritual and temporal power did not lie in the same hands, let alone in the same places. Hawaiian "priests" were known as **kahunas** ("men who know the secrets"), and were the masters of ceremonies at temples called **heiaus**. A *heiau* consisted of a number of separate structures set on a rock platform (*paepae*). These might include the *hale mana* ("house of spiritual power"), the *hale pahu* ("house of the drum") and the *anuʻu* ("oracle tower"), from the top of which the *kahunas* conversed with the gods. Assorted *kiʻi akua*, wooden images of different gods, stood on all sides, and the whole enclosure was fenced or walled off. In addition to the two main types of *heiau* – **luakinis**, dedicated to the war god Kū, which held *leles* or altars used for human sacrifice, and **māpeles**, peaceful temples to Lono, an errant former ruler of the Big Island who had become deified as patron of the annual *makahiki* (renewal) festival – there were also *heiaus* to such entities as Laka, goddess of the *hula*. Devotees of Pele, on the other hand, did not give their protectress formal worship at a *heiau*. Most *heiaus* were built for some specific occasion, and did not remain in constant use; the largest on all the islands, Piʻilanihale near Hāna on Maui (see p.205), is thought to have been constructed by chief Piʻilani around 1570 to celebrate his conquest of the island.

Hawaiian religion in the form encountered by Cook was brought to the islands by the Tahitian warrior-priest Paʻao, who led the last great migration to Hawaii. Paʻao is also credited with introducing the complex system of **kapu** – the Hawaiian version of the Polynesian *tabu*, or *taboo* – which circumscribed the daily lives of all Hawaiians. Some of its restrictions served to augment the power of the kings and priests, while others regulated domestic routine or attempted to conserve natural resources. Many had to do with food. Women were forbidden to prepare food or to eat with men; each husband was obliged to cook for himself and his wife in two separate ovens and to pound the *poi* in two distinct calabashes. The couple had to maintain separate houses, as well as a *Hale Noa*, where a husband and wife slept together. Women could not eat pork, bananas or coconuts, or several kinds of fish. Certain fish could only be caught in specified seasons, and a *koa* tree could only be cut down once two more were planted in its place.

No one could tread on the shadow of a chief; the highest chiefs were so surrounded by *kapus* that some would go out only at night. The ruling chiefs did not necessarily possess

RELIGION

245

the highest spiritual status. One of Kamehameha's wives was so much his superior that he could only approach her on all fours.

The only crime in ancient Hawaii was to break a *kapu*, and the only punishment was death. It was possible for an entire *ahupua'a* to break a *kapu* and incur death, but that penalty was not always exacted. One way guilty parties could avoid execution was by hotfooting it to a *pu'uhonua*, or "place of refuge." Maui is thought to have had at least six of these, perhaps one per *ahupua'a*, including examples at Lahaina, Kahukuloa, and Hāna.

The Hawaiian environment

*Of all the places in the world, I should like to see
a good flora of the Sandwich Islands.*

Charles Darwin, 1850

Much of the landscape in Hawaii seems so unspoiled and free from pollution that many visitors remain unaware of how fragile the environmental balance really is. Native life forms have had less than two millennia to adapt to the arrival of humans, while the avalanche of species introduced in the last two centuries threatens to overwhelm the delicate ecosystems altogether.

Hawaii is a unique ecological laboratory. Not only are the islands isolated by a "moat" at least 2000 miles wide in every direction, but having emerged from the sea as lifeless lumps of lava they were never populated by the diversity of species that spread across the rest of the planet.

Those animals that found a foothold evolved into specialized forms unknown elsewhere. Of more than 10,000 species of insects found in the islands, for example, 98 percent are unique to Hawaii, while at least 5,000 species are thought to remain unidentified. Recent discoveries include the tiny "happy-face spiders" of Maui's rainforests, whose markings are now familiar from postcards sold all over the state.

Such species are particularly vulnerable to external threats; half of Hawaii's indigenous plants, and three-quarters of its birds, are already extinct, while 73 percent of all the species in the US classified as threatened or endangered are unique to the islands. More than one hundred species of Hawaiian plants now have fewer than twenty remaining individuals in the wild.

The arrival of life

During the first seventy million years after the Hawaiian islands started to rise from the ocean, new plants and animals arrived only by sheer happenstance, via a few unlikely routes. Such were the obstacles that a new species established itself only once every 100,000 years. Some drifted, clinging to flotsam washed up on the beaches; others were borne on the wind as seeds or spores; and the odd migratory bird found its way here, perhaps bringing insects or seeds. The larvae of shallow-water fish from Indonesia and the Philippines floated across thousands of miles of ocean to hatch in the Hawaiian coral reefs.

Of **birds**, only the strongest fliers made it here; the *nēnē*, Hawaii's state bird, is thought to have evolved from a Canada goose injured during its annual migration and forced to remain on the islands. Its descendants adapted to walking on raw lava by losing the webbing from their feet.

No land-based amphibians or reptiles reached Hawaii, let alone large land mammals. At some point a hoary bat and an intrepid monk seal must have gotten here, as these were the only two mammals whose arrival predated that of humans.

Each species mutated from a single fertilized female to fill numerous ecological niches with extraordinary speed. Hundreds of variations might develop from a single fruit fly or land snail, and many species adapted themselves to conditions in specific areas of individual islands. One lone blown-astray finch, for example, evolved into more than fifty separate species of honey-creeper. Maui examples include the bright scarlet 'i'iwi, with its black wings, orange legs, and salmon-colored sickle-shaped bill, perfect for sipping nectar, and the 'apapane, which also has a red body and black wings but has a short, slightly curved black bill.

Although the Hawaiian environment was not entirely free of competition, many **plants** prospered without bothering to keep up their natural defenses. Thus there are nettles with no stings, and mints with no scent. Conversely, normally placid creatures turned savage: caterpillars content to munch leaves elsewhere catch and eat flies in Hawaii. These evolutionary changes have taken place so fast that five species of banana moth have evolved in the 1500 years since the Polynesians brought the banana to the islands.

As each new island emerged, it was populated by species from its neighbors as well as stragglers from farther afield. This process can still be seen on the Big Island, where Hawaii's last remaining stand of pristine rainforest still attempts to spread onto the new land created by Kīlauea. Although lava flows destroy existing life, fresh lava is incredibly rich in nutrients. Water collects in its cavities in the rock, and seeds or spores soon gather. The basic building block of the rainforest is the hāpu'u tree fern. Patches of these grow and decay, and in the mulch the 'ōhi'a lehua gains a foothold as a gnarled shrub; in time it grows to become a gigantic tree, forcing its roots through the rock. After several hundred years, the lava crumbles to become soil that will support a full range of rainforest species. In addition, lava flows swirl around higher ground, or even random spots, to create isolated "pockets" of growth that quickly develop their own specialized ecosystems.

The Polynesian world

The first humans to arrive on the Hawaiian scene swiftly realized that the islands lacked the familiar comforts of their South Seas homelands. Many of what might seem quintessentially Hawaiian species, such as coconut palms, bananas, *taro* and sugar cane, were in fact brought from Tahiti by the Polynesians, who also introduced the islands' first significant mammals – goats, dogs and pigs.

The settlers set about changing the island's physical environment to suit their own needs. They constructed terraces and irrigation channels in the wetland valleys, planted coconuts along the shoreline, and built fishponds out into the ocean. While their animals wrought destruction on the native flora, the settlers also had a significant impact on the bird population. Around twenty species of flightless birds, for example, swiftly became extinct. Forest birds were snared so their feathers could be used to make cloaks, helmets and *leis*; bright red feathers came from the *'i'iwi* bird, while yellow became the most prized color of all, so yellow birds such as the *mamo* and *'ō'ō* grew progressively rare. The *nēnē* was hunted for food, and the *'auku'u* heron, the curse of the fishponds, was driven from its native habitat.

On the whole, however, the Hawaiians lived in relative harmony with nature, with the *kapu* system helping to conserve resources. It was the arrival of foreigners, and the deluge of new species that they introduced, that really strained the ecological balance of Hawaii. Among the first victims were the Hawaiians themselves, decimated by the onslaught of foreign diseases.

Foreign invaders

The ships of the European explorers were explicitly intended to play the role of Noah's Arks. They carried food plants and domestic animals around the world in order to adapt newly discovered lands to the European image, and present their benighted natives with the necessary accoutrements of civilization. Hawaii's first cattle, for example, were presented to Kamehameha the Great by Captain George Vancouver of the *Discovery* in February 1793 and allowed to run wild on the Big Island. They ate through grasslands and forests, as well as through the crops of the Hawaiians. When they were eventually rounded up and domesticated, it formalized the change in land usage they had already effected. Horses had a similar initial impact, and wild goats remain a problem to this day.

Foreign plants, too, were imported, ranging from the scrubby mesquite trees of the lowlands (now known as *kiawe*) to the Mexican cacti that dot Upcountry Maui and the strawberry guava that runs riot along the forest trails of 'Ohe'o Gulch.

Along with such deliberate introductions came the stowaways, such as rats and forest-choking weeds. An especially unwelcome arrival was the **mosquito**. Scientists have pinpointed the exact moment it turned up, in 1826, when the whaling vessel *Wellington* emptied its rancid water casks into a stream near Lahaina prior to filling up with fresh water; they've even decided from which Peruvian river the water, and the mosquito larvae it contained, was originally drawn.

Another spectacular disaster was the importation to Hawaii of the **mongoose** by sugar plantation owners in the hope that it would keep down the rat population. Unfortunately, this plan failed to take into consideration the fact that rats are nocturnal and mongooses are not. The rodents continued to thrive while the mongooses slept, having gorged themselves on birds' eggs during the day. Only Kauai, where the mongoose never became established – myth has it that an infuriated docker threw the island's consignment into the sea after he was bitten – now retains significant populations of the many Hawaiian birds which, in the absence of predators, had decided it was safe to build their nests on the ground.

Wild pigs have had an especially ravaging effect. It is said that for every twenty humans in Hawaii, there lurks a feral pig. Though tourists are unlikely to spot one, their impact on Hawaiian rainforests has been devastating. For the ancient Hawaiians, the pig god Kama'pua'a was the embodiment of lusty fertility, ploughing deep furrows across the islands with his mighty tusks. His modern counterparts combine the strongest characteristics of the Polynesian pigs brought by early settlers with those of later European imports. Rooting through the earth, eating tree ferns, eliminating native lobelias and greenswords, and spreading the seeds of foreign fruits, the pigs have in most places destroyed the canopy that should prevent direct sunlight and heavy raindrops from hitting the forest floor. In addition, they have created muddy wallows and stagnant pools where mosquitoes thrive – the resultant avian malaria is thought to be the major single cause of the extinction of bird species. Fences to keep out the pigs have been erected in many of Maui's remotest areas, creating an enclave, for example, of the upper reaches of Kīpahulu Valley.

Unwanted alien species continue to arrive. Among those reported in the last few years of the twentieth century are the **coqui frog** from Puerto Rico, which has already achieved population densities in excess of 10,000 individuals per acre in several locations on Maui, and the Madagascar **giant day gecko**, a foot-long orange-spotted lizard now established on Oahu. Environmentalists fear that Hawaii's next likely arrival will be the **brown tree snake**. Originally found in the Solomon Islands, it has been hitch-hiking its way across the Pacific since World War II, sneaking into the holds of ships and planes, then emerging to colonize new worlds that have never seen a single snake. In Guam it has already established itself in concentrations of up to 30,000 individuals per square mile, happy to eat virtually anything, and wiping out the local bird populations.

Issues and prospects

The state of Hawaii has a short and not very impressive history of legislating to conserve its environment, and what little has been achieved so far appears to be jeopardized by Republican moves to rein in the powers of the Endangered Species Act. One positive development is that the whole state has been officially declared a **humpback whale sanctuary**, though the Navy is dragging its heels about certain areas just offshore from its installations, and there has been much opposition from local fishermen.

Throughout Hawaii, a resurgence of interest in what are seen as native Hawaiian values has dovetailed with the influx of New Age *haoles* to create an active environmental movement, which has had plenty of issues to occupy its attention. In particular, conservationists are struggling to combat the disappearance of Hawaii's indigenous **wildlife**. There have been some high-profile successes, such as the preservation of the extraordinary silversword plants of Haleakalā (see p.190), and the breeding of *nēnē* geese in the national parks on both Maui and the Big Island. However, the rarest bird species survive only in isolated mountain-top sanctuaries such as Kīpahulu Valley. So long as they stay at least 3500 feet above sea level, the mosquitoes can't reach them; nonetheless, birds such as the ʻōʻō aʻā honey-creeper are becoming extinct at an alarming rate. Activists concerned about the destruction of Hawaiian plants by casually imported newcomers point out that all passengers *leaving* Hawaii for the US are subjected to stringent inspections, to prevent Hawaiian species from reaching the mainland, but there are no equivalent checks on arriving passengers.

The greatest debates of all, however, have revolved around **tourism**. The power of the development lobby has for the last few decades been great enough to override environmental objections to the growth of resorts across all the islands. Anyone who believes that conserving the earth's resources is inherently a good thing is liable to have trouble accepting the kind of conspicuous consumption reflected in the fact that a single hotel devours seven percent of the Big Island's energy each year. There are also concerns that the resorts are damaging their immediate environment: the combination of golf courses and coral reefs may be ideal for vacationers, but that won't last if fertilizer and silt washed down from the greens and fairways end up choking the reef to death. However, it now looks as though the era of resort building is drawing to a close, albeit due more to economic factors than environmental pressure.

Hula and
Hawaiian music

I f your idea of Hawaiian music is Elvis doing the limbo in *Blue Hawaii*, you won't be disappointed by the entertainment offered in most of Maui's hotels. A diet of *Little Grass Shack* and the *Hawaiian Wedding Song*, with the occasional rendition of *Please Release Me* in Hawaiian, is guaranteed. However, the island also boasts its own lively contemporary music scene, and it's still possible to see performances of its most ancient form, *hula*, which embraces elements of theater and dance.

Hula

Although the ancient Hawaiians were devotees of the poetic chants they called **meles**, they had no specific word for "song." *Meles* were composed for various purposes, ranging from lengthy genealogies of the chiefs, put together over days of debate, through temple prayers, to lullabies and love songs. When the chanted words were accompanied by music and dance, as was often the case, the combined performance was known as **hula**.

Musical instruments included gourds, rattles, small hand or knee drums made from coconuts, and the larger *pahu* drums made by stretching shark skin over hollow logs. As a rule the tonal range was minimal and the music monotonous, though occasionally bamboo pipes may also have been played. Complexity was introduced by the fact that the dance, the chant and the music were all likely to follow distinct rhythmic patterns.

The telling of the story or legend was of primary importance; the music was subordinate to the chant, while the feet and lower body of the dancers served mainly to keep the rhythm, and their hand movements supplemented the meaning of the words. Dancers would be trained in a *hālau hula*, a cross between a school and a temple dedicated to Laka, and performances were hedged around by sacred ritual and *kapus*.

The first Christian missionaries to reach Hawaii saw *hula* as a lascivious manifestation of the islands' lack of morality. The religious subtleties of the so-called "genital *hula*" dances, for example, which celebrated the genitals of leading members of the *ali'i*, were lost on visiting whalemen.

In consequence, *hula* was largely suppressed for a century. It only returned to public performance at the coronation of the "Merrie Monarch," King David Kalākaua, in February 1883. By then the process of adapting music and dance to suit foreign tastes had started; the grass skirt, for example, was imported to Hawaii from the Gilbert Islands in the 1870s. As a 1923 magazine article complained, "real Hawaiian *hula* has little in common with the coarse imitations served up to sight-seers, magazine readers, and the general public."

Today *hula* persists in two forms. The first, *kahiko*, is closer to the old style, consisting of chanting to the beat of drums; the dancers wear knee-length skirts of flat *ti* leaves, and anklets and bracelets of ferns. *'Auana* is the modern style, featuring musicians playing Western-style instruments.

HULA

Slack-key and steel guitar

The roots of contemporary Hawaiian music lie in a mixture of cultural traditions brought from all over the world by nineteenth-century immigrants. In particular, Spanish and Mexican *paniolos* introduced the guitar, while the *braginha* of the Portuguese plantation workers was adapted to become the Hawaiian *ukelele*. King David Kalākaua had his own ukulele group, and co-wrote Hawaii's national anthem, *Hawaii Pon'ī*, while his sister Queen Lili'uokalani composed the haunting *Aloha 'Oe*, since covered by Elvis Presley among others.

The next step toward creating a distinctive Hawaiian sound came roughly a century ago, when the conventional method of tuning a guitar was abandoned in favor of **slack-key** tuning (*kī hō'alu* in Hawaiian), in which a simple strum of the open strings produces a harmonious chord. Next came the realization that sliding a strip of metal along the strings produced a glissando effect; an Oahu student is credited with inventing the **steel guitar**, as played by early virtuosos such as Sol Ho'opii.

English words were set to Hawaiian melodies, and the resultant *hapa-haole* music was by World War I the most popular music form in America. The craze for all things Hawaiian took several decades to die down, though it grew progressively more debased. By the time of the nationwide *tiki* craze of the 1950s, when mass tourism was just taking off and Polynesian-themed restaurants were opening all across the United States, pseudo-Hawaiian music such as Martin Denny's cocktail-jazz stylings was still topping the charts.

The modern generation

The sound created by the newest generation of Hawaiian musicians is a fascinating hybrid, drawing on the tradition of the ancient *meles*, but influenced by mainstream rock, country and even reggae music. It combines political stridency with sweet melodies, and powerful drum beats with gentle *ukelele* tinklings.

The first prominent name in the movement was **Gabby Pahinui**, an exponent of classic slack-key guitar who in the final years before his death in 1980 achieved international fame through his recordings with Ry Cooder. His success encouraged others to stop tailoring their music to suit mainland tastes, and it soon became apparent that there was a market for recordings in the Hawaiian language.

Among the biggest names on the contemporary scene are the Maui-based duo **Hapa** – Barry Flanagan, originally from New Jersey, and Keliʻi Kanealiʻi – who combined slack-key guitar instrumentals with soaring harmonies on the huge-selling album *Hapa*, blended ponderous rock with traditional chant on their version of U2's *Pride (In The Name of Love)*, and then riffed their way to heaven with the affectionate spoof *Surf Madness*. Having started out as the house band at Lahaina's *Cheeseburger in Paradise* restaurant, they now own *Hapa's Brew Haus* in Kīhei (see p.150) and *Hapa's Café* in Lahaina (see p.113). Another Maui performer, the *kumu hula* (*hula* teacher) **Keliʻi Reichel**, has produced several successful CDs of his exquisite alto singing, of which the first, *Kawaipunahele*, is probably the best, though *E Ō Mai* boasts an enjoyable rendition of the theme from *Babe*. Look out, too, for concert appearances by **Amy Gilliom**; her crystal-clear voice brings out all the beauty of her classic Hawaiian-language material, while she and her partner, guitar virtuoso Wille K, also make a great quick-fire comedy duo.

Finally, visitors may be surprised to encounter the Hawaiian-reggae fusion known as **Jawaiian**, in which the traditional beat of the *pahu* drum is accompanied by a thunderous electrified bass. Reggae is very popular with young

IZ (MAY 20 1959–JUNE 26 1997)

In the summer of 1997, the contemporary Hawaiian music scene lost the man who was in every sense its biggest star. Israel Kamakawiwo'ole, who started out singing in the Makaha Sons of Niihau and then went solo in 1990, died of respiratory difficulties in a Honolulu hospital. During his twenty-year career, "Iz" came to epitomize the pride and the power of Hawaiian music. His extraordinary voice adapted equally well to rousing political anthems, delicate love songs, pop standards and Jawaiian reggae rhythms, while his personality and his love for Hawaii always shone through both in concert and on record. Like his brother Skippy before him – also a founding member of the Makaha Sons – Iz eventually succumbed to the health problems caused by his immense size. At one point, his weight reached a colossal 757 pounds; he needed a fork-lift truck to get on stage, and could only breathe through tubes. His strength in adversity did much to ensure that he was repeatedly voted Hawaii's most popular entertainer, and after his death he was granted a state funeral, with his body lying in state in the Capitol. His enduring legacy will be the music on his four solo albums – *Ka Ano'i* (1990), *Facing Future* (1993), *E Ala Ē* (1995), and *'n Dis Life* (1996) – while his haunting rendition of *Hawai'i 78* (featured on *Facing Future*) has become the signature song of the Hawaiian sovereignty movement.

Hawaiians, but the home-grown groups don't tend to have the hard edge of the touring Jamaican bands who often perform on the islands. **Ho'ikane**, from the Big Island, is among the best; the group is credited with being the first to introduce an up-to-date dance-hall sound. Other performers include **Titus Kinimaka** – a pro surfer from Kauai's leading *hula* family – and **Butch Helemano**, who has at least nine albums to his name.

Books

An extraordinary number of **books** have been written about Hawaii and all matters Hawaiian, though you're likely to come across most of them only in bookstores on the islands themselves. Because most of the publishers listed below are US-based, they're especially hard to find abroad. The best place to buy books on Maui itself is the huge Borders in the Maui Marketplace in Kahului.

History

Gail Bartholomew, *Maui Remembers* (Mutual Publishing). Large-format paperback history of Maui, with lots of early photographs and entertaining stories.

Gavan Daws, *Shoal of Time* (University of Hawaii Press). Definitive if dry single-volume history of the Hawaiian Islands, tracing their fate from European contact to statehood.

Noel J. Kent, *Hawaii: Islands Under the Influence* (University of Hawaii Press). Rigorous Marxist account of Hawaiian history, concentrating on the islands' perennial "dependency" on distant economic forces.

Lili'uokalani, *Hawaii's Story by Hawaii's Queen* (Mutual Publishing). Autobiographical account by the last monarch of Hawaii of how her kingdom was taken away. Written in 1897 when she still cherished hopes of a restoration.

Gananath Obeyesekere, *The Apotheosis of Captain Cook* (Princeton University Press/Bishop Museum Press). An iconoclastic Sri Lankan anthropologist reassesses Captain Cook from an anti-imperialist – but, according to most authorities, historically inaccurate – perspective.

A. Grenfell Price (ed), *The Explorations of Captain James Cook in the Pacific* (Dover). Selections from Cook's own journals, including entries about his first landfall on Kauai and his ill-fated return to the Big Island.

Marshall Sahlins, *How Natives Think . . . About Captain Cook, for example* (University of Chicago Press). An impassioned and closely argued response to the Obeyesekere book, reviewed above. Sahlins is currently considered to be ahead on points.

Ancient Hawaii

Nathaniel B. Emerson, *Unwritten Literature of Hawaii – The Sacred Songs of the Hula* (Charles E. Tuttle Co). Slightly dated account of ancient Hawaii's most important art form. Published in 1909, its wealth of detail ensures that it remains required reading for all students of the *hula*.

Samuel M. Kamakau, *The People of Old* (Bishop Museum Press, 3 vols). Anecdotal essays, published in Hawaiian as newspaper articles in the 1860s. Packed with fascinating information, they provide a compendium of Hawaiian oral traditions. Kamakau's longer *Ruling Chiefs of Hawaii* (Bishop Museum Press) details all that is known of the deeds of the kings.

David Malo, *Hawaiian Antiquities* (Bishop Museum Press). Nineteenth-century survey of culture and society, written by a Maui native who was brought up at the court of Kamehameha the Great.

Valerio Valeri, *Kingship and Sacrifice; Ritual and Society in Ancient Hawaii* (University of Chicago Press). Detailed academic analysis of the role of human sacrifice in establishing the power of the king – an aspect of Hawaiian religion many other commentators gloss over.

Contemporary Hawaii

Michael Kioni Dudley and Keoni Kealoha Agard, *A Call for Hawaiian Sovereignty* (Nā Kāne O Ka Malo, 2 vols). The first of these short books attempts to reconstruct the world view of the ancient Hawaiians; the second is the clearest imaginable account of their dispossession.

Randall W. Roth (ed), *The Price of Paradise* (Mutual Publishing, 2 vols). Assorted experts answer questions about life and society in Hawaii, in short essays that focus on economic and governmental issues. Of most interest to local residents or prospective migrants, but a useful introduction to ongoing island debates, which sadly has now become somewhat dated.

Haunani Kay Trask, *From a Native Daughter: Colonialism and Sovereignty in Hawaii* (University of Hawaii Press). A stimulating and impressive contribution to the sovereignty debate, from one of Hawaii's best-known activists.

Travelers' tales

Isabella Bird, *Six Months in the Sandwich Islands* (University of Hawaii Press). Enthralling adventures of an Englishwoman in the 1870s, who unfortunately made only the briefest of visits to Maui.

Mark Twain, *Letters from Hawaii* (University of Hawaii Press). Colorful and entertaining accounts of nineteenth-century Hawaii, though ironically Twain enjoyed Maui so much he never found the time to write about it. Much of the best material was reworked for inclusion in *Roughing It* (Penguin UK and US).

Fiction

W. S. Merwin, *The Folding Cliffs* (Alfred Knopf). A compelling, visually evocative blank-verse retelling – in more than three hundred pages – of the story of Koolau the Leper, by one of America's leading contemporary poets.

Paul Theroux, *Hotel Honolulu* (Houghton Mifflin US, Hamish Hamilton UK). This funny and very entertaining slice of reportage brilliantly captures the flavor of life in modern Hawaii, packed with tourists passing through as well as local charac-

ters; there's even a cameo appearance from Iz himself (see p.259).

Kathleen Tyau, *A Little Too Much is Enough* (Farrar, Straus & Giroux US, The Women's Press UK). Atmospheric and amusing account of growing up as a Chinese-Hawaiian, with an appetizing emphasis on food.

Sylvia Watanabe, *Talking to the Dead* (Doubleday US, The Women's Press UK). Short, haunting evocation of village life in West Maui, in the days before the resorts.

Natural sciences

Garrett Hongo, *Volcano* (Vintage Books). The "Volcano" of the title is the Big Island village where Hongo was born; the book itself is a lyrical evocation of its physical and emotional landscape.

Arthur C. Medeiros and Lloyd L. Loope, *Rare Animals and Plants of Haleakalā National Park* (Hawaii Natural History Association). Fascinating illus-

trated booklet that will give you at least a sporting chance of identifying the weird life forms you encounter in Haleakalā.

Frank Stewart (ed), *A World Between Waves* (Island Press). Stimulating collection of essays by authors such as Peter Matthiessen and Maxine Hong Kingston, covering all aspects of Hawaiian natural history.

Language

The **Hawaiian language** is an offshoot of languages spoken elsewhere in Polynesia, with slight variations that arose during the centuries when the islands had no contact with the rest of Polynesia. Among its most unusual features is the fact that there are no verbs "to be" or "to have," and that, although it has no word for "weather," it distinguishes between 130 types of rain and 160 types of wind.

Although barely two thousand people speak Hawaiian as their mother tongue, it remains a living language and has experienced a revival in recent years. While visitors to Hawaii are almost certain to hear Hawaiian-language songs, it's rarely spoken in public, and there should be no need to communicate in any language other than English. However, everyday conversations tend to be sprinkled with Hawaiian words, and you'll also spot them in many local place names.

The Hawaiian alphabet

Hawaiian only became a **written language** when a committee of missionaries gave it an alphabet. The shortest in the world, it consists of just twelve letters – *a, e, h, i, k, l, m, n, o, p, u,* and *w* – plus two punctuation marks. When the missionaries were unable to agree on the precise sounds of the language, they simply voted on which letter to include – thus *k* beat *t*, and *l* beat *r*.

Hawaiian may look hard to **pronounce**, but in fact with just 162 possible syllables – as compared to 23,638 in Thai – it's the least complicated on earth. The letters *h*, *l*, *m* and *n* are pronounced exactly as in English; *k* and *p* are pronounced approximately as in English but with less aspiration; *w* is like the English *v* when it follows an *i* or an *e*, and the English *w* when it follows a *u* or an *o*. At the start of a word, or when it follows an *a*, *w* may be pronounced like a *v* or a *w*.

The **glottal stop** (') creates the audible pause heard in the English "oh-oh." Words without macrons (¯) to indicate stress are pronounced by stressing alternate syllables working back from the penultimate syllable. Thanks to the frequent repetition of syllables, this is usually easier than it may sound. "Kamehameha," for example, breaks down into the repeated pattern *Ka–meha–meha*, pronounced *Ka–mayha–mayha*.

a	*a* as in above	*ē*	*ay* as in day
e	*e* as in bet	*ī*	*ee* as in bee
i	*y* as in pity	*ō*	*o* as in hole (but
o	*o* as in hole		slightly longer)
u	*u* as in full	*ū*	*oo* as in moon
ā	*a* as in car		

Note that, strictly speaking, the word Hawaii should be written Hawai'i, with the glottal stop to show that the two "i"s are pronounced separately. However, this book follows the convention that words in common English usage are written without their Hawaiian punctuation. Maui itself is unique among the islands in that its correct name features neither a macron nor a glottal stop, while all the other island names – Hawaii, Oahu, Kauai, and so on – appear in their familiar English form.

Glossary

'A'ā rough lava

Ahupua'a basic land division, a "slice of cake" from ocean to mountain

'Āina land, earth

Akua god, goddess, spirit, idol

Ali'i chief, chiefess, noble

Aloha love, hello, goodbye.

'Aumākua personal god or spirit; totem animal

'Elepaio bird

Hala tree (pandanus, screw pine)

Halāu long house used for *hula* instruction; also a *hula* group

Hale house, building

Hana work

Haole (white) non-native Hawaiian, whether foreign or American resident

Hapa half, as in *hapa haole*, or half-foreign

Hāpu'u tree fern

Heiau ancient place of worship

Honua land, earth

Hui group, club

Hula dance/music form (*hula 'auana* is a modern form, *hula kahiko* is traditional)

Imu pit oven

Kahuna priest(ess) or someone particularly skilled in any field; *kahuna nui* chief priest

Kai sea

Kālua to bake in an *imu* (underground oven)

Kama'āina Hawaiian from another island; state resident

Kāne man

Kapa the "cloth" made from pounded bark, known elsewhere as tapa

Kapu forbidden, taboo, sacred

Kapu Moe prostration

Kaukau food

Keiki child

Kiawe thorny tree, mesquite

Ki'i temple image or petroglyph

Kīpuka natural "island" of vegetation surrounded by lava flows

Koa dark hardwood tree

Kōkua help

Kona leeward (especially wind)

Lānai balcony, terrace, patio

Lau leaf

Lehua or **'Ōhi'a Lehua** native red-blossomed shrub/tree

Lei garland of flowers, feathers, shells or other material

Liliko'i passion fruit

Limu seaweed

Lomi Lomi massage or raw salmon dish

Luakini temple of human sacrifice

Lū'au traditional Hawaiian feast

Mahalo thank you

Mahimahi white fish or dolphin fish (not the mammal)

Makai direction: away from the mountain, toward the sea

Malihini newcomer, visitor

Mana spiritual power

Mauka direction: away from the sea, toward the mountain

Mele ancient chant

Menehune in legend, the most ancient Hawaiian people, supposedly dwarfs

Mu'umu'u long loose dress

Nēnē Hawaiian goose – the state bird

Nui big, important

'Ohana family

'Ōhelo sacred red berry

'Ōhi'a Lehua see *Lehua*

'Ono delicious

'Ō'ō yellow-feathered bird

'Ōpae shrimp

Pāhoehoe smooth lava

Pali sheer-sided cliff

Paniolo Hawaiian cowboy

Pau finished

Pili grass, used for thatch

Poi staple food made of *taro* root

Poke raw fish dish

Pua flower, garden

Pūpū snack

Pu'u hill, lump

Taro Hawaiian food plant

Tsunami tidal wave

Tūtū grandparent, general term of respect

Wahine woman

Wai water

Wikiwiki hurry, fast

INDEX

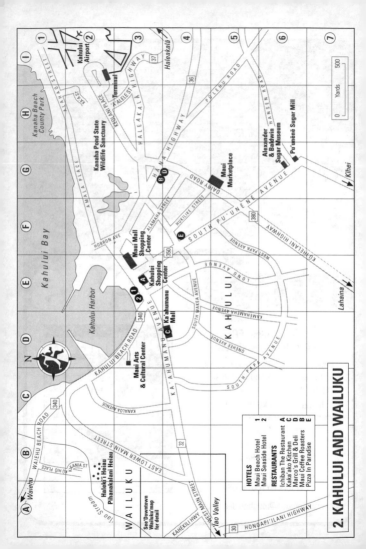

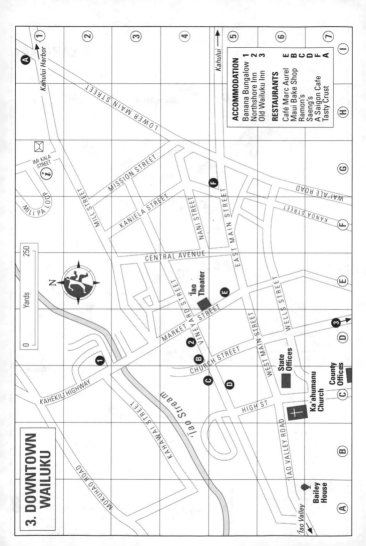

3. DOWNTOWN WAILUKU

N

0 — 250 Yards

↑ Kahului Harbor

↑ Kahului

ACCOMMODATION
Banana Bungalow 1
Northshore Inn 2
Old Wailuku Inn 3

RESTAURANTS
Café Marc Aurel E
Maui Bake Shop B
Ramon's C
Saeng's D
A Saigon Cafe F
Tasty Crust A

LOWER MAIN STREET

MILL PA LOOP

IMI KALA STREET

MILL STREET

MISSION STREET

KANIELA STREET

NANI STREET

CENTRAL AVENUE

MARKET STREET

VINEYARD STREET

'Iao Theater

CHURCH STREET

EAST MAIN STREET

WAI'ALE ROAD

KANOA STREET

WELLS STREET

WEST MAIN STREET

State Offices

County Offices

Ka'ahumanu Church

HIGH ST

'Iao Stream

KAHEKILI HIGHWAY

KAHAWAI STREET

MOKUHAU ROAD

'IAO VALLEY ROAD

Bailey House

'Iao Valley ↓

Kahului →

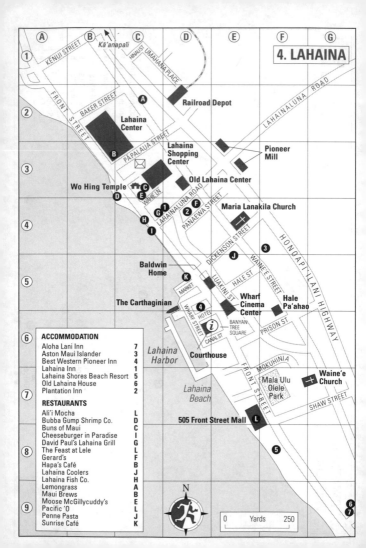

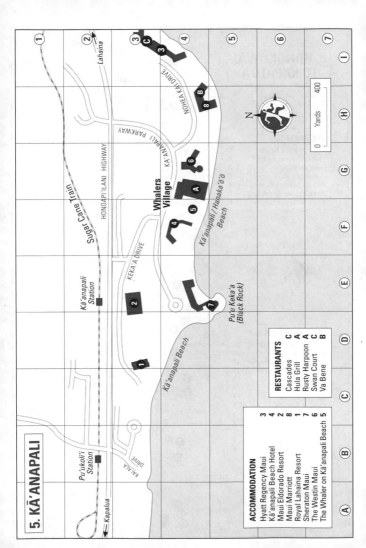

5. KĀʻANAPALI

Puʻukoliʻi Station

Kaʻanapali Station

Sugar Cane Train

HONOAPIʻILANI HIGHWAY

KAIALA DRIVE

KEKAʻA DRIVE

KAʻANAPALI PARKWAY

NOHEA KAʻI DRIVE

Whalers Village

Kapalua

Lahaina

Kāʻanapali Beach

Puʻu Kekaʻa (Black Rock)

Kāʻanapali / Hanaka ʻōʻō Beach

N

0   Yards   400

ACCOMMODATION

Hyatt Regency Maui	3
Kāʻanapali Beach Hotel	4
Maui Eldorado Resort	8
Maui Marriott	2
Royal Lahaina Resort	1
Sheraton Maui	6
The Westin Maui	6
The Whaler on Kāʻanapali Beach	5

RESTAURANTS

Cascades	C
Hula Grill	A
Rusty Harpoon	A
Swan Court	C
Va Bene	B

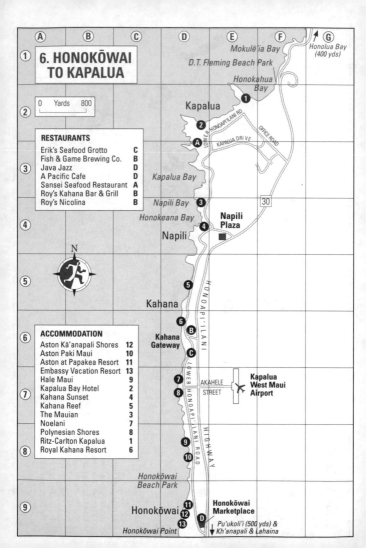

6. HONOKŌWAI TO KAPALUA

0 Yards 800

RESTAURANTS

Erik's Seafood Grotto	C
Fish & Game Brewing Co.	B
Java Jazz	D
A Pacific Cafe	D
Sansei Seafood Restaurant	A
Roy's Kahana Bar & Grill	B
Roy's Nicolina	B

ACCOMMODATION

Aston Kā'anapali Shores	12
Aston Paki Maui	10
Aston at Papakea Resort	11
Embassy Vacation Resort	13
Hale Maui	9
Kapalua Bay Hotel	2
Kahana Sunset	4
Kahana Reef	5
The Mauian	3
Noelani	7
Polynesian Shores	8
Ritz-Carlton Kapalua	1
Royal Kahana Resort	6

N

Mokulē'ia Bay

Honolua Bay (400 yds)

D.T. Fleming Beach Park

Honokahua Bay

Kapalua

LOWER HONOAPI'ILANI RD

KAPALUA DRIVE

OFFICE ROAD

Kapalua Bay

30

Napili Bay

Napili Plaza

Honokeana Bay

Napili

HONOAPI'ILANI

Kahana

Kahana Gateway

LOWER HONOAPI'ILANI ROAD

AKAHELE STREET

Kapalua West Maui Airport

HIGHWAY

Honokōwai Beach Park

Honokōwai

Honokōwai Marketplace

Pu'ukoli'i (500 yds) & Kā'anapali & Lahaina

Honokōwai Point

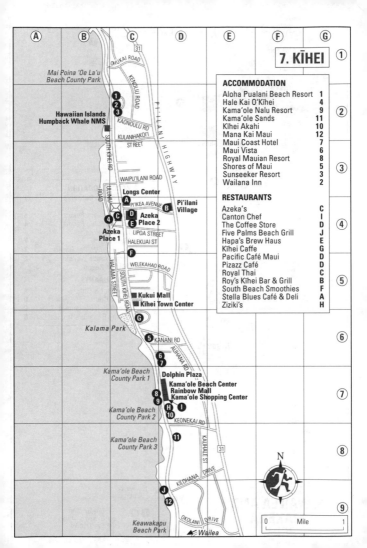

7. KĪHEI

ACCOMMODATION

Aloha Pualani Beach Resort	1
Hale Kai O'Kīhei	4
Kama'ole Nalu Resort	9
Kama'ole Sands	11
Kīhei Akahi	10
Mana Kai Maui	12
Maui Coast Hotel	7
Maui Vista	6
Royal Mauian Resort	8
Shores of Maui	5
Sunseeker Resort	3
Wailana Inn	2

RESTAURANTS

Azeka's	C
Canton Chef	I
The Coffee Store	D
Five Palms Beach Grill	J
Hapa's Brew Haus	E
Kīhei Caffe	G
Pacific Café Maui	D
Pizazz Café	D
Royal Thai	C
Roy's Kīhei Bar & Grill	B
South Beach Smoothies	F
Stella Blues Café & Deli	A
Ziziki's	H

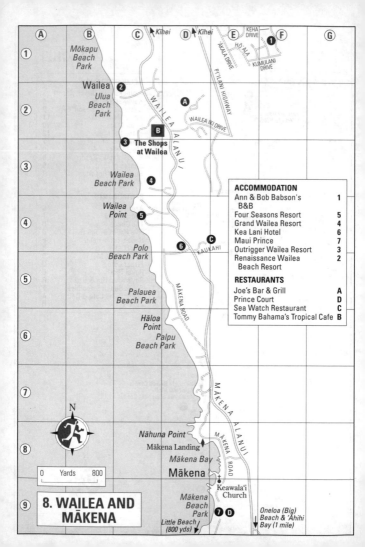

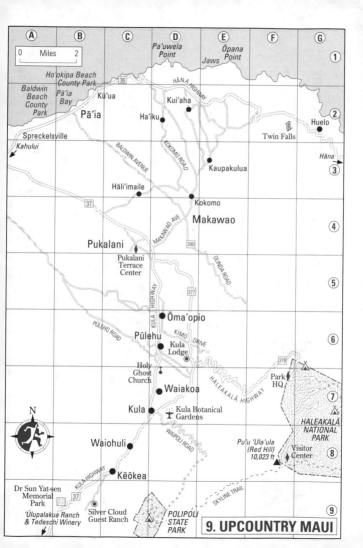

9. UPCOUNTRY MAUI

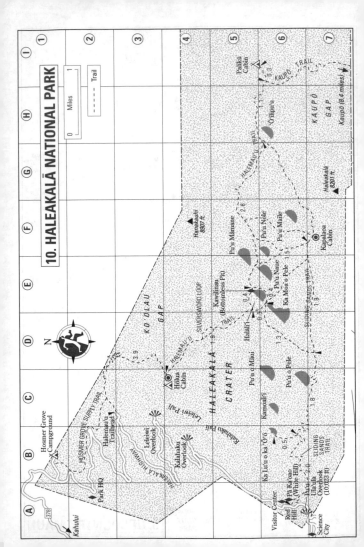

10. HALEAKALĀ NATIONAL PARK

Miles

- - - - Trail

N

KO·OLAU GAP

HALEAKALA CRATER

KAUPŌ GAP

Kahului

378

Hosmer Grove Campground

HOSMER GROVE SUPPLY TRAIL

Halemau'u Trailhead

HALEAKALA HIGHWAY

Leleiwi Overlook

Kalahaku Overlook

Park HQ

Kalahaku Pali

Leleiwi Pali

Hōlua Cabin

HALEMAU'U TRAIL

SILVERSWORD LOOP

3.9

Hamatauhi 8507 ft

Pu'u o Māui

Kamoali'i

Pu'u o Pele

HALEMAU'U TRAIL

1.9

Halāli'i

Kawilinau (Bottomless Pit)

0.4

0.2

Pu'u Māmane

Pu'u Naue

Ka Moa o Pele

0.4

2.6

Pu'u Nole

Pu'u Maile

1.5

Ōilipu'u

HALEMAU'U TRAIL

Paliku Cabin

0.3

KAUPO TRAIL

Kapalaoa Cabin

Haleakala 8201 ft

Kaupō (8.4 miles)

SLIDING SANDS TRAIL

1.3

1.9

Visitor Center

Red Hill

Pā Kā'oao (White Hill)

Ka Lu'u o ka 'O'ō

Ulaʻula Overlook (10,023 ft)

Pa'u

SLIDING SANDS TRAIL

0.5

1.8

Science City

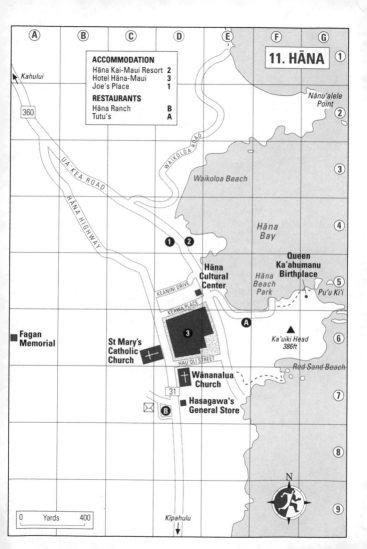

11. HĀNA

ACCOMMODATION
Hāna Kai-Maui Resort 2
Hotel Hāna-Maui 3
Joe's Place 1

RESTAURANTS
Hāna Ranch B
Tutu's A

Kahului

360

Nānu'alele Point

WAIKOLOA ROAD

UA'KEA ROAD

HĀNA HIGHWAY

Waikoloa Beach

Hāna Bay

1 2

KEANINI DRIVE

Hāna Cultural Center

KEAWA PLACE

Queen Ka'ahumanu Birthplace

Hāna Beach Park

Pu'u Ki'ī

A

Fagan Memorial

St Mary's Catholic Church

3

Ka'uiki Head 386ft

HAU'OLI STREET

Red Sand Beach

Wānanalua Church

31

B

Hasagawa's General Store

N

0   Yards   400

Kīpahulu